Uneven Ground

American Indian Sovereignty and Federal Law

Uneven Ground

American Indian Sovereignty and Federal Law

BY DAVID E. WILKINS
AND K. TSIANINA LOMAWAIMA

UNIVERSITY OF OKLAHOMA PRESS : NORMAN

ALSO BY DAVID E. WILKINS

American Indian Sovereignty and the U.S. Supreme Court: The Masking of Justice (Austin, 1997)

(with Vine Deloria, Jr.) *Tribes, Treaties & Constitutional Tribulations* (Austin, 1999)

ALSO BY K. TSIANINA LOMAWAIMA

They Called It Prairie Light: The Story of Chilocco Indian School (Lincoln, 1994)

Library of Congress Cataloging-in-Publication Data

Wilkins, David E. (David Eugene), 1954–
    Uneven ground : American Indian sovereignty and federal law / by David E. Wilkins and K. Tsianina Lomawaima.
        p.   cm.
    Includes bibliographical references and index.
    ISBN 0–8061–3351–1 (hc : alk. paper)
    1. Indians of North America—Legal status, laws, etc.   2. Indians of North America—Government relations.   3. Sovereignty.   I. Lomawaima, K. Tsianina, 1955–   II. Title.

KF8205 .W533 2001
323.1'197073—dc21

                                                                2001027138

The paper in this book meets the guidelines for permanence and durability of the Committee on Production Guidelines for Book Longevity of the Council on Library Resources, Inc. ∞

1   2   3   4   5   6   7   8   9   10

Contents

TABLES

Acknowledgments

David Wilkins thanks, as always, his family for their love and support: Evelyn, Sion, Niłtooli, and Nazhone. Tsianina Lomawaima thanks Hartman. Both authors thank Kathy Lewis for her skilled editing of the manuscript.

Earlier versions of some of the chapters in this book appeared in the following publications, and the authors gratefully acknowledge permission to use these materials: "Tribal-State Affairs: American States as 'Disclaiming' Sovereigns," *Publius: The Journal of Federalism* 28, no. 4 (Fall 1999); "Quit-Claiming the Doctrine of Discovery: A Treaty-Based Reappraisal," *Oklahoma City University Law Review* 23, nos. 1 and 2 (Spring and Summer 1998); "With the Greatest Respect and Fidelity: A Cherokee Vision of the 'Trust' Doctrine," *Social Science Journal* 34, no. 4 (1997); "Convoluted Essence: Indian Rights and the Federal Trust Doctrine," *Native Americas* 14, no. 1 (1997); and "The U.S. Supreme Court's Explication of 'Federal Plenary Power': An Analysis of Case Law Affecting Tribal Sovereignty, 1886–1914," *American Indian Quarterly* 18, no. 3 (Winter 1994).

The authors respectfully dedicate this work to Vine Deloria, Jr. He inspired and encouraged us to reexamine these doctrines in a systematic way rather than simply accept their validity at face value; and he remains the centrally motivating voice for the development of American Indian Studies.

Uneven Ground

American Indian Sovereignty and Federal Law

INTRODUCTION

When the Pilgrims landed on the coast of what would one day be called New England, desperate to replenish their dwindling supplies (especially of beer), they had no intention of settling; they were headed for the mouth of the Hudson River, in what was termed Virginia. But they found unexpected gifts of cleared fields, granaries full of corn, and no people. The Pilgrims knew Indian people existed and inhabited these coasts but had little accurate information about them. As a consequence the Pilgrims feared Indians. Imagine their surprise when they were greeted by Samoset, who had learned English from cod fishermen, with "Welcome, Englishmen." Sometime later, they were met by Squanto, or Tisquantum, who had been captured by English captain Thomas Hunt, had escaped from slavery in Spain to England, and had guided a subsequent trans-Atlantic voyage—a sojourner who had returned home. Surely this was a sign from God to his chosen people that they had found a rightful home. God further expressed his divine wishes in ensuing decades, as to which population should prosper. Pilgrims certainly suffered those first harsh winters, but native populations were decimated by infectious epidemic diseases to which many Europeans had developed immunities.

The situation, of course, looked quite different to the Wampanoag, Narragansett, Pequot, and other native communities. Decades of intermittent contact with European fishing fleets and mutual trade, raids, and hostilities had built a foundation of knowledge about these newcomers. Some native people had been captured and returned, like Squanto, bringing firsthand accounts of European cities, industries, customs, and tastes. With these contacts came epidemic diseases. The area that would become known as Plimoth Plantation was deserted by the native Patuxets when the Pilgrims arrived in 1620 because of a devastating series of illnesses that swept through between 1617 and 1619. Native political, economic, social, and religious life had been damaged, no doubt, but was not moribund. Significant native populations remained and caused the English no small amount of grief, as Indians resisted expanding immigrant populations and expansive English claims to jurisdiction over lands and peoples.[1]

The contest among the diverse English colonies and diverse native nations of this newly named New England would be repeated, in many times and many places, across the American continent. Local details varied, but the contests were similar—they all involved peoples asserting and defending their sovereign rights. The contest remains today. What is at stake? Important questions of identity, jurisdiction, powers of government, and rights to make decisions are involved, and all are bound up in the notion of sovereignty. A sovereign nation defines itself and its citizens, exercises self-government and the right to treat with other nations, applies its jurisdiction over the internal legal affairs of its citizens and subparts (such as states), claims political jurisdiction over the lands within its borders, and may define certain rights that inhere in its citizens (or others).

The United States of America declared itself an independent and sovereign nation with the successful revolt against Britain and the ratification of the Constitution as a governing document. Does the United States today, as an international superpower, possess an unlimited sovereignty? Certainly not. The United States is bound, as a nation, by the terms of its treaties with other sovereign nations (including hundreds of treaties with Indian nations); federal powers are balanced with state powers in what we know as the federalist system; the Constitution reserves certain rights and powers to the people, rather than vesting those powers in the government. In the real world, sovereignty operates within constraints.

American Indian tribes are sovereign nations. Their sovereignty is inherent, pre- or extraconstitutional, and is explicitly recognized in the Constitution. What do these terms mean? Inherent sovereignty inheres in self-governing human groups—various scholars no doubt define different criteria of political organization as requisite for sovereign status. Tribes existed before the United States of America, so theirs is a more mature sovereignty, predating the Constitution; in that sense, tribal sovereignty exists "outside" the Constitution. The drafters of the Constitution, in express wording in the commerce clause, recognized Indian nations as something distinct from the United States. The relevant constitutional phrasing will be discussed in greater detail as we proceed; suffice to say for now that this clause and the treaty and property clauses add a constitutional basis to understandings of tribal sovereignty. Are tribes today unlimited sovereigns? Certainly not. The political realities of relations with the federal government, relations with state and local governments, competing jurisdictions, complicated local histories, circumscribed land bases, and overlapping citizenships all constrain their sovereignty.

The relationship between American Indian tribes and the U.S. federal government is an ongoing contest over sovereignty. At stake are fundamental questions of identity, jurisdiction, power, and control. Who defines tribes? The federal government, through the process of recognition? Or states? Or tribes themselves? In the contemporary world, the federal government officially recognizes over 560 American Indian tribes and Alaska Native villages. A few tribes are state-recognized, but not federally recognized. Some groups claim Indian identity but have no standing in law. Many tribes maintain tribal courts and police forces; others are under federal jurisdiction; some are under state or local law enforcement jurisdiction; many reservations are tangled in a complicated web of interlocking jurisdictions depending on the ethnicity of the victim and/or perpetrator or the seriousness of the offense. Tribes have certain powers of self-government: the right to establish criteria for tribal membership, for example, or to elect governing councils, or to tax on-reservation businesses and persons. Some tribes have their own departments of education and run their own schools. Some reservations are incorporated into public school districts and thus are subject to the rulings of state departments of education. Some communities are served by the federal school system operated by the Bureau of Indian Affairs (BIA): the possibilities for self-determination, for local decision-making in education, vary widely across these diverse circumstances.

How did we get to the current state of affairs? What has led to the current complexity of federal-tribal-state relations? Local histories are pertinent, but all tribes have been subject to certain developments in federal Indian policy and certain interpretations and applications of federal Indian law. Law and policy are the concerns of this book, as we trace the development of the contest between federal and tribal sovereigns; the contest has been joined at particular moments by the states, as well. Within law and policy, we focus on six doctrines of law, plus certain clauses within state organic acts and constitutions known as "disclaimer" clauses. All of these doctrines have been and continue to be central principles of legal interpretation, especially legal interpretation that focuses on sovereignty (disclaimer clauses have not played such an important role, but we argue that they might). What do they all have in common? They have all over time been marked by inconstancy, indeterminacy, and variability in interpretation.

Inconstancy, indeterminacy, and variability characterize the uneven ground of federal Indian policy. The course of Indian policy has not proceeded along some smooth racetrack, but has pitched and bumped over the rutted tracks that the conflicting interests of tribes, states, federal agencies, railroads, energy and industrial barons, homesteaders, tourists, and casual visitors have carved across Indian Country. Of course, there is another meaning of "uneven ground" that also applies. Relations of power among native and non-native groups have shifted over time as well, favoring one, then another.

When the United States was first established, tribes were politically and militarily powerful and recognized as sovereigns through the treaty-making process, among others. Through the 1800s, tribal fortunes waned, and some powers of sovereignty were diminished by military defeats, economic marginalization, removal and relocation, continued ill health and epidemic episodes among tribal populations, shrinking land bases, and many colonial practices. Arguably, the nadir of tribal sovereignty occurred around the turn of the nineteenth to the twentieth century. In the 1920s and 1930s, tribal leaders, Indian people, and their allies successfully fought to reassert some measures of tribal sovereignty. These advances, especially under the administrations of President Franklin Roosevelt, Secretary of Interior Harold Ickes, and Commissioner of Indian Affairs John Collier, were eroded during the years after World War II, but were not entirely overturned or forgotten. Civil rights activism of the 1960s and growing political and legal action by Indian people and tribes resulted in tremendous political, social, and educational gains.

The federal government inaugurated policies of tribal self-determination and self-governance in the early 1970s in order to recognize the distinctive cultural, political, and economic rights of tribal nations and to encourage greater political independence of tribes. The gains for tribes have not gone unchallenged, however. There is firm evidence that since the late 1980s the United States Supreme Court has become more conservative and has veered away from the congressional policy of tribal self-determination. The Court's opinions from this era hearken back to nineteenth-century policies of coercive assimilation and acculturation (Pommersheim 1995; Wilkins 1992).[2] Assimilation was also a federal goal throughout much of the twentieth century, but enforcement was occasionally less overt than nineteenth-century practices: the difference, for example, between native people going to jail for playing cards on a Sunday and tribes spending millions of dollars fighting lengthy court battles to protect native religious freedoms.

Since the Republican Party ascended to power in both houses of Congress in 1994, the Congress has also become more conservative. Legislative conservatism, augmented by the disputed presidential election of George W. Bush in 2000 and the late twentieth century resurgence of states' rights, threatens tribal economic growth, political development, and social progress. Tribes increasingly compete with states for a share of federal dollars, or, in some cases, tribal governments must seek funding directly from states when Congress devolves program funds to the states under block grants (Wilkins 1994a, sec. F, 2). States seek to regulate and profit from casino gaming on Indian lands; treaty rights to hunt, fish, shellfish, or gather are hotly contested by states as well as by hunters and anglers; traditional religious practices have been denied protection; tribal courts struggle for jurisdiction with state and federal courts; and tribal economic development struggles under the weight of decades of federally deferred maintenance and underfunding. How do we account for the inconsistency, the apparent collision course between tribal self-determination/self-government and assaults on tribes by states, agencies, Congress, and the courts?

We believe the collision between tribes and other political, administrative, and corporate entities results from different understandings of the status of tribes. Tribes believe they are, and operate as, nations who held inherent sovereign status when they met and first dealt with European sovereigns, later succeeded by the sovereign government of the United States. Tribes today continue to wield important powers that descend from their inherent sovereign powers. The federal and state governments have sometimes acknowledged, sometimes ignored, and sometimes attacked the status of tribes as sovereigns.

We hold that America's indigenous nations occupy a distinctive political/legal status within the United States as separate sovereigns. Tribal rights are based in the doctrine of inherent sovereignty, affirmed in hundreds of ratified treaties and agreements, acknowledged in the commerce clause of the U.S. Constitution, and recognized in ample federal legislation and case law. The Constitution acknowledges tribal sovereignty in the commerce clause by charging Congress with the responsibility to regulate trade with Indian tribes. "The Indian Commerce Clause by its own terms acknowledges tribes as sovereigns, sovereigns other than states for which the federal government needs delegated authority to regulate" (Pommersheim 1995, 121). The Constitution, however, does not precisely define or delimit tribal sovereignty. As a consequence, through time, questions of the exact parameters of tribal sovereignty have arisen as state actions, federal laws, and court interpretations have restricted or enhanced it. Some of the important questions that have arisen include:

Do tribes possess a nation-to-nation political relationship with the federal government, or are they merely another "minority," defined as ethnic groups?[3]

Are tribes distinct, independent communities, or are they "domestic, dependent nations," as Chief Justice John Marshall defined them in 1831 and 1832?

Does Congress have only those powers over tribes that tribes have granted, or is congressional authority over tribes complete and unhindered, what some scholars term "plenary"?

Do tribes exercise some measures of external sovereign power—in other words, do they have powers to deal with other governments—or do they retain only limited internal sovereignty—that is, only some powers over their own lands and people?

Who has the power to modify or break treaties between tribes and the United States government; and who has the responsibility to enforce those treaties?

Are tribes inferior, superior, or equal to the political status of the states?

Why are so many states consistently hostile to expressions of tribal sovereignty?

Are tribes exempt from congressional laws unless they are specifically written in, or are tribes subject to congressional law unless they are specifically exempted?

Why do these questions have varying, even conflicting answers? One reason is because of the diversity and sheer number of tribes. Another reason is that federal policies and practices toward Indian tribes and peoples have proceeded from many sources: from congressional laws; executive orders; bureaucratic regulations of agencies such as the Office or Bureau of Indian Affairs and other divisions of the Department of the Interior, the Department of Education, or the Department of Agriculture; and court decisions and interpretations. Because all these streams are tributary to the river of what has been collectively termed "Indian policy," the course of Indian policy has not been consistent. Within the federal government, Congress has not always agreed with the Supreme Court, the president has not always agreed with Congress, and bureau chiefs have often had their own particular visions or agendas. In the larger national context, federal Indian policy has not necessarily been endorsed by the various states. In the historical long term, of course, much of federal Indian policy and many individual state actions have proceeded with complete disregard for tribal input or opinion. From 1775 to the present, federal and state intentions toward tribes have changed direction in various ways. One could argue that indeterminacy, or inconsistency, is a hallmark of the tribal-federal relationship.

Much scholarly attention has focused on what in the past prompted, and now perpetuates, federal indeterminacy toward tribes (Deloria and Lytle 1984; Nagel 1996; Newton 1993). The federal government has been unable, or unwilling, to maintain a consistent policy orientation—some policies and practices over the years have favored the breakup of tribes and the assimilation of Indians, while others respect tribal sovereignty. Our goal in this book is to reach some understanding of the contest between sovereigns, between tribes and the United States. To that end, we examine the tribal-federal relationship, and the tribal-states relationship, through the lens of six critical doctrines of U.S. law: the doctrine of discovery, the trust doctrine, the doctrine of plenary power, the reserved rights doctrine, the doctrine of implied repeals, and the doctrine of sovereign immunity. We also discuss the disclaimer clauses that enjoin states from interference in the federal-tribal political relationship. We have several goals, as we argue for the recognition of tribes as inherent sovereigns.

First, we want to present a comprehensive overview written for the layperson or interested student; a reader should not need a law degree to understand this book. Second, we want to outline the history of each of these doctrines, to illustrate their point of origin, the times in which each was conceived, and the forces that have shaped the doctrines since. We believe in the maxim that those who ignore history are condemned to repeat its mistakes. Our third goal is to make particular arguments for defining or implementing these doctrines today and into the future. Toward that goal, we assemble a range of evidence from federal agency actions, congressional laws and committee hearings, court decisions and interpretations, and tribal petitions, constitutions, laws, and courts. We believe that the evidence clearly indicates that a great deal of Indian policy rests on a foundation of racism, ethnocentrism, repression of tribal histories, inappropriate policy-making by judicial bodies, and inaccurate historical understandings.

Given this context, it is critically important to recognize that legal doctrines are not "facts"; they demand analysis, and analysis sometimes (but not always) demands doctrinal reconfiguration. We hope that better understandings of Indian history, Indian law, and Indian perspectives will strengthen respect for tribes as sovereigns.[4] Our ultimate goal is that the analyses presented here will motivate all levels of government, tribal, state, and federal—especially Congress and the courts—to give careful consideration to the doctrines discussed here and make an informed decision on whether to support, reexamine, or reconsider each doctrine.

The doctrine of discovery is the first to be considered. We outline the competing definitions or legal senses of the term. This doctrine has been popularly interpreted to mean that the act of "discovery" conveyed legal title to, and ownership of, American soil to European nations, a title that devolved to the United States. We term this sense or definition of discovery "expansive." Expansive discovery implies that native nations have a right to lands as occupants, or possessors, but that they are incompetent to manage those lands and need a benevolent guardian—such as the federal government— who holds legal title. A closely allied second definition, which we call "absolute," denies Indian tribes even a possessory title or rights of use to their lands; it equates "discovery" with complete conquest. The expansive and absolute notions of discovery either view tribes as mere tenants or strip tribes and Indian individuals of their complete property rights. We propose that an accurate definition of discovery—which we term "preemptive"—granted the "discovering" nations an exclusive, preemptive right to purchase Indian land, if a tribe agreed to sell any of its territory. We examine the historic record, the "actual state of affairs" as European and native nations negotiated and implemented land transfers, to argue that discovery did nothing more than grant an exclusive and preemptive right to buy, if tribal owners were inclined to sell.

We examine three classes of evidence in the course of our argument for the preemptive definition of the discovery doctrine. First, pragmatic realities of colonial interaction among native nations and Spain, France, Great Britain, and the United States indicate that all these political "sovereigns" had to recognize indigenous title to land. Second, analysis of treaties illustrates how the United States further confirmed indigenous land rights after the Revolutionary War. Third, relevant Supreme Court decisions are analyzed for appropriate and inappropriate constructions of the discovery doctrine.

In the second chapter, we address the trust doctrine. The United States' relationship with Indian tribes has been defined in myriad ways, using the terms "trust," "trust doctrine," "trust duty," "trust relationship," "trust responsibility," "trust obligation," "trust analogy," "ward-guardian," and "beneficiary-trustee." Most of these terms are synonymous, except that the "guardian-ward" relationship is substantively different than the "trustee-beneficiary" relationship. The chapter first examines possible origins of the various "trust" concepts, then illustrates the multiple definitions of trust, looking at how different federal governmental branches have interpreted trust and how interpretations have shifted over time. Common to many definitions of "trust" is the notion of federal *responsibility* to *protect or enhance* tribal assets, which raises two important questions. Does the federal government, as "trustee" of Indian tribes' assets, have a responsibility to manage *in the best interests* or for the benefit of tribes? We argue that it does. Two, is that responsibility legally mandated or does it operate as a lesser moral "force"? We argue for legal force. After delineating countervailing views of trust, we ask which definition of trust is most appropriate to protecting tribal interests. We argue for an indigenous vision of trust. We closely examine the historic moment of Removal in the 1830s, using as our model the experience of the Cherokee people. The indigenous vision of trust authorizes and allows both parties—the United States and the tribe—to do only what is diplomatically agreed or consented to. Any unilateral action that adversely affects either party violates the trust. Based on an indigenous, reciprocal vision of trust, tribes believe that tribal and federal rights, properties, and sovereignty are equally entitled to deep and profound respect.

Chapter 3 examines the doctrine of plenary power, which constitutes a paradox at the heart of the tribal-federal relationship. On the one hand, the United States sometimes claims plenary power—absolute and unlimited power—over tribes, their resources, and Indian affairs. On the other hand, the United States sometimes understands plenary power as exclusive or preemptive power, which supports the inherent sovereignty of American Indian nations. This paradox is termed "irreconcilability" in Indian law and policy. We propose that breaking down the definition of "plenary" into its component parts makes it possible to reconcile the seemingly contradictory federal impulses toward jurisdictional monopoly and jurisdictional multiplicity. Plenary power as an *exclusive* power of Congress (not a power of the executive or judicial branches of the federal government, nor a power of the states) is a constitutionally based and appropriate understanding of the term. *Preemptive* plenary power, when Congress preempts the action of states toward tribes, is also constitutionally based and appropriate. *Unlimited and absolute* plenary power over tribes is insupportable, however. We present two arguments against unlimited-absolute plenary power: that such a definition creates a constitutional impasse and that the United States frequently recognizes tribes' sovereign rights. Our discussion of plenary power, accordingly, proceeds hand in hand with a discussion of tribal sovereignty.

The doctrine of reserved rights is the fourth doctrine to be considered here. Rights reserved through treaties are sometimes seen as "special rights" that set Indians apart in inappropriate, even unconstitutional, ways. States, local governments, and non-native citizens have sometimes reacted strongly against reserved rights, such as treaty-based rights to fish in "usual and accustomed places" in the Pacific Northwest; the treaty-guaranteed rights of Chippewa tribal members to spear-fish for walleye on ceded lands in Wisconsin; and the Makah decision to revive their cultural tradition, and treaty right, of whaling. As we begin a new century, states continue their efforts to block or regulate gaming on Indian lands. The question at hand is one of power. Do Indian tribes reserve all those powers and rights that they have not expressly surrendered, or do they exercise only those rights that have been expressly delegated to them by act of Congress? Following the precedents set by Vine Deloria, Jr. (1996), and Charles Wilkinson (1987), we propose a judicially supported and historically accurate vision of the reserved rights doctrine. Reserved rights are those rights that a tribe never expressly surrendered. Importantly, *all rights* are reserved except those specifically given up in a treaty or similar agreement. Tribes do not exercise rights because Congress granted them rights, but because of tribes' original and inherent sovereignty. Tribal sovereignty has some limitations that have arisen over the last few centuries (as do all sovereigns),[5] but we assert that it should erode no further than what tribes have expressly allowed. We develop our argument based on analysis of the Tenth Amendment to the Constitution and judicial decisions. After detailed consideration of the political principle of federalism, we conclude that tribal reserved rights will be vulnerable to state and federal attack until, or unless, reserved rights attain a status comparable to the Tenth Amendment.

The doctrine of implied repeals is at center stage in chapter 5, which discusses the power to change or terminate treaties (termination of treaties, legally, is called "abrogation"). Treaties are, by definition, bilateral or multilateral agreements; it takes at least two to engage in this form of diplomacy. Treaties begin when two or more nations enter into the treaty-negotiation process. How treaties might end has been a critical issue in tribal-federal relations. Who has the power to abrogate treaties or change their provisions: the political branches (Congress or the president) or the Supreme Court? The Supreme Court has never claimed this power; it has consistently recognized that only the political branches may modify or abrogate treaties. In several cases, however, the U.S. Supreme Court has acted to quash or dramatically modify Indian treaty rights without congressional authorization or tribal consent. The Supreme Court has justified its actions in these cases on the basis of what is called the doctrine of "implied repeal." What does this term mean? The Court occasionally must decide cases where treaty language disagrees with, or contradicts, the language of later congressional or state statutes. The Court may abrogate a previously existing treaty because a later law contains provisions perceived to be so contrary to, so irreconcilable with, those of the earlier treaty that only one of the two can stand in force. This is known as "repeal" of the earlier treaty. The Court, in essence, assumes the power to act in a political arena—Congress's arena of authority over Indian affairs—without a directive from Congress to do so.

We argue against this exercise of "implied repeals" by the Court based on an extensive analysis of legal cases, including the *Lone Wolf* case. The power to abrogate or modify Indian treaties may *only* be exercised by the Congress, and then only after the legislative branch has expressly and unequivocally stated its intent to alter or annul the diplomatic arrangement between the United States and a particular tribal nation. When the Supreme Court hands down opinions that by implication sever specific Indian treaty rights, and does so without a specific legislative mandate directing the termination of the treaty right, the Court has vastly overstepped its juridical power. In such instances, the Court violates the Constitution and acts contrary to the acknowledged trust relationship to tribes.

In the sixth chapter, we examine the often fractious relations among tribes and states in the context of the disclaimer clauses, inserted in many state enabling acts and constitutions, which explicitly prohibit states from interfering in the tribal-federal political relationship. When the U.S. Constitution was ratified, relations with tribes were firmly situated as the responsibility of Congress; in other words, official political relations with tribes were federalized. As new states entered the Union, especially in the West, they were required in their organic acts and constitutions to disclaim jurisdiction over Indian property and persons forever. In chapter 6 we examine "disclaimer clauses," explain the factors that have enabled states to assume some jurisdictional presence in Indian Country, point out the key issues where disclaimers continue to carry significant weight, and explain the vacillating role of the federal government, which has sometimes protected tribes from states and sometimes fostered state intrusions into tribal life. We argue that the federal government should reclaim its role as the lone constitutional authority to deal with indigenous nations. Disclaimer clauses are an important but often overlooked tool in the arsenal available to tribes to assert their own sovereignty against state threats and to privilege the tribal government-to-federal government relationship over any inappropriate intrusion by the states.

The doctrine of sovereign immunity is the last doctrine of federal Indian law we examine. In 1998, an editorial in the *New York Times* declared that "Senator Slade Gorton has once again declared war on the Indian." This declaration of war raises a number of troubling questions. What was the "war" about? Why was Senator Gorton, who was defeated in his reelection bid in 2000 in part because a number of Indian tribes in the region mounted a well-funded lobbying effort to oust him, the lead protagonist? What had prompted him on other occasions to wage "war" against native people? And what do the states and the federal government have to say?

To sum up, the war was about tribal sovereignty. Gorton, among others, was concerned that tribes, as sovereign governments, were immune to certain kinds of legal prosecution. This characteristic of sovereign governments—including federal, state, local, and tribal governments—is called "sovereign immunity." Tribes' inherent sovereignty and sovereign immunity were apparently deep affronts to Gorton's vision of America. Ex-Senator Gorton and others who deny the legal, political, and historical status of tribes as sovereigns are committed to reducing tribal nations to polities with no sovereignty, limited or otherwise, or perhaps even to oblivion. Some argue that tribes should have no standing at all, as governments, and that Indian individuals should be distinguished by nothing more than a particular "ethnicity," rather than a treaty-based political relationship with the United States. In chapter 7, we discuss the history of this doctrine and develop our arguments in support of tribal sovereign immunity based on court decisions, examples of when various governments have waived their immunity, and the fact that tribes do not exercise immunity in ways that fundamentally differ from those of other governments.

When we set out to write this book, we hoped to accomplish more than a mere recitation of historic moments, government actions, policymakers' beliefs, and judicial interpretations. We hope to help reinsert, and strengthen, an indigenous perspective in federal Indian policy and law. We hope that a detailed analysis of these founding and enduring principles of Indian law and policy, and constitutional doctrines, will provide an opportunity for critical evaluation. These doctrines and principles deserve critical analysis; some merit reconsideration, and others, firmly grounded in diplomacy and bilateral relations, merit support. We scrutinize these doctrines in order to educate, provoke, and motivate lawyers, judges and justices, congresspeople, state lawmakers, the executive agencies, and all American citizens to respect the Constitution, to respect tribes, and to respect themselves.

CHAPTER ONE

"THE LAW OF NATIONS": THE DOCTRINE OF DISCOVERY

Again, were we to inquire by what law or authority you set up a claim [to our land], I answer, none! Your laws extend not into our country, nor ever did. You talk of the law of nature and the law of nations, and they are both against you.

CORN TASSEL (Cherokee),
speech to U.S. commissioners seeking a peace treaty, 1785

One version of the European notion of a doctrine of discovery proposes that explorers' "discovery" of land in the Americas gave the discovering European nation—and the United States as successor—absolute legal title to, and ownership of, American soil. This popular and debilitating definition of discovery reduces Indian tribes to mere tenants, whose legal claims to their aboriginal homelands are secondary to the claims of the "discoverers." We call this sense of the doctrine of discovery the "expansive" definition. As recently as 1986, a federal district court recognized the European expansive doctrine of discovery as "a legal fiction,"[1] meaning that despite its use in popular language it has no foundation in law. Nevertheless, the expansive doctrine and an even more extreme definition of discovery meaning "absolute" title remain entrenched doctrines within federal Indian policy and law. The discovery doctrine, under both expansive and absolute guises, perpetuates a second-class national status for tribal nations and relegates individual Indians to a second-class citizenship status, because it strips tribes and individuals of their complete property rights. In these popular definitions, the doctrine granted full legal title (that is, full ownership) to American lands to the "discovering" European nations.[2] A less complete but still superior title was "inherited" by the United States of America, reducing tribes to mere "tenants."

We propose that an accurate definition of the doctrine of discovery is one that grants "discovering" European nations an exclusive, preemptive right to be the first purchaser of Indian land, should a tribe agree to sell any of its territory. Our definition of preemption is based on what Chief Justice John Marshall termed the "actual state of things" during the colonial and early American period.[3] A close examination of historic realities, the "actual state of affairs" as European and native nations negotiated and implemented land transfers, reveals that discovery did nothing more than grant an exclusive and preemptive right to buy, if tribal owners were inclined to sell. We call this definition the "preemptive" doctrine of discovery.

The absolute and expansive definitions, which imbue the doctrine of discovery with the power to assign land ownership unilaterally to European "discoverers," have come under increasing and well-deserved scrutiny by indigenous and nonindigenous scholars and commentators.[4] It is critically important to challenge these definitions because the discovery principle represents one leg of a framework of power. Discovery, along with the doctrines of plenary power and the trust principle,[5] among others to be discussed in the pages ahead, is part of a legal structure that generally privileges the powers of the federal government over the powers of tribes. These doctrines have often been defined and interpreted by American courts in ways that serve the interests of the United States, supporting its claim to be superior, politically and territorially, to indigenous nations.[6]

However, each of these problematic legal rules—plenary power, the trust principle, and discovery—has contrary meanings that support and enhance tribal sovereignty.[7] The contradictory essence of these important concepts makes this area of study simultaneously exciting and frustrating. The contrary definitions must be stated clearly, and the legal and historic basis in fact for each must be considered carefully. This chapter discusses the historic realities of European-native negotiation of land transfers and shows that those transfers, especially as they were accomplished through the treaty process, did not assume that a "doctrine of discovery" had vested land ownership in the "discovering" nations. The competing definitions of discovery are considered in turn and analyzed in terms of the legal justifications for their use. First, the expansive definition of discovery asserts that indigenous nations have an occupancy or possessory right to lands, but that they are incompetent to manage those lands and require a benevolent guardian who holds full legal title to native lands. This definition invokes a sense of the "benevolent paternalism" supposedly exercised toward tribes by European, and later the U.S., governments. Second, the absolute definition of discovery equates discovery with complete conquest. It denies any possibility that indigenous nations possessed aboriginal title, or even use and occupancy rights, to their lands. This definition implies no need for U.S. respect for native land rights. Finally, a third definition of discovery, as a preemptive doctrine granting an exclusive right of first purchase, is argued for as the legally and historically most authentic understanding of the term.

We examine three classes of evidence as we argue for the preemptive definition of the discovery doctrine. First, the actual political and diplomatic relations between native nations and Spain, France, Great Britain, and the United States constitute compelling evidence. The pragmatic realities of colonial interaction indicate that all these political "sovereigns" had to recognize indigenous title to land. Second, after the Revolutionary War, the new federal government of the United States continued European practices of treaty-making with Indian tribes. Detailed analysis of treaty language and treaty negotiations illustrates how the United States further confirmed indigenous land rights. Third, relevant Supreme Court decisions are analyzed for appropriate and inappropriate constructions of the discovery doctrine. Although the decision in *Johnson v. McIntosh* in 1823 articulated a definition of discovery that allegedly vested in the United States a legal title superior to that of the tribes, later decisions (*Worcester v. Georgia* and *Mitchel v. United States*) persuasively argued otherwise. We conclude that since the political branches of the federal government—the Congress and the executive—are constitutionally charged with establishing and maintaining the treaty relationship and with overseeing federal Indian policy, it is time for an important and long overdue corrective to be issued. The federal government should explicitly disavow the absolute and expansive definitions of the discovery doctrine and should turn away from legacies of conquest and benevolent paternalism.

COMPETING DEFINITIONS OF DISCOVERY

The first two definitions of the doctrine of discovery are dangerous in the current world because discovery, defined as conquest or as benevolent paternalism, belittles the autonomy of tribes. The doctrine deprives tribal nations, even as they enter the twenty-first century, of full legal ownership of the lands they have inhabited since time immemorial. As such, tribes are stripped of their most basic resource and are relatively powerless politically and economically compared to the federal government.

Absolute Definition: Discovery as Conquest

In its most brazen and negative sense, discovery is equated with conquest, with the complete subjugation of indigenous nations. In this sense, "discovery" has been a legal weapon in the service of the colonial juggernaut. In the case of *Tee-Hit-Ton v. United States*, 348 U.S. 272 (1955), the discovery principle was used to deny indigenous nations any legal title to their lands. *Tee-Hit-Ton* considered the legal standing of what has been termed "aboriginal title," a term that assumes that indigenous nations "owned" their lands in a way that European law could acknowledge through its notion of "title," meaning the written documents recording land boundaries. Proceeding from the Constitution's Fifth Amendment guarantee that the United States government would compensate any legal landowners (title-holders) if the government took or condemned their lands, the Court asked the question: does the United States owe compensation, under the terms of the Fifth Amendment, to indigenous nations if their land is taken by the United States? In other words, can tribes be considered legal landowners, in the sense of possessing a recognized title? The legal question rested on how to interpret or define the notion of aboriginal title. The Court had to decide whether aboriginal title constituted a legal title; if it did, then tribes should be compensated under the Fifth Amendment if that title was taken by the United States. In *Tee-Hit-Ton* the Supreme Court ruled that "Indian occupation of land without government recognition of ownership creates no rights against taking or extinction by the United States protected by the Fifth Amendment or any other principle of law" (348 U.S. 272 [1955], 285). The Constitution's Fifth Amendment protections were denied to tribes in this decision; tribal ownership of land was only deemed real if it was "recognized" by the U.S. government. Indigenous nations had no land rights based on their indigenous and original occupation of those lands.

The historic and legal evidence in this chapter demonstrates that the Court's conclusion in *Tee-Hit-Ton* represents the extreme application of the "discovery as conquest" interpretation of the discovery doctrine and that it is wholly without merit. The discovery principle, in this instance, is symbiotically linked with the equally problematic doctrine of conquest, another European-derived legal principle. The doctrine of conquest theoretically transfers ownership of territory from a state defeated in warfare to the victorious state. The conquest doctrine has been utilized by European colonial powers to justify their territorial acquisitions in much of Africa, parts of Asia, and portions of the Western Hemisphere throughout the last centuries. For example, Justice Stanley F. Reed described America's alleged conquest of Indians thus in *Tee-Hit-Ton v. United States* (1955): "Every American schoolboy knows that the savage tribes of this continent were deprived of their ancestral range by force and that, even when the Indians ceded millions of acres by treaty in return for blankets, food and trinkets, it was not a sale but the conquerors' will that deprived them of their land."[8] Reed's statement is one of the most glaring misrepresentations of fact ever uttered by a Supreme Court justice. Little in the historical record corroborates Justice Reed's contention—in fact, federal Indian policy and the history of treaty-making give ample evidence to the contrary. Article 3 of the 1787 Northwest Ordinance (1 St. 50, 1789) was one of the first major congressional policy pronouncements that stated that good faith, justice, and humanity—not military conquest—were the appropriate political and moral principles guiding the federal government's dealing with tribal nations. The federal government turned its back on the conquest doctrine when it chose to pursue a policy of purchasing Indian lands via treaties and agreements. Despite these facts, some justices have disputably argued that conquest provides a legal basis for the federal government's claims to title to Indian Country.

Expansive Definition: Discovery as Benevolent Paternalism

In 1831 Chief Justice John Marshall crafted a definition of discovery as benevolent paternalism in *Cherokee Nation v. Georgia*, 30 U.S. (5 Pet.) 1 (1831). In this definition of discovery (which bears a strong resemblance to certain interpretations of the federal trust doctrine, discussed in chapter 2) indigenous nations are imagined to be like children or wards, incompetent to manage their own territorial affairs. Tasks of land management, consolidation, and sales are left to the federal "guardian," who is empowered to act on behalf of the tribal wards because of their alleged technical and cultural shortcomings.

Although it can be forcefully argued that the so-called guardian-ward relationship is not synonymous with the more commonly asserted trustee-beneficiary relationship, the two relationships share a crucial assumption: that tribal nations do not possess full legal title to their territory but have merely a possessory or occupancy interest. The Indian occupancy or possessory right might have been recognized or established by aboriginal possession, treaty, congressional act, executive order, or purchase or by action of some other sovereign. Regardless, Indian nations are not seen as full legal owners, in the sense of title-holders. They hold an exclusive right of occupancy, but only rarely hold the ultimate fee to the land.[9]

Contemporary judicial interpretation, based on the expansive definition of the discovery principle, presumes that the federal government holds the ultimate title to Indian lands, subject to the Indian right of occupancy (possessory interests). That is to say, Indians retain rights to use and occupy their lands until such time as the federal government opts to purchase it, if the tribes have "recognized" title. Federal case law vacillates on the precise meaning of the Indian possessory title. Some opinions hold that it is a "mere" right of occupancy, while others refer to it as a "sacred" right of occupancy, but there is a general consensus that while Indian title is an exclusive right of occupancy, it does not involve an ultimate fee to the land (Cohen 1972, 293). Until such time as the federal government grants the actual fee-title to a tribe or individual Indian, the Indian title, it is said by those who support this perspective, cannot be sold without explicit authorization from the federal government.

Preemptive Definition: An Exclusive Right of First Purchase

The two previous definitions have, over the last one hundred years, evolved into the "dominant paradigm" defining Indian versus federal title to land. However, a critical reading of European and early American land policies, the literal language of European and early

American treaties, U.S. congressional directives, and specific comments from American officials vividly shows that the doctrine of
discovery is more correctly defined as an exclusive preemptive rule
that limited the rights of the discoverers or their successors and
that entailed no limitation on the preexisting land title of tribes.

Close examination of land policies and treaty language of the
Spanish, French, and English sovereigns points to the historic, "real
life" limitations on the parameters of the discovery doctrine. Taken
together with numerous examples from the American period, these
colonial era cases illustrate how a preemptive right to first purchase, with no inherent limitations on tribal land title, constitutes
a realistic and pragmatic definition of the discovery doctrine.

INDIGENOUS LAND TITLE AS RECOGNIZED BY
EUROPEAN AND U.S. POWERS

Of the various European nation-states that colonized North America, Spain, France, and Great Britain exerted the most lasting influence upon tribes and federal Indian policy. Their respective Indian
policies, crafted according to each nation's unique mix of religious,
cultural, economic, and political factors, have been chronicled elsewhere and are not repeated here.[10] Each nation developed distinctive colonial policies, but they shared common ground because of
the strengths of native nations: "Indian cooperation was the prime
requisite for European penetration and colonization of the North
American continent."[11]

This is not to say that the competing European powers always
sought out the cooperation of indigenous peoples or that the level
of violence was not high. Violence was endemic, even epidemic.
Acknowledging the necessity of cooperation with tribes means
acknowledging historic reality. If tribes had not been willing and
able to negotiate a plethora of diplomatic arrangements with various competing intruders, the violence would likely have been
worse. If European nations and the United States had not recognized
the necessity of negotiation, the important extant treaty legacy of

each of these states with tribal nations would not have evolved to the degree it did. As Robert A. Williams, an Indian legal scholar, shows in his recent study, "in the seventeenth and eighteenth century Encounter era, European colonists often found themselves outnumbered and outflanked with a bare foothold on the North American continent. During much of this period, whites in their small colonial settlements were not the dominant power on the continent. They soon learned that their survival, flourishing, and expansion could be better secured through cooperative relationships with surrounding Indian tribes rather than through wars and conflict" (Williams 1997, 20–21).[12]

Spanish Recognition of Indian Title

In the 1530s the Catholic king of Spain asked Francisco de Vitoria, a prominent Spanish theologian, to address the rights of the Spanish in the New World. By extension, de Vitoria also addressed what rights, if any, the indigenous peoples retained in the face of Spanish colonialism. Spanish administrators were already reaping the political and economic benefits of destructive policies such as the *requerimiento* (a formal document of conquest), the *encomienda* (a system of enslavement of indigenous people, who were assigned to a colonial overseer or enslaver, known as the *encomendero*), and the related *repartimiento* (a system of wage assessments the Spanish Crown levied on Indian communities) (Gibson 1988, 96–102).

When de Vitoria delivered his lecture in 1532 entitled "On the Indians Lately Discovered," he confirmed that the indigenous peoples possessed natural rights and that as free people they were the "true owners" of the land they inhabited. De Vitoria jettisoned the doctrine of discovery, which had been used by Spanish explorers—with the pope's blessing—to justify Spanish land claims and to deny the Indians' aboriginal claims to their lands. He overturned the discovery doctrine as a basis on which the Spanish could claim legal title to inhabited Indian land.

De Vitoria's lectures were not entirely a pro-Indian manifesto. He asserted that the Law of Nations required Indians to allow the Spanish the right to travel through Indian lands and to trade with them (Williams 1990). His comments on the discovery doctrine, however, merit close attention here. Since Indians owned the land, the Spanish Crown could not claim title through discovery. Title by discovery was valid only where property was vacant and owners did not exist. In the absence of a just war, only the voluntary consent of the Indians could justify the confiscation of Indian land (Deloria and Lytle 1983, 2–3; Williams 1990, 96–108).

The negotiation of treaties was the most practical procedure, at least in North America, that the Spanish and other European nations used to secure the goodwill and consent of tribes. Treaties accomplished many purposes: to establish peace, friendship, trade, and military alliance; to delineate territorial boundaries and land cessions; and to secure European footholds on the frontier against other European competitors. As Dorothy Jones (1988) and Robert A. Williams (1997) show, the majority of these treaty arrangements were steeped in indigenous understandings of diplomacy: "The protocols and ceremonies of this indigenous North American language of diplomacy were rarely European because it was a language grounded in indigenous North American visions of law and peace between different peoples. The hierarchical, feudal symbols of seventeenth- and eighteenth-century European diplomacy simply did not translate well on the North American colonial frontier" (Williams 1997, 31).

Spain negotiated a multitude of treaties with southeastern (Choctaw, Creek, Seminole) and southwestern (Navajo, Apache) tribal nations from the early 1700s through the early 1800s. The Navajos, for example, signed four treaties with the Spanish, from 1706 to 1819 (and six with the Mexican government, from 1822 to 1844). One purpose of these diplomatic arrangements was to recognize the territorial boundaries of the Navajo Nation (Wilkins 1999, 73). The treaties, in fact, did not stipulate Spanish land ownership of Indian lands, though the Crown did claim sovereignty or dominion (jurisdiction or control) vis-à-vis other European nations, and sometimes over indigenous peoples as well. A claim of sovereignty, however, does not equate with a claim of ownership—it is a claim of political jurisdiction, not an assertion of land title.

A treaty negotiated on May 31 and June 1, 1784, between Spain and the Talapuchys (Seminoles), Natchez, and Chickasaws, verifies the distinction between political jurisdiction and land ownership. The preamble states that the parties desired "unanimously to obliterate the remembrance of the evils caused by the last war, and to make all the subjects of Catholic majesty enjoy the fruits of peace, to conclude and cement, on the most solid foundations, the friendship and good union which the Spanish nation proffers to the Talapuchy tribes" (U.S. Congress 1832, 278). The first articles contain the major goals of the treaty: (1) to maintain an "inviolable peace and fidelity," (2) to encourage "commerce permanent and unalterable," and (3) to establish a firm military alliance, with the Talapuchys agreeing to arrest any person entering their country "with the insidious idea of inducing us to take up arms" against the king of Spain. The concluding provision, Article 13, deals specifically with Indian title, and the Spanish negotiators unequivocally acknowledged the Indians' territorial rights: "As the generous mind of his Catholic Majesty does not exact from the nations of Indians any lands to form establishments, to the prejudice of the right of those who enjoy them, in consequence, and with a knowledge of his paternal love towards his beloved nations, we promise, in his royal name, the security and guarantee of those which they actually hold, according to the right of property with which they possess them, on condition that they are comprehended within the lines and limits of his Catholic Majesty, our sovereign" (ibid., 279). Although the ubiquitous paternalistic language directs the Indians to acknowledge the sovereignty of the Spanish king, this article recognizes full indigenous ownership of their lands.

A few years later, in 1790, the Spanish Crown negotiated another treaty of friendship, with the Chickasaws and Choctaws. The three nations promised to "love one another reciprocally" and to act as

staunch allies should any other party attempt to interfere. The
treaty also demarcated the boundaries of the Spanish Crown (in
La Florida and Louisiana) and the territory of the two tribes. Article 4 stated that "the Spanish nation declares and acknowledges
that all the lands to the east of the said dividing line of the 2d article belong lawfully and indisputably to the Chickasaw and
Choctaw nations, promising to support them therein with all their
power" (ibid., 280).

French Recognition of Indian Title

France's policy toward tribal nations and lands differed substantively from both Spain's and Great Britain's. In 1897 Frances Parkman, a prominent historian, wrote this pithy, if oversimplified,
summation of the three competitors' views of Indian tribes: "Spanish civilization crushed the Indian; English civilization scorned and
neglected him; French civilization embraced and cherished him"
(Wade 1988, 20). On the whole, most commentators agree with
Parkman's assessment, particularly as he alludes to the French willingness to interact closely with Indian peoples. As Mason Wade
described it: "The French, with their lack of racial prejudice, were
able to achieve a much closer relationship with the Indians than
any other European colonists in North America" (ibid.).[13]

The French were active in North America from the time of
Jacques Cartier's travels in the Northeast in 1534 to their final
defeat by the English in the French and Indian War in 1763. In the
Treaty of Paris, which contained the terms of peace, French Canada
and lands east of the Mississippi were ceded to Great Britain
(Nugent 1994, 817). French fur traders, Jesuit missionaries, and sol-
diers, who probably never totaled more than 70,000 as late as 1759,
inhabited the vast area from Quebec to the Great Lakes and south
to New Orleans, Louisiana. In part because of their small numbers,
but also because of concerted governmental policy and their emphasis on trade rather than permanent settlement, the French tended
to get along with many tribes. A major advantage of this generally

peaceful coexistence was that there were few contentious encounters over land. As Cyrus Thomas noted in his analysis of French
policy toward Indian lands: "A somewhat thorough examination
of the documents and histories relating to French dominion in
Canada and Louisiana fails to reveal any settled or regularly
defined policy in regard to the extinguishment of the Indian title
to land" (Thomas 1899, 545). An example of a land transaction in
colonial Illinois in the early 1700s exemplifies French concern with
Indian title. A French man wished to purchase property from a
married French couple. The purchaser of the deeded property was
advised that the deed was valid unless the Indians—the original
owners—decided to retake the property. A caveat such as this
would most likely not have been found in contemporary land
exchanges among the English (Gitlin 1994, 108).

Throughout the vast territory they explored, trapped, and sparsely
settled, the French apparently made no recorded efforts to claim
Indian land based on the doctrine of discovery, although in their
treaty negotiations (like the Spanish) they encouraged signatory
tribes to refer to the French king as their "sovereign," and they tried,
unsuccessfully, to place the tribes in a subject status. France des-
perately needed various tribes as trade, political, and military allies
in the economic wars—most notably the fur trade—against their
primary competitors, the British. Political exigency did not support
the false belief that tribes were their subjects. These circumstances,
in fact, compelled the French in the late 1500s and early 1600s into
a number of unrecorded trade and military pacts with the tribes of
northeastern North America (Abenaki, Micmac, Nipissing, Huron,
Montagnais, Maliseet, Passamoquoddy, and Algonquian) against
the powerful Iroquois Confederacy, whose tribes traded from their
territory in northern New York, first with the Dutch and later with
the English (Delage 1993, 95).

The extant treaty record between the French and indigenous
nations is, unfortunately, quite slight, but a few treaties were formally recorded in French and later translated into English.[14] A
majority of the early French/indigenous alliances were conducted

in the traditional manner. These delicate multicultural negotiations were prolonged conferences where the leaders of both parties discussed the key points in detail and at length, exchanged presents and other items, and participated in tribally appropriate cultural ceremonies to seal the arrangement. On December 13, 1665, Gov. Chevalier Seigneur de Tracy and others representing France signed a treaty of peace with leaders of several member nations of the Iroquois Confederacy (Onondaga, Cayuga, Seneca, and Oneida). The treaty was negotiated at Quebec. None of its provisions involved any French claims to Indian lands. In an attached note entitled "Ratification by the Senecas of the preceding treaty," it was stated that the French had "discovered their Country" and that the Senecas were to be considered "faithful subjects." This assertion of sovereignty was immediately counterbalanced by the statement that "it might please his Majesty to continue it [their lands] to them." The French wanted the Indians to consider themselves French subjects for alliance purposes, but knew that any attempt to claim title to Indian lands would have been met with disbelief and fierce resistance.[15]

Some years later, in 1688, the Onondagas, Cayugas, and Oneidas agreed to remain neutral in the latest war between the French and the English. Their "declaration of neutrality" impressively described these tribal nations' title to their lands. The nations stressed that "they held their country directly of God, and had never been conquered in war, neither by the French nor the English, and that their intention was only to observe a perfect neutrality" (O'Callaghan 1855, vol. 9, 384–85).

British Recognition of Indian Title

Unlike France, Britain and its American colonies were more interested in permanent settlement than in trade and political alliances with the tribes. Commerce, of course, played a crucial role in tribal/British affairs, but it was intimately connected to English colonization goals. While there was a measure of intermixture between tribes and the British, at least in early diplomatic negotiations, segregation of white and native societies was more the norm, and the British aimed to replace tribes with white colonists (Prucha 1962).[16] Simple replacement was not easily realized, however, and British policy toward tribal nations evolved in unpredictable and ad hoc ways over a 200-year period.

One somewhat predictable aspect of British Indian policy was that "it allowed no special place for the American Indian, who was regarded as a kind of non-person" (Jacobs 1988, 5). Notwithstanding this ethnocentric perspective, as the historian Dorothy Jones points out in her article "British Colonial Indian Treaties," in the 175 treaties negotiated between Britain and Indian tribes from 1607 (with the Powhatan Confederacy of Virginia) to 1775 (with the Iroquois of Ohio, the Shawnees, and the Delawares and the Virginia colonies), a "new kind of diplomacy took shape" when the British and the tribes met on the frontier in treaty negotiations. This diplomacy "developed its own protocols and ceremonies, and these were rarely European" (Jones 1988, 185).

The establishment of peace and the negotiation of military or trade alliances were the most common treaty goals, especially from 1700 to 1763, when the French and Spanish still had designs on North America. Treaties devoted to Indian land cessions confirmed the reality that the negotiating tribes were the true owners of the soil. The British Crown's or colonists' "purchase" of Indian territory via treaties or deeds clearly acknowledged that the doctrine of discovery did not limit Indian land rights, but did constrain inter-European claims in North America. For example, in a peace treaty between Governor Richard Nicolls of New York and the Esopus Indians, dated October 3, 1665, the tribe ceded a tract of land to the governor in exchange for blankets, powder, and other implements. Article 5 stated that "the said Sachems and their Subjects now present do for and in the names of themselves and their heirs forever, give, Grant, alienate and confirme all their Right and Interest, Claime or demand to a certaine Parcell of Land . . . to bee given, granted and confirmed unto the said Richard Nicolls . . . to hold and Enjoy the same as his free Land and Possession against any Clayme hereafter to bee made by the said Sachems or their Subjects" (Vaughan 1985, 307–10). This provision unequivocally places title in the hands of the Esopus, prior to the transfer to Governor Nicolls.

A multitude of troubles, however, marred the smooth transfer of Indian land title to the English, including the chaotic mix of English economic, moral, and political motives, conflicting policies among the individual colonies, and the international competition from Spain and France. In addition, individual colonists, land speculating companies, colonial governments, and the Crown itself rarely shared common interests or attitudes toward the tribes.

With chaos reigning supreme by the mid-1700s, the British government decided it was time to impose more structure on Indian affairs by centralizing Indian policy in the hands of the Crown. Tribes were dissatisfied as well and had complained frequently to British and colonial authorities about the unmasked pressures bearing on Indian lands. When Iroquois leaders met the colonial delegates at the Albany Conference in June 1754, they candidly stated their grievances. The sale of liquor was troublesome to the Iroquois Confederacy, but their greatest concern was the unscrupulous scramble for their land. "We understand that there are writings for all our lands, so that we shall have none left but the very spot we live upon and hardly that" (Horowitz 1978, 169). The Albany delegates responded with a structured plan, written by Benjamin Franklin, but heavily influenced by the Iroquois Confederacy's system of government. The plan proposed to unite the colonies under a general government, with a president general and Grand Council, which would manage the affairs of the United States in matters of defense and commerce with the Indians. The premature plan failed, however, because the colonial assemblies were not yet prepared to surrender any sovereignty to establish a central government (ibid.).

British officials recognized the pressing need for more centralized authority and predictable policy, if they wanted Indian tribes to remain their allies. Accordingly, in 1755–56, the Crown created northern and southern departments of Indian affairs, headed respectively by superintendents William Johnson and Edmond Atkin. The superintendents, rather than individual colonies, had full command of political relations with Indian tribes. Johnson's jurisdiction included the powerful Iroquois Confederacy, and he was expected to ease the concerns of the Indians "with respect to the Lands which have been fraudulently taken from them" and to address other grievances including trade (Horowitz 1978, 179).

The year 1763 proved significant for British/French/Indian relations. By the Treaty of Paris, ending the Seven Years' War with France, the English claimed all of French Canada and North America east of the Mississippi, as well as Spanish Florida. England was now the dominant European power in eastern North America. Tribal nations, many of whom had allied with the French, distrusted the encroaching English. In the spring of 1763, Indians throughout the Ohio Valley and the Great Lakes launched assaults against the British and captured a number of forts. The assault, "traditionally attributed to the ambition of the Ottawa leader Pontiac, was in fact a wide-ranging attempt to establish a native position of power at a time of uncertainty and change, and although the British retook their posts by 1765, the natives' point was made. In later calculations, the English would weigh Indian perceptions and demands more heavily" (West 1994, 118).

As a direct result of this flexing of indigenous military muscle, the Crown issued the royal proclamation of October 7, 1763. The proclamation recalled all settlers from west of the crest of the Appalachian Mountains, forbade emigration there until further notice, and authorized *only* licensed government agents to trade with the Indians (Jacobs 1988). The most important measure in the proclamation regarding Indian title to lands was the establishment of a boundary line between British and Indian territories—a clear delineation of Indian ownership of Indian Country. The reality of tribal resistance to British encroachment motivated the idea of the boundary line. The proclamation nullified the preposterous theory that the "sea to sea" land claims common to colonial charters had any real force in the world (ibid., 10).

Unfortunately, the royal proclamation only substituted one theory for another: the north-south boundary line separating Indian land from Anglo settlements never became a reality. Surveys were never completed, and the boundary proved impossible to enforce. Colonists, land speculators, and fur traders agitated for access to and ownership of more Indian territory. Pressures were so great that in the 1768 Treaty of Fort Stanwix, which modified the proclamation, the Iroquois nations ceded a large tract of land to Britain. Despite the exception of the Fort Stanwix treaty, Britain was trying to slow frontier expansion. In 1773 an act was passed that forbade any new grants to speculators. In 1774 the Quebec Act closed the entire area north of the Ohio River to all but the most limited trade and settlement. The *idea* of a boundary line was a fundamental tool of both British and American policymakers. Although American colonists breached "the line" in reality, policymakers were trying to recognize tribal lands and to assure the tribes that their remaining territory would be protected from intrusion. It remains an important concept of federal Indian policy and law even today.

U.S. Recognition of Indian Title

In its earliest years, the United States may have preferred an absolute or expansive definition of the discovery doctrine, but the historical record tells us that was an unrealistic hope. For a brief period from 1784 to 1787, the federal government spoke haughtily of claiming the Indians' country by "right of conquest," especially the country of tribes who had sided with Great Britain in the war.[17] Despite such extravagant claims, the tribes maintained that they had not been conquered and that their lands rightfully remained in their possession. A close reading of recorded statements of indigenous leaders, of the literal language of the early treaty record from the 1780s through the early 1800s, and of the policy pronouncements of congressional committees, the president, and highly placed federal officials demonstrates that in reality, when the federal government dealt with tribes, it exercised an exclusive, preemptive right to be the first purchaser of any lands tribes might choose to sell.

When the thirteen colonies declared their independence from Great Britain they claimed that the king of England had "endeavored to bring on the inhabitants of our frontiers the merciless Indian savages, whose known rule of warfare is an undistinguished destruction of all ages, sexes, and condition" (Declaration of Independence). Although the colonists misrepresented the realities of colonial warfare, their claim did acknowledge, in a graphic way, tribal sovereignty and independence. The early republic unhappily had to recognize that virtually all Indian nations allied with Great Britain against the upstart colonies. The colonists, after all, were endeavoring to acquire Indian lands, through fair means or foul; the Crown had made at least feeble attempts, through the 1763 proclamation, to protect Indian ownership and land tenure.

The American defeat of the British and their Indian allies was confirmed by the Treaty of Paris, drawn up in 1782 and signed on September 3, 1783. Britain not only granted the new nation its independence, but also ceded jurisdictional claims and preemptive rights to a tremendous expanse of land stretching in the north to the St. Lawrence River and the Great Lakes, in the west to the Mississippi River, and in the south to the thirty-first parallel (West 1994, 123). Despite the expansive breadth of the Treaty of Paris, not all tribal nations had allied with the British, and not all British allies had participated in treaty negotiations—what was to happen to them in the new republic?

During the American republic's fragile formative years, the central government keenly wished to maintain peace with tribal nations, to clarify its title to land its citizens occupied, and to assure tribes that their territorial rights and boundaries would be respected, lest the tribes align with Spain or Great Britain. The United States knew it had to appease the tribes and assured the Indians that their lands would be protected. In the first weeks after the Treaty of Paris was signed, evidence indicates that the United States did not assume an expansive definition of the discovery doctrine. Less than three

weeks after the treaty, Congress formally forbade white settlement
on Indian lands outside state jurisdiction and regulated the sale of
Indian land. Like the royal proclamation of 1763, this legislation
declared that no purchase of Indian land by states or individuals
would be valid without the express sanction of the Congress. Congress meant to reassure the tribes that their preexisting land rights
would be protected from persons or companies bent on their appropriation (Prucha 1962, 32). This congressional action is among the
first important evidence that the fledgling nation exercised a
restricted vision of the discovery doctrine. The United States had
assumed Britain's obligations as the preeminent sovereign with the
right of first purchase of Indian land—no more, and no less.

Tribal nations during this same period, at a minimum, worked
to maintain a fixed boundary between their lands and those of
European nation-states and the United States and to secure formal
acknowledgments of their independent status, their jurisdictional
control over aboriginal territories, and their access to an unimpeded
flow of European manufactured goods (Jones 1982, 44). As already
mentioned, there is evidence that some American policymakers
immediately after the Revolutionary War felt that they could dic-
tate terms to those tribes who had allied militarily with Great
Britain. In a letter written to James Duane on September 7, 1783, just
four days after the Treaty of Paris was signed, George Washington,
commander in chief of the Continental Army, chastised several
tribes for having joined with Britain, but hastened to add that the
federal government was magnanimous enough to forgive them:

> But as we prefer Peace to a State of Warfare, as we consider
> them [tribes] as a deluded people; as we perswade [sic] our-
> selves that they are convinced, from experience, of their error
> in taking up the Hatchet against us, and that their true Inter-
> est and safety must now depend upon *our* friendship. As the
> Country, is large enough to contain us all; and as we are dis-
> posed to be kind to them and to partake of their Trade, we
> will from these considerations and from motives of Compn.,

[*sic*: compassion] draw a veil over what is past and establish a boundary line between them and us beyond which we will *endeavor* to restrain our People from Hunting and Settling. (Prucha 1990, 1; emphasis in the original)

Even in this mild rebuke of tribes, Washington articulated the need for a boundary line to separate Indian territory from American. Nevertheless, he also clearly wanted the Indians to understand that the Americans would request additional land cessions to accommodate the land-hungry population and the increasing flow of European immigrants. Washington understood that orderly westward expansion depended on peaceful dealings with the tribes. "I am clear in my opinion," noted Washington, "that policy and economy point very strongly to the expediency of being upon good terms with the Indians, and the propriety of purchasing their Lands in preference to attempting to drive them by force of arms out of their Country" (Prucha 1990, 2).

Policy, economy, and propriety were not the only reasons to recognize native title and to purchase lands. Any unilateral federal claims to Indian territory under the doctrines of discovery and conquest were bound to spark significant indigenous resistance. In addition, after the Revolutionary War, Great Britain diplomatically supported indigenous land rights. As Jones notes: "When the northern and western Indians asserted that the [1768] Fort Stanwix line was the only proper boundary between their lands and that of white America, British officials backed the assertion. The officials assured the Indians that *Americans had no claim whatsoever to land beyond the Ohio, since King George would not and could not have given to the Americans what he had no right to give*" (Jones 1982, 142; emphasis added).

In 1786 the Shawnee Chief Kekewepellethe addressed expansive United States claims to native lands: "and as to the land, God gave us this country, we do not understand measuring out the land, it is all ours" (Prucha 1994, 51). Ultimately, the fear of war compelled American policymakers to abandon their pretentious claims to Indian soil based on an expansive doctrine of conquest. Concern over negative world opinion of the new republic, the probability of intense tribal resistance, and the costs of warfare in dollars and lives reinforced Secretary of War Henry Knox's views that the United States should operate its Indian policy from principles of humanity and honorable intentions—not conquest. Neither an expansive sense of discovery nor an absolute definition of the term was part of his discourse. As a result, U.S. relations with native nations, especially and particularly land transactions, were carried out through the treaty process, and it is to treaties that we turn next.

THE CONFIRMATION OF INDIGENOUS LAND RIGHTS IN AMERICAN INDIAN TREATIES

The negotiation, ratification, and proclamation of Indian treaties affirmed the political status of indigenous nations as distinctive sovereigns exercising inherent sovereign powers. The treaty relationship means that tribal nations enjoy a nation-to-nation relationship with the United States that can be termed "extraconstitutional." Tribes existed as sovereigns before the Constitution, the founding document of the United States, was drafted. Tribes predate the Constitution, so in a legal sense they have an existence "outside" the Constitution. No other racial/ethnic group in America signed treaties with the federal government; hence American Indians have a unique political status in this country that distinguishes them from other "minority" groups.

The unique triumvirate of rights articulated in treaties further distinguishes Indians from all other groups and individuals in the United States. The triumvirate includes corporate rights such as self-government, individual rights such as eligibility for allotments, and property rights such as rights to hunt, fish, and gather (Deloria 1994). Indian treaties are, of course, susceptible to the political machinations of the political and judiciary branches, but they are according to the Constitution the supreme law of the land until they are expressly disavowed by Congress. Treaties express the core foundation of rights enjoyed by tribal nations. Many treaties, as legal documents, functioned to transfer land titles from native nations to the United States. Land cessions from tribes to the United States were the basis for the vast expansion of federal territory in the nineteenth century. What treaties say about land, and how they articulate notions of land ownership and land transfer, constitutes critical evidence as we evaluate the different definitions of discovery. Because of significant changes in the political landscape, treaties negotiated before the War of 1812 and those after it will be considered as two separate groups. Between the Revolutionary War and the War of 1812, tribes had the diplomatic backing of Great Britain, which supported their territorial rights. Defeat in the War of 1812 removed Britain as a major political player along the United States' western frontier. It makes sense, then, to group U.S. treaties with tribes in terms of these two distinct political eras. Segregating treaties in this way also reinforces the validity of a restricted notion of the discovery principle. We might expect the nascent American nation to curtail its claims while Britain was still a power to be reckoned with, but even the treaties negotiated with tribes *after* the War of 1812 do not claim more than a preemptive right to buy any lands that tribes wish to sell.

Revolutionary War to the War of 1812

Most of the treaties negotiated between tribes and the United States between the Revolutionary War and the War of 1812 were designed to restore peace on the frontier and in the interior.[18] The first major Indian land cession treaty was the Treaty with the Wyandots and other tribes at Fort Harmar on January 9, 1789 (7 Stat., 28).[19] This treaty was negotiated by the sachems and warriors of the assembled tribes, on the one part, and by Commissioner Arthur St. Clair, governor of the Northwest Territory, for the United States. Article 2 established a permanent boundary line between the tribes and the United States, and the Indians ceded a tract of land in exchange for federal protection and $6,000 worth of goods.

According to the treaty, the tribes "release, quit claim, relinquish and cede to the said United States all the land . . . above described, so far as the said Indians formerly claimed the same; for them the said United States to have and to hold the same in true and absolute propriety forever" (ibid., Article 2).

In Article 3, the United States announced that it relinquished and quit claim to all the lands the tribes reserved (in other words, retained or kept for themselves) under Article 2. The only claims the United States had to the reserved Indian lands were based on the doctrine of discovery; but here discovery clearly entailed preemption, not ownership. The restricted sense of discovery is manifest in the language of the closing section: "But the said nations, or either of them, *shall not be at liberty to sell or dispose of the same, or any part thereof, to any sovereign power, except the United States; nor to the subjects or citizens of any other sovereign power, nor to the subjects or citizens of the United States*" (ibid., Article 3; emphasis added). If the United States felt it actually "owned"—in the sense of possessing full legal title to—Indian lands under the doctrine of discovery, then the treaty language should have reflected that. The lands "reserved" by the Indians would have been assumed to be lands already "owned" by the United States, and the treaty language would only have to stipulate that the United States was relinquishing its claims to the tribes. Instead, the government's negotiators insisted on including language in the treaty that if the tribes chose to sell any part of their reserved lands, they must sell to no other sovereign "except the United States." This language reflects an understanding that tribes *had* owned the lands they were ceding to the United States and that they *still* owned the lands they were reserving. The only right the United States could assert was the preemptive right to buy those reserved lands if the tribe ever decided to sell them. This treaty language exemplifies a classic preemptive definition of the doctrine of discovery.

Several months later, on June 15, 1789, Secretary of War Henry Knox reported to President Washington concerning the Wabash and other Indians who lived northwest of the Ohio River (U.S.

Congress 1832, 12–14). Knox forcefully advised that justice and dignity, rather than force of arms, should guide principles of federal Indian policy. He also acknowledged the Indians' ownership rights to their property in remarkably unclouded language: "The Indians being the prior occupants, possess the right of soil. It cannot be taken from them unless by their free consent, or by the right of conquest in a case of a just war. To dispossess them on any other principle, would be a gross violation of the fundamental laws of nature, and of that distributive justice which is the glory of a nation.... The principle of the Indians' right to the lands they possess being thus conceded, the dignity and interest of the nation will be advanced by making it the basis of the future administration of justice towards the Indian tribes" (ibid., 13).

Some scholars, including Francis P. Prucha, a noted historian of federal Indian policy, contend that "the right of soil" Knox acknowledged here was little more than a right of occupancy, which "permitted occupants to enjoy the usufruct of the land as long as they occupied it" (Prucha 1994, 226). The United States, Prucha asserts, held the fee-simple right of absolute dominion over the land based on the discovery principle. The historical evidence cited above does not support his contentions. Scholars such as Dorothy Jones (1982), also a historian, paint a more realistic picture. By the post-revolutionary period the United States was forced to acknowledge that it had a curtailed sovereignty because tribes had preexisting territorial rights.

More evidence to corroborate a restricted, preemptive definition of the discovery principle is found in a September 27, 1792, treaty of peace and friendship between the Wabash and Illinois tribes and the United States. Brig. Gen. Rufus Putnam negotiated on behalf of the federal government. After the two tribal nations agreed to perpetual peace and placed themselves under the protection of the United States, Article 4 affirmed their unabridged land rights. "The United States solemnly guaranty to the Wabash, and the Illinois nations, or tribes of Indians, all the lands to which they have a just claim; and no part shall ever be taken from them, but by a fair purchase, and to their satisfaction. *That the lands originally belonged to the Indians; it is theirs, and theirs only. That they have a right to sell, and a right to refuse to sell. And that the United States will protect them in their said just rights*" (U.S. Congress 1832, 338; emphasis added). This unequivocal language shows that the United States was fully cognizant of the Indians' unencumbered title to their territory. When President Washington communicated this treaty to the Senate for ratification on February 13, 1793, he urged the Senate to add an exclusive preemption statement to the fourth article that would grant the United States first opportunity to purchase any lands the Indians might, in the future, decide to sell. Political maneuvering within the Senate committee, the decimation of signatory Wabash chiefs by smallpox (Prucha 1994), and more warfare thwarted the insertion of a "first purchaser" clause.

The powerful Iroquois Confederacy also participated in treaties that confirmed their undivided title to their lands. The Treaty with the Six Nations (7 Stat., 44) in the fall of 1794 is one such document. In Article 2, the United States acknowledged the lands reserved to the Cayugas, Onondagas, and Oneidas in their treaties with New York State "to be their property; and the United States will never claim the same, nor disturb them or either of the Six Nations, nor their Indian friends residing thereon and united with them, in the free use and enjoyment thereof: *but the said reservations shall remain theirs until they choose to sell the same to the people of the United States, who have the right to purchase*" (ibid.; emphasis added). The federal government here secured the right of preemption it had been unable to gain in the earlier Wabash/Illinois treaty. Thomas Jefferson explained what exclusive preemption meant: "I consider our right of preemption of the Indian lands, not as amounting to any dominion, or jurisdiction, or paramountship whatever, but merely in the nature of a remainder after the extinguishment of a present right, which gave us no present right whatever, but of preventing other nations from taking possession, and so defeating our expectancy; *that the Indians had the full, undivided and independent sovereignty as long as they choose to keep it, and that this might be forever*" (Prucha

1994, 227; emphasis added). The right of exclusive preemption expressed in these and other treaties, as endorsed by Congress and the president, is a wholly different entity from the notion of absolute proprietorship or fee-simple title that Chief Justice John Marshall proposed in his interpretation of the doctrine of discovery.

Analysis of a pivotal treaty—the Treaty of Greenville (7 Stat., 49)—provides another set of historical and political data that defangs the absolute and expansive notions of discovery. This treaty was negotiated after American troops led by Gen. Anthony Wayne defeated Indian forces at the Battle of Fallen Timbers on the Maumee River. The Indians had learned that their former ally, Great Britain, would no longer assist them, and one might expect that the United States would take advantage of the situation to assert a more expansive notion of land claims. Despite the favorable military and political climate, the literal language of the treaty laid no federal claims to absolute sovereignty or proprietorship over the lands retained by the Indian nations. Although the signatory tribes ceded an enormous amount of land to the United States,[20] including the southern part of Ohio and lands in present-day Indiana, a permanent boundary line was established between the tribes' reserved lands (north of the Ohio, east of the Mississippi, and south of the Great Lakes) and those of the United States.

More importantly, the language of Article 5 reiterated earlier treaties. The tribes were the only legitimate proprietors of their remaining territory, and the United States sought assurances that it would have preemptive rights to purchase tribal lands in the future:

> The Indian tribes who have a right to those lands, are quietly to enjoy them, hunting, planting, and dwelling thereon so long as they please, without any molestation from the United States; but when those tribes, or any of them, shall be disposed to sell their lands, or any part of them, they are to be sold only to the United States; and until such sale, the United States will protect all the said Indian tribes in the quiet enjoyment of their

lands against all citizens of the United States, and against all other white persons who intrude upon the same. And the said Indian tribes again acknowledge themselves to be under the protection of the said United States and no other power whatever. (ibid., Article 5)

In Article 4, the United States promised to relinquish its claim to remaining tribal lands, but the government was relinquishing its exclusive right of preemption, not ownership of the Indians' land. The United States, to reassure the tribes and clarify exactly what they were relinquishing, stated in the first section of Article 5:

To prevent any misunderstanding about the Indian lands relinquished by the United States in the fourth article [the lands retained by the tribes], it is now explicitly declared, that the meaning of that relinquishment is this. The Indian tribes who have a right to those lands, are quietly to enjoy them, hunting, planting, and dwelling thereon so long as they please, without any molestation from the United States; but when those tribes, or any of them, shall be disposed to sell their lands, or any part of them, they are to be sold only to the United States; and until such sale, the United States will protect all the said Indian tribes in the quiet enjoyment of their lands against all citizens of the United States, and against all other white persons who intrude upon the same. (ibid.)

One other treaty negotiated before the War of 1812 contains this exclusive purchase provision. In an agreement with the Sac and Fox Indians on November 3, 1804 (7 Stat., 84), Article 4 states emphatically that the United States would never interfere with the Indians' land rights and that the government would "protect" the tribes in the enjoyment of their lands against all others. "And the said tribes," it was declared, "do hereby engage that they will never sell their lands or any part thereof to any sovereign power, *but the United States*, nor to the citizens or subjects of any other sovereign power, nor to the citizens of the United States" (ibid., Article 4; emphasis added).

If the United States literally "owned" all of America under an absolute or expansive doctrine of discovery, why would the government insist on a preemptive clause in treaties that insured the first option to purchase tribal lands? The answer is that the doctrine of discovery did not directly bear on the tribes' actual property rights. The best the United States could hope for—and so insisted upon—was that the signatory tribes would consent to give the federal government first purchase rights. As we have seen, the tribes agreed to this clause on a number of occasions.

After the War of 1812

When the United States acquired a massive territory from France through the Louisiana Purchase in 1803, new opportunities arose for national development, western expansion, and Indian policy experimentation. Although President Jefferson had occasionally proposed removal of eastern Indian tribes to lands west of the Mississippi, he was more keen on their being civilized and assimilated into American culture (Horsman 1988, 36). Tribes, on the contrary, were increasingly willing to go to war to stem the tide of whites into their country. By 1805, the Shawnee Prophet Tenskwatawa, and his brother Tecumseh, sought to unite indigenous resistance throughout the Ohio Valley, the Great Lakes Country, and the Old Southwest (Mississippi and Alabama). They hoped to stifle Anglo advancement and to restore traditional Indian life. Most of the Indians ultimately joined forces with Great Britain in the War of 1812 against the United States. Tecumseh's followers fought in at least 150 engagements against the Americans, but the United States emerged victorious. Tecumseh's death at the Battle of the Thames in October 1813 signaled the end of effective Indian resistance between the Ohio and the Mississippi rivers (Edmunds 1996, 621).

In Mississippi and Alabama, the Upper Creeks, many of whom had taken to the Prophet's message, also fought valiantly to protect their lands from further intrusions. They, too, were defeated. Andrew Jackson led a combined force of American troops and Cherokee and Lower Creek allies to victory at the Battle of Horseshoe Bend in 1814. In the subsequent Treaty of Fort Jackson, concluded on August 9, 1814, the Creeks—even the Lower Creeks who had remained neutral or sided with Jackson—were forced to cede more than twenty-two million acres of land, including parts of western Georgia and much of Alabama (7 Stat., 20). The United States considered this enormous land cession to be "an equivalent for all expenses incurred in prosecuting the war to its termination" (ibid.).

Notwithstanding the British and native defeat in 1814, Great Britain insisted as a "sine qua non" (an indispensable condition) of a treaty of peace (the Treaty of Ghent, 8 Stat., 218) that the United States extend peace to "the Indian allies of Great Britain, and that the boundary of their territory be definitively marked out as a permanent barrier between the dominions of Great Britain and the United States" (U.S. Congress 1832, 708). The United States treaty delegation, led by John Q. Adams, initially refused to concede a permanent Indian territorial boundary as laid out by the British. The Americans argued that recognition of such a large territory "would comprehend [i.e., affect] a great number of American citizens, not less, perhaps, than a hundred thousand" (ibid., 709). The British delegation, led by Gambier, retorted that they were not "prepared to abandon the Indian nations to their fate" and that their Indian allies should also be directly involved in the peace negotiations as a "principle of public law" (ibid., 714).

Adams responded by describing what he termed the "humane and liberal policy" of the United States toward tribes, but the policy would not allow the tribes to participate in these particular treaty negotiations. Even here, as they denied native nations a seat at the table where their futures were being discussed, the Americans restrained themselves to a restricted definition of preemptive land claims:

> Under that system the Indians residing within the United States are so far independent that they live under their own

customs, and not under the laws of the United States; that their rights upon the lands where they inhabit or hunt, are secured to them by boundaries defined in amicable treaties between the United States and themselves; and that whenever those boundaries are varied, it is also by amicable and voluntary treaties, by which they receive from the United States ample compensation for every right they have to the lands ceded to them. *They are so far dependent as not to have the right to dispose of their lands to any private persons, not to any Power other than the United States,* and to be under their protection alone, and not under that of any other Power. Whether called subjects, or by whatever name designated, such is the relation between them and the United States. (ibid., 716; emphasis added)

The British emphatically maintained that they would sign a treaty only if "the Indian nations are included in it, and restored to all the rights, privileges, and territories which they enjoyed in the year 1811" (ibid., 718). The United States was still unwilling to recognize the rights of tribes as "independent nations," fearing that the tribes might realign with the British. Such action, said the Americans, "would place them [the tribes] effectually and exclusively under her [British] protection, instead of being, as heretofore, under that of the United States" (ibid., 720).

The British delegation quickly challenged the Americans' "novel and alarming pretension" (a pretension that Britain itself had used when it suited): that Indian nations were to be considered the subjects of the United States, and Indian territories were subject to the disposal of the federal government. "Pretensions such as these," said the British delegation, "Great Britain can never recognize" (ibid., 722). Britain finally had to concede, however, that the United States would not consent to the tribes as direct parties in the peace negotiations. Instead, Britain settled for an article requiring that the United States recognize the rights and possessions of tribes that existed prior to 1811, and the United States accepted. Hence, Article 9 of the Treaty of Ghent, dated December 24, 1814, states:

The United States of America engage to put an end, immediately after the ratification of the present treaty, to hostilities
with all the tribes or nations of Indians with whom they may
be at war at the time of such ratification, and forthwith to
restore to such tribes or nations, respectively, all the possessions, rights, and privileges which they may have enjoyed,
or been entitled to . . . provided always, that such tribes or
nations shall agree to desist from all hostilities against the
United States of America, their citizens and subjects, upon
the ratification of the present treaty being notified to the such
tribes or nations, and shall so desist accordingly. (ibid.,
747–48)

Although tribes did not participate as sovereigns in these negotiations, both the United States and Great Britain honored their preexisting rights, including their territorial rights. Other treaties
negotiated between the United States and Indian tribes in the years
after the War of 1812 continued to recognize and confirm tribes'
rights to land. For example, in the treaty concluded at Portage des
Sioux on the Mississippi, tribes and the federal government agreed
to end hostilities and establish perpetual peace, and the United
States reassured the tribes that their preexisting treaties were recognized and reconfirmed (Kappler 1904, 79–85). In a series of
treaties with the Potawatomies, the Piankeshaws, and the Teton and
Yankton Sioux, among others, the United States and the tribes, anxious to reestablish peace and friendship, agreed that "every injury
or act of hostility by one or other of the contracting parties against
the other, shall be mutually forgiven and forgot" and that the parties "recognize, re-establish, and confirm, all and every treaty, contract, or agreement, heretofore concluded" (Treaty with the Piankeshaws, 7 Stat., 124).

The federal peace and friendship espoused in the Portage des
Sioux treaties conform with the other tenets of federal Indian policy that would remain firmly in place into the 1830s and beyond:
(1) recognition of Indian land rights by the establishment of clear

boundaries for Indian Country; (2) the use of formal treaties as the principal means of dealing with tribal nations; (3) regulation of Indian trade by the federal government as a means of maintaining an exclusive relationship with the tribes, but also to protect the Indians from being defrauded; (4) expenditures by the United States designed to promote the "civilization" and education of Indians; and (5) a series of trade and intercourse acts—first enacted in 1790 and made permanent in 1834—to restrain the actions of whites and provide justice to the Indians (Prucha 1962, 2–3).

The evidence from treaties, discussed above, supports the preemptive definition of the discovery doctrine, but we do not need to rely on treaty evidence alone. The federal government recognized tribal ownership of Indian land in the trade and intercourse acts as well. Just as in earlier treaties, the language of congressional legislation envisioned the United States as a protector of Indian interests in their lands and as first in line to buy land should a tribe choose to sell. Section 12 of the 1834 Trade and Intercourse Act declared that "no purchase, grant, lease, or other conveyance of land, or of any title or claim thereto, from any Indian nation or tribe of Indians, shall be of any validity in law or equity, unless the same shall be made by treaty or convention entered into pursuant to the Constitution" (4 Stat., 729). The 1834 law permanently codified previous temporary laws by defining "Indian Country" as all land west of the Mississippi (and not within the states of Missouri or Louisiana or the territory of Arkansas) and all lands east of the Mississippi "not within any state to which the Indian title has not been extinguished" (ibid.).

Just as Spain, France, and England had recognized indigenous land title in earlier centuries, the United States from 1776 through the early 1800s adhered to a restricted notion of any land claims based on the doctrine of discovery. Abundant evidence from treaties negotiated both before and after the War of 1812 points to the U.S. conception of itself as the preemptive "first purchaser" of Indian lands, not as the ultimate proprietor of any and all lands stretching into the unknown West. Congressional trade and intercourse acts also assumed a federal right to purchase Indian lands, but not the automatic federal ownership *prior to* purchase.

Treaties are instruments negotiated by the executive branch of the federal government; acts of Congress are instruments of the legislative branch. The third branch of the U.S. government, the judiciary, also exercises important powers in the republican system of checks and balances, and it has wielded tremendous influence over the historic course of American Indian law and policy. Our analysis so far of the doctrine of discovery has considered evidence from treaties, treaty negotiations, congressional acts, and policy pronouncements. To be complete, we must also consider judicial interpretations, or so-called legal constructions, of the doctrine of discovery.

U.S. SUPREME COURT INTERPRETATIONS OF DISCOVERY

The Constitution empowers Congress as the appropriate branch of government to exercise exclusive authority in the policy field of Indian affairs. Congress fulfills its constitutional mandate by generating legislation and establishing tribally specific and general policies that will democratically guide the political relationship between tribal nations and the federal government—a relationship rooted in treaty arrangements. Alongside Congress, the executive branch, at least until 1871,[21] had a role in negotiating and proclaiming the treaty arrangements that provide the ongoing diplomatic linkages between tribes and the United States. The Supreme Court's role in Indian affairs is restrained by the force of congressional exclusive authority (also called plenary power, discussed in more detail in chapter 3). One of the Court's primary roles in Indian affairs, especially insofar as Indian land rights are involved, should be to interpret treaty language, especially ambiguous language, in a way that comports with both the tribes' and the United States' understanding of how the two peoples' affairs can best be carried out in a perpetual state of fairness, justice, and informed consent.

The Supreme Court is the ultimate arbiter of U.S. law and, like the law itself, has a history. Enmeshed in contemporary politics, swayed by social trends, constituted of individual personalities, the Court has evolved over generations of judicial interpretation and reinterpretation. Precedents have been set and followed, and sometimes ignored or overturned. Like the Devil who can quote Scripture to suit his own purposes, a legal analyst can—indeed, *must*—pick and choose the time, the place, the case, the justice, the opinion or the dissent, in order to build an argument. In the next few pages, we build our case against judicial misconstructions of the discovery doctrine and for historically appropriate constructions of discovery. As the following paragraphs reveal, certain personalities have dominated judicial interpretation of American Indian law, and none has been so instrumental as Chief Justice John Marshall, who served from 1801 to 1835.[22]

Judicial Misconstructions of Discovery

In 1823, the United States Supreme Court rendered a stunning ruling in *Johnson v. McIntosh*, 21 U.S. (8 Wheat.) 543 (1823), that attempted to redefine the political contours of the indigenous/federal relationship dramatically. The Court, in a decision crafted by Chief Justice Marshall, hoped to elevate the federal government to a superior proprietary position relative to tribal nations. At issue in the case were transfers of Indian land title. In two separate land transactions, in 1773 and 1775, the Illinois and Piankeshaw tribes had ceded title to the plaintiffs, Joshua Johnson, et al. The defendant, William McIntosh, had purchased title from the United States in 1818. The lands that McIntosh bought were part of the territory that Johnson et al. had originally purchased from the tribes. The purpose of the case was to decide whose title was valid. The question should have been whether private individuals could purchase Indian land, or whether only the national government had that authority. This question assumes that tribes possessed title to their lands, but considers who has the authority to buy any lands the tribes might choose to sell. In fact, Chief Justice Marshall chose to pose a much broader question: whether tribes *possessed a title* that could be conveyed to whomever they chose.

The previous actions of European sovereigns, as well as treaties negotiated and affirmed by the United States government, attested that tribes held a title equal to the fee-simple title of whites. Marshall and the Court, however, for political reasons, refused to recognize that tribal or aboriginal title was unaffected by the claims of European and U.S. "discoverers." The Court apparently feared that such a holding would have nullified state and federal land grants derived from Indians. The Court did not go to the extreme of asserting that the doctrine of discovery completely vanquished Indian title, since this would have left the tribes with no enforceable interests whatsoever. Instead, Marshall craftily reached a political and legal compromise that avoided a vision of Indian title either as aboriginally intact and untouched by the claims of "discoverers" or as completely superseded by "discoverers'" claims of ownership. Marshall's articulation of an expansive doctrine of discovery in *McIntosh* allowed that tribes were the "rightful occupants of the soil," but that their legal claim to their lands was less than— secondary to—the claim of the United States. He also suggested that the "complete sovereignty" of independent tribal nations was significantly "impaired" by the imperious claims of the federal government. Tribes were also unilaterally informed in this decision that they no longer possessed the power to sell their lands to others should they choose.[23] In short, the Marshall Court reduced indigenous groups from landowners to occupants only: their "occupancy title" was legally inferior to the federal government's claims of ownership.

At the heart of the decision was Marshall's distorted, historically inaccurate, and legally fictitious construction of the doctrine of discovery. According to Marshall, the principle meant that the "discovering" European nations (and the United States, as heir to Great Britain's rights of discovery in North America) had gained a superior (read: expansive) title to *both* unoccupied and occupied indigenous lands. "Thus," said Marshall, "has our whole country been granted by the crown while in the occupation of the Indians. These grants purport to *convey the soil as well as the right of dominion* to the grantees" (ibid., 579; emphasis added). Marshall was rewriting history to suit the federal government's needs. As the preceding analyses show, no previous sovereign—including Great Britain—had acted as if it had a superior title to Indian land. European nations did claim to be the "sovereign," in the sense of being the premier political entity vis-à-vis other competitor states, and at times even in their relationship to tribes, but this did not translate into sole proprietorship or ownership of all land.

Even in Marshall's time, the preponderance of historic evidence supported a recognition of Indian ownership of the soil that rested in the tribes until they chose to sell that soil to a bidding European sovereign. Indian title, while understood as substantively different from the fee-simple title of Europeans, nevertheless was a historically recognized reality. The position taken by the British during the negotiation of the Treaty of Ghent could not be explained otherwise.

Capping off his imaginative opinion, Marshall ruled that the United States, by stepping into Great Britain's shoes after the Treaty of Paris, had gained an exclusive and virtually "absolute" legal title to all of America (ibid., 588). The historical record shows that what the United States had gained after the 1783 Paris treaty and the 1814 Treaty of Ghent, contrary to Marshall's creative assertions, was merely an exclusive status vis-à-vis other European sovereigns. The United States only gained title to those lands Great Britain had already purchased from the Indians; it had not secured the "absolute" title to the rest of America. As Milner Ball, a leading constitutional historian, showed in his analysis of *McIntosh*, "in the case of the Europeans and Indians, however, incorporation— the humanitarian rule after conquest—was impossible. The Indians had not been conquered, and they would not mingle" (Ball 1987, 27). While acknowledging that Marshall used some language in the *McIntosh* opinion that can be construed to mean that the idea

of conquest was applied to indigenous-European/American relations, Ball and other scholars (Berman 1978; Shattuck and Norgren
1991) point to language employed elsewhere by Marshall. Marshall argued even more persuasively, in another part of *McIntosh*,
and in *Worcester v. Georgia*, 31 U.S. (6 Pet.) 515 (1832), that the conquest doctrine had to do with the way Europeans dealt *with one
another* "as they attempted to assert and defend territorial claims"
(Ball 1987, 28 n. 132). Marshall did not propose that the conquest
doctrine applied to the relations between European and native
nations. As he stated in *Worcester v. Georgia*, "In this view, perhaps,
our ancestors, when they first migrated to this country, might have
taken possession of a limited extent of the domain, had they been
sufficiently powerful, without negotiation or purchase from the
native Indians. But this course is believed to have been nowhere
taken. A more conciliatory mode was preferred, and one which
was better calculated to impress the Indians who were then powerful, with a sense of the justice of their white neighbors" (31 U.S.
[6 Pet.] 515 [1832], 578–80). In other words, treaty negotiation, not
military coercion, was the foundation of U.S. Indian policy.

This nonconquest view was upheld by the Supreme Court in
Mitchel v. United States, 34 U.S. (9 Pet.) 711 (1835), where Justice
Henry Baldwin declared that "by thus holding treaties with these
Indians, accepting of cessions from them with reservations, and
establishing boundaries with them, the King [of England], waived
all rights accruing by conquest or cession, and thus most solemnly
acknowledged that the Indians had rights of property which they
could cede or reserve" (34 U.S. [9 Pet.] 711 [1835], 749). The United
States, said Baldwin, could not assume the right of conquest
because it had renounced conquest policy when it chose to continue
the treaty relationship with tribes that Great Britain, Spain, and
France had begun (ibid., 754).

Marshall himself seemed well aware of the absurdity of con-
structing the discovery principle as expansively as he had done in
McIntosh, but he found it expedient to rationalize from a policy and
philosophical perspective: "However extravagant the pretension

of converting the discovery of an inhabited country into conquest may appear, if the principle has been asserted in the first instance, and afterwards sustained; if a country has been acquired and held under it; if the property of the great mass of the community originates in it, it becomes the law of the land, and cannot be questioned" (ibid., 591). Even extravagant pretensions, in Marshall's own words, become law and "cannot be questioned" if enough property is at stake. Despite Marshall's seemingly autocratic pronouncement, this "law" would be questioned.

The discovery principle as an international rule was not questioned by Spain, France, and England because they shared imperial and cultural premises. They had devised the principle as a mechanism to eliminate, or at least reduce, international conflicts. The discovery doctrine was certainly questioned, however, and openly defied, by indigenous nations who had occupied their lands for millennia. "Ownership of land was, of course, the basic question at issue between Indians and Europeans in North America, as it was between the Europeans who contended with each other for possession. There was a fundamental difference in these two contests, however. The Europeans agreed on the conditions and prerogatives of ownership, and fought over the right to exercise them. The Indians not only opposed the Europeans' efforts, they denied utterly the validity of the underlying concepts" (Jones 1982, 18). Sir William Johnson learned this lesson directly in his dealings with the Iroquois: "The Indians were sometimes bitter, sometimes cynical, and frequently outspoken about the European assumption that unceded Indian land could be bartered back and forth at European conference tables" (ibid., 72). The Indians were amused, said Johnson, by the actions of both the French and the British "with stories of their upright intentions, and that they made War for the protection of the Indians' rights, but that they plainly found it was carried on to see who would become masters of what was the property of neither the one nor the other" (ibid.). The same tribal view could be taken of *McIntosh*. The fact that tribal nations were extraconstitutional sovereigns at the time of the *McIntosh* decision is a further argument against its impairment of their proprietary rights. Since tribal nations were not parties in the *McIntosh* litigation—though they were indirectly involved, having sold the land to both the non-Indian parties—an argument can be made that the precedent is not binding upon them. Indian tribes were not participants in the case; therefore, they had not consented to be bound by the Court's holding.

Historically Appropriate Judicial Constructions of Discovery

The fairly consistent actions of Spain, France, Great Britain, and even the United States, both before and after the *McIntosh* ruling, strongly suggest that these governments only *sometimes* attempted to force the view that tribes were simple occupants, with a diminished title to their ancestral lands. On the whole, the record of treaties, legislative actions, and sovereign and presidential pronouncements indicates that tribes were the actual owners of the soil and that European/American sovereigns went to great lengths to purchase Indian title peacefully before claiming ownership.

McIntosh is sandwiched between ample treaty precedent, statutory law, and sovereign pronouncements pointing to a more accurate understanding that the discovery doctrine merely gave the alleged "discoverer" the right to be the exclusive purchaser of any land tribes were willing to sell. The preemptive theory of discovery as an exclusive right appeared in the two major Supreme Court cases that immediately succeeded *McIntosh*: *Worcester v. Georgia*, 31 U.S. (6 Pet.) 515 (1832), and *Mitchel v. United States*, 34 U.S. (9 Pet.) 711 (1835). In *Worcester*, also authored by Marshall, the court made clear that discovery did not restrict the rights of Indians to their territory:

> America, separated from Europe by a wide ocean, was inhabited by a distinct people, divided into separate nations, independent of each other and of the rest of the world, having institutions of their own, and governing themselves by their own laws. It is difficult to comprehend the proposition that

the inhabitants of either quarter of the globe could have rightful original claims of dominion over the inhabitants of the
other, or over the lands they occupied; or that the discovery
of either by the other should give the discoverer rights in the
country discovered which annulled the preexisting rights of
its ancient possessors. (31 U.S. [6 Pet.] 515, 542–43)

In this case, Marshall went even further in his historical analysis of discovery in what appears to be an effort to correct the effron-
tery he had issued in the *McIntosh* ruling:

The great maritime powers of Europe discovered and visited
different parts of this continent at nearly the same time. The
object was too immense for any one of them to grasp the
whole, and the claimants were too powerful to submit to the
exclusive or unreasonable pretensions of any single poten-
tate. To avoid bloody conflicts, which might terminate disas-
trously to all, it was necessary for the nations of Europe to
establish some principle which all would acknowledge, and
which should decide their respective rights as between themselves. This principle, suggested by the actual state of things,
was "that discovery gave title to the government by whose
subjects or by whose authority it was made, against all other
European governments, which title might be consummated
by possession." *This principle, acknowledged by all Europeans,
because it was the interest of all to acknowledge it, gave to the
nation making the discovery, as its inevitable consequence, the sole
right of acquiring the soil and of making settlements on it.* It was
an *exclusive principle* which shut out the right of competition
among those who had agreed to it; not one which could
annul the previous rights of those [like tribes] who had not
agreed to it. *It regulated the right given by discovery among the
European discoverers, but could not affect the rights of those already
in possession, either as aboriginal occupants, or as occupants by
virtue of a discovery made before the memory of man.* It gave the
exclusive right to purchase, but did not found that right on a

denial of the right of the possessor to sell. (ibid., 543–44; emphasis added)

Marshall continued by challenging one of the basic myths about the discovery era. Some commentators maintained that the king of England's charters to the original colonies entailed a conveyance of the actual soil to the newly established colony. Marshall explicitly denied this interpretation. He declared that

> the extravagant and absurd idea that the feeble settlements made on the sea-coast, or the companies under whom they were made, acquired legitimate power by them to govern the people, or occupy the lands from sea to sea, did not enter the mind of any man. They were well understood to convey the title which, according to the common law of European sovereigns respecting America, they might rightfully convey, and no more. *This was the exclusive right of purchasing such lands as the natives were willing to sell. The crown could not be understood to grant what the crown did not affect to claim, nor was it so understood. . . . These colonial grants and charters merely asserted a title against Europeans only, and were considered as blank paper so far as the rights of the native were concerned.* (ibid., 546; emphasis added)

Three years later, in *Mitchel v. United States*, the Supreme Court further denied the *McIntosh* precedent, and amplified *Worcester*, by disavowing that the doctrine of discovery vested absolute ownership of America in the discovering states. Justice Henry Baldwin did not disclaim the doctrine as explicitly as Marshall had done, but his description of Indian title easily supported Marshall's *Worcester* views. For instance, Baldwin noted that "friendly Indians were protected in the possession of the lands they occupied, and were considered as owning them by a perpetual right of possession in the tribe or nation inhabiting them" (34 U.S. [9 Pet.] 711 [1835], 745).

Baldwin expanded on his notion of Indian title: "it is enough to consider it as a settled principle, that their right of occupancy is considered as sacred as the fee simple of the whites" (ibid., 746). It logically followed that if Indians held their lands with a sacred title, comparable to fee-simple, then they must also possess the power to transfer the title, that is, to sell those lands. In a statement directly at odds with the *McIntosh* holding that Indians lack the power to convey their lands, the *Mitchel* court held that "the Indian right to the lands as property was not merely of possession, that of alienation was concomitant; both were equally secured, protected, and guarantied by Great Britain and Spain" (ibid.).

How do we explain the Court's rulings in *Worcester* and *Mitchel*, which run contrary to *McIntosh* and to the other noted Marshall decision, *Cherokee Nation v. Georgia* (30 U.S. [5 Pet.] 1 [1831])? In *Cherokee Nation*, Marshall held that tribes were domestic dependent nations whose relationship with the United States resembled that of a guardian to a ward. *Worcester*, handed down immediately after *Cherokee Nation*, involved several Congregational missionaries who were in Cherokee Territory at Cherokee request and under the protection of federal statutory and treaty law. In fact, although Marshall used virtually the same treaty and statutory documentation in *Worcester* that he had used in *Cherokee Nation*, he was actually ruling on different issues. *Cherokee Nation* involved the relationship of tribes to the federal government; in *Worcester* the Court was clarifying the relationship between tribes and the states. Marshall was most emphatic: tribes retained sufficient sovereignty to protect themselves and their lands from state intrusion, since the relationship between tribes and the United States was rooted in tribal sovereignty, international law, ratified treaties, and the U.S. Constitution.[24] Noted legal analyst Jill Norgren, who has closely analyzed the "Cherokee Cases" under discussion here, also points out that the Supreme Court feared that its ruling in *Cherokee Nation* might well have exacerbated Georgia aggression and violence against the Cherokee people (Norgren 1996, 118). The Court took the opportunity in *Worcester* to back away from the language of conquest used in *McIntosh* and, in Justice Joseph Story's words, "to wash its [the Court's] hands clean of the iniquity of oppressing the Indians and disregarding their rights" (quoted in ibid.).

There are two plausible explanations for the *Mitchel* holding, which denied absolute discovery and upheld a preemptive definition of the doctrine. The first hinges on the fact that since the Seminoles' sale of land to Mitchel had been made with the consent of a European sovereign (Spain), the purchasers of the Indian land thereby gained a superior title to any that the United States could assert. The Spanish king, via his North American governors, had given his explicit sanction to the Indian deeds. As a result, the United States was bound by the law of nations and by its treaty with Spain to recognize this land transaction. As Justice Baldwin put it: "They [the deeds] are drawn up in great form; contain a perfect recognition of the Indian grants, and give to them all the validity which he [the Spanish governor] could impart to them. They are made in the name of the king, executed and attested in all due formality, and their authenticity proved as public documents, and by the testimony of witnesses to the official documents" (34 U.S. [9 Pet.] 711, 728 [1835]). In this reading, the Court's interpretation did not consider Indian title as a primary issue at all.

The second possible explanation for the ruling involves the fact that Mitchel et al., in contrast to the plaintiffs in *McIntosh*, had the benefit of several congressional laws that required the federal government to execute the provisions of the Spanish-American treaty of 1819. Later laws allowed individuals to institute claims against the United States for losses they may have sustained (ibid., 716). The Court, in this instance, was deferring to the will of the legislature, which had enacted laws to protect individual property rights, especially those recognized by a European sovereign. Once again, native or aboriginal title was not the pivotal issue being considered.

CONCLUSION

Historic evidence demonstrates that ownership of the North American continent rested quite evidently in the hands of indigenous peoples. Contrary to assumptions that ultimate legal title to occupied Indian lands passed upon "discovery" to a European nation-state or the United States as successor, the historical record shows that legal ownership resided fully in the hands of tribal nations. Indian tribes retained complete ownership of their respective territories until such time as they formally ceded their claims to land in a consensual treaty arrangement with one of the competing European nations or, later, with the Americans.

The doctrine of discovery, when defined as an absolutist concept designed to regulate European/American affairs, was a colonial metaphor that gave the quickest and most powerful European nation the upper hand over other European claims as they colonized various parts of the world, including North America (and disregarded any aboriginal land rights). The doctrine of discovery, when defined as an exclusive principle of benevolent paternalism or, as it was in the *McIntosh* decision, as an assertion of federal ownership of fee-simple title to all the Indian lands in the United States, is a clear legal fiction that needs to be explicitly stricken from the federal government's political and legal vocabulary. A doctrine of discovery that purports to assign instantaneous ownership of Indian lands to European/American nations, and that hopes to reduce Indians to a status as simple tenants in their aboriginal homelands, runs contrary to common sense and to the force and continued vitality of tribal sovereignty. It is also inimical to congressional and executive policy pronouncements and Supreme Court precedent and is directly at odds with the bulk of extant European and U.S. treaty provisions, which abundantly demonstrate that tribes possessed full and complete legal title to their lands. Federal abandonment of the demeaning and unjust legal fiction contained in the absolute and expansive definitions of discovery, and congressional, presidential, and judicial endorsement of a preemptive discovery doctrine, would be a significant first step in reformulating Indian policy so that policy is based on justice, humanity, and "the actual state of things."

CHAPTER TWO

"With the Greatest Respect and Fidelity": The Trust Doctrine

And here we beg leave to ask of our father that, in future transactions of a public nature between the United States and our nation, the American Government will not require of our nation any thing which, as our protectors and guardians, they will not, after due deliberation, advise us to comply with; and having no doubt of the magnanimity and benignity of the Government, we shall return home satisfied, and report to our nation the result of our mission to this. With the greatest respect and fidelity, we subscribe our names.

CHEROKEE DEPUTATION,
December 13, 1817

In 1992 noted Lakota legal scholar, author, and political commentator Vine Deloria, Jr., analyzed the disturbing 1988 decision of the Supreme Court in *Lyng vs. Northwest Indian Cemetery Protective Association*, 485 U.S. 439 (1988). The Court had devastatingly held that neither the federal government's trust doctrine nor the First Amendment's religious freedom clause was sufficient to stop the destruction of the sacred sites—and hence the religion—of three small northern California tribes. For Deloria, *Lyng* raised an important question: "What is the nature of the trust responsibility of the federal government toward American Indians and what primacy does it have in the pyramid of federal values and decision making?" (Deloria 1992, 287).

The United States' relationship with Indian tribes has been defined in complex and myriad ways. In fact, a number of terms are used to describe the relationship between the governments of tribes and of the United States: trust, trust doctrine, trust duty, trust relationship, trust responsibility, trust obligation, trust analogy, ward-guardian, and beneficiary-trustee. In the following discussion we look at whether or not the terms and phrases listed are synonymous—is the trust *relationship*, for example, equal to the trust *responsibility*? We argue that it is. Is the "guardian-ward" relationship substantively different than the "trustee-beneficiary" relationship? We argue that it is.

Common to many, but not all, definitions of "trust" is the notion of federal *responsibility* to *protect or enhance* tribal assets (including fiscal, natural, human, and cultural resources) through policy decisions and management actions. Two important issues are at stake. One, does the federal government, as "trustee" of Indian tribes' assets, have a responsibility to manage *in the best interests* of tribes, that is, for tribal benefit? Two, is the trust responsibility legally mandated or does it only carry a lesser moral "force"? Some argue that trust means "best management"; in other words, federal actions must benefit tribes and respect tribal wishes. Others argue that federal powers to manage Indian assets and Indian lives are unlimited by *any* legal constraints, let alone any notions of "best management." They debate whether or not trust is a legally enforceable doctrine that might constrain federal action regarding tribal funds, property, or political and civil rights. So a major issue in discussing trust is determining whether legal, or moral, or any force at all constrains federal powers over Indian affairs. Different interpretations of trust disagree on this issue. The force of trust has varied in real-world applications based on the issue involved (questions of jurisdiction have played out differently than questions of congressional appropriations), on the tribe involved (federally recognized, state-recognized, nonrecognized, or terminated), and on the origin of the trust (whether it is specifically or only implicitly spelled out in an Indian treaty, an agreement, a congressional statute, an executive order, or a judicial decree).

Ambiguities in interpretation arise for other reasons as well. Scholars do not even agree on when, or why, the doctrine originated. Did the trust concept originate in the "discovery era" of Europe's commercial and religious excursions to the Americas, or is it an outgrowth of the Marshall Court's critically important Indian law cases of the 1820s and 1830s? Or, as Francis P. Prucha (1985) has asserted, is the trust doctrine merely a figment of the fertile imagination of the 1975–77 American Indian Policy Review Commission (U.S. Congress 1977, vol. 1, chapter 4)?

Complicating the issue more is the fact that each of the federal government's three branches (executive, legislative, and judicial) has coined and implemented sundry definitions of the trust doctrine over time (Newton 1982; "Rethinking the Trust Doctrine" 1984). It is a question for debate whether the Bureau of Indian Affairs is solely responsible for enforcing the federal trust or whether every federal agency (and each branch) is also required to uphold the federal government's pledges to tribes. Several decades ago, the noted scholar of federal Indian law Felix Cohen wrote that the similarly contested term "wardship" (which is not synonymous with "trusteeship") had varied meanings numbering "two to the tenth power minus one, that is to say, 1023" (Cohen 1972, 170, n. 289). The assorted and conflicting definitions of "trust" might number as high or higher.

This chapter begins by examining possible origins of the various "trust" terms and concepts. Then we illustrate the multiple definitions of "trust" through examples, looking at how different federal governmental branches have interpreted the term over time. After delineating these countervailing views, we focus on a central question: what is the essence of the trust concept from an indigenous viewpoint? In other words, which definition of trust is most appropriate to protecting tribal interests? One of the main goals of this chapter is to argue for an indigenous vision of trust, one that appropriately conforms to native understandings and political realities.

Deloria and others decry the fact that there is no agreed-upon definition of the federal-tribal "trust relationship." The contest over the trust doctrine's meaning puts tribes at risk. They cannot be assured that their rights will be protected by—or from—their "trustee," the federal government. This is troublesome for pragmatic, intergovernmental, and public policy reasons. Inconsistency leaves tribes uncertain about how their status is being interpreted by various government agencies and what their relationship to the U.S. government is based upon.

ORIGINS OF TRUST

A minority of commentators (Green 1975; Prucha 1985, 91–92) assert that the United States' "trust responsibility" is a relatively recent notion and may not even be a legal principle, except in the narrow sense outlined by explicit treaty provisions. They argue that the "trust responsibility" is only a moral obligation—not a legal one—on the part of the federal government. According to this interpretation, the federal government might feel an ethical responsibility to manage tribal assets such as land or natural resources for tribal benefit, or in accordance with tribal directives, but there is no legal mandate to do so. In contrast, the majority of political and legal scholars, jurists, and federal policymakers assert that the federal trust responsibility is an ancient and entrenched (although ambiguous) legal doctrine that permeates the tribal-federal relationship.[1]

Did the trust concept originate in the "discovery era" of Europe's commercial and religious excursions to the Americas? Vine Deloria, Jr., has linked the doctrines of discovery and trust in an intriguing and useful way. As long as the federal government asserts claims to Indian lands based on the doctrine of discovery, Deloria believes, then the government willingly assumes a role as protector of

Indian nations. As the tribes' protector from all enemies—foreign as well as domestic—the federal government "must defend the Indian tribes against intrusions by other Christian nations, and it must adjust its domestic law and the behavior of its citizens to ensure that its institutions and its citizens do not intrude upon the activities and the political rights of the Indian nations" (U.S. Senate 1994b, 75–76). "Rights" claimed as a discoverer (or as an heir to a discoverer) carry with them responsibilities as a protector.

Is the trust doctrine an outgrowth of the Marshall Court's critically important Indian law cases of the 1820s and 1830s? We have seen in the prior chapter on the discovery doctrine that the Marshall Court decisions from this era contradict one another regarding the doctrine of discovery, regarding whether or not tribes held title to their lands, and regarding whether or not tribes were sovereign nations. But Marshall seemed clearer on the question of federal responsibility toward tribes, although he never explicitly used the "trust" concept in his opinions. For example, in *Johnson v. McIntosh* (1823) Marshall ruled that federal courts would not recognize the validity of a private sale of Indian lands to non-Indians. In other words, individuals could not buy land directly from Indian tribes unless the federal government was involved or approved the transaction. More famously, in *Cherokee Nation v. Georgia* (1831) Marshall said that tribes were not foreign nations but could "more correctly, perhaps, be denominated domestic, dependent nations" whose "relation to the United States resembles that of a ward to his guardian." Many commentators suggest that this and other phraseology in the decision formed the basis of the doctrine of federal trusteeship in Indian affairs (Hall 1981, 34).

Prucha argues for a much more recent origin of what he terms "trust responsibility." He believes that "trust relationship" and "trust responsibility" are altogether different terms. Prucha asserts that the United States legitimately acts as a "trustee" for Indian land and other natural resources, "which all agree are legally incumbent upon the federal government" when those are spelled out in treaties (Prucha 1985, 101). He distinguishes this legal sense of treaty-specific "trustee" from the expanded view that he traces to the federally established American Indian Policy Review Commission in the late 1970s. According to the commission: (1) the trust responsibility of American Indians covers protection and enhancement of Indian trust resources and tribal self-government and the provision of economic and social programs needed to raise the standard of living of the Indians to a level comparable to the non-Indian society; (2) it extends through the tribes to the Indian members, whether on or off the reservation; and (3) it applies to all federal agencies, not just those charged specifically with administration of Indian affairs (U.S. Congress 1977, 11–12). Prucha asserts that the American Indian Policy Review Commission overstated the scope of trust. Trust, in his view, is limited to the specific wording in Indian treaty provisions that spell out a clear and legal fiduciary responsibility on the part of the federal government in specific places and over specified times. It is not a generally applied principle governing all federal-tribal interactions.

We acknowledge all of these sources as tributaries to the notion of trust that has evolved over the generations: the notion of trust began in the discovery era—it is no recent "invention" as Prucha claims—but it has been shaped to fit different eras of Indian policy.

NONBENEFICIAL OR UNCONSTRAINED THEORY OF THE TRUST DOCTRINE

We turn our attention first to the recent phenomenon of growing resentment from what we term, for lack of a better phrase, the "anti-trust" segment. An anti-trust interpretation denies that the trust doctrine carries any legally enforceable federal obligation to "best manage" Indian affairs. In this view, the federal government simply wields ultimate power over Indian affairs, managing however it sees fit, and often to the detriment of tribal interests. These commentators have argued that the trust doctrine had, and still has, more use as a rhetorical than a legal principle. In other words, the notion of trust has been used to "give moral color to depredations of [i.e., visited upon] tribes [by others]" (Ball 1987, 62). Federal authority, in this view, is more appropriately understood as "an assertion of unrestrained political power over Indians, power that may be exercised without Indian consent and without substantial legal restraint" (Coulter and Tullberg 1984, 203). Trust, then, carries no responsibility for acting in tribal best interests or for considering tribal opinions at all. Trust is a "metaphor for federal control of Indian affairs without signifying any enforceable rights of the tribal 'beneficiaries' " (Krauss 1983, 447). This perspective further suggests that the "beneficial management" interpretation of the trust doctrine is an "illusion unsupported by legal authority"; that in reality Congress has become "the source of largely unrestrained federal power to regulate all aspects of tribal existence—from the management and disposal of Indian land and resources, to the imposition of federal criminal jurisdiction over tribal members, even the dissolution of tribal government" (Shattuck and Norgren 1991, 116). In sum, "the trust doctrine has proved to be a pliable instrument of nearly unlimited federal control and neglect" (ibid., 118).

An example of this "nonbeneficial" theory of trust (and concomitantly unconstrained theory of federal powers) is found in *United States v. Sioux Nation* (448 U.S. 371 [1980]). The U.S. attorney made the startling oral argument that the trustee relationship "carries both *obligations* but also *unusual powers*, the power to dispose [of Indian land] against the will [of the Indian tribe] and without exercising the power of eminent domain" (United States 1980, 46; emphasis added). In response, a justice acerbically asked: "The Constitution itself recognizes Indian tribes as sovereigns, does it not?" Legal counsel responded, remarkably, by asserting: "Yes, but the Constitution *perhaps* also recognizes the dependent status of Indian tribes, their inability to alienate their land which accordingly, if it must be done in their interest, may occasionally have to be done against their will by their guardian" (ibid.; emphasis added). Counsel's hedge against reality is encapsulated in the word "perhaps": in fact the Constitution says nothing about tribes as dependents or about tribes' abilities, or inabilities, to alienate land.

The nonbeneficial theory of trust not only flies in the face of tribal "will," but also attempts to rewrite the Constitution.

Another example of an "anti-trust" interpretation that brooks no constraints whatsoever on the exercise of federal powers over Indian affairs is found in the 1988 *Lyng* case mentioned earlier. The Supreme Court held that the United States Forest Service had the right to construct a 6-mile road segment that would admittedly "destroy the . . . Indians' ability to practice their religion." In this case involving the construction of a logging road through areas sacred to three small northern California tribes, Justice Sandra Day O'Connor wrote (in the majority opinion) that Indian religious rights could not be allowed to "divest the Government of its right to use what is, after all, *its* land" (485 U.S. 439, 453 [1988]; emphasis in the original). In O'Connor's opinion, federal powers over federal lands could not and should not be restrained by any tribal concerns, even religious freedom.

In contrast to the "anti-trust" commentators are those who could be labeled "pro-trust," who forcefully argue that the trust responsibility does create "legally enforceable duties for federal officials in their dealings with Indians" (Chambers 1975, 1215). A legally enforceable notion of the trust doctrine "has great significance in that it provides a check (albeit sometimes minimal) on federal and state actions which may endanger Indian rights" (Hall 1981, iv). The trust doctrine, according to the "pro-trust" interpretation, has been articulated and added to over time in several distinctive ways: (1) in ratified treaties and agreements with tribes; (2) in the international law doctrine of trusteeship (first broached in papal bulls and related documents when European states encountered non-Western societies and assumed a protective and insulating role over these peoples and their territories); (3) in general congressional policies and specific acts applicable to all Indian tribes (such as the 1819 Civilization Act and the 1921 Snyder Act); (4) in presidential policy pronouncements, such as executive orders, and finally; (5) in federal court judicial opinions describing the federal government's fiduciary responsibility to tribal peoples.

The trust doctrine, in this view, "emanates from the unique relationship between the United States and Indians in which the Federal Government undertook the obligation to insure the survival of Indians. . . . Its broad purpose . . . is to protect and enhance the people, the property, and the self-government of Indian tribes" (U.S. Congress 1977, 126). Here the federal trust duty is best characterized as a trustee-beneficiary relationship and not as a guardianward relationship (ibid., 127). Charles F. Wilkinson, a major proponent of this interpretation of trust, asserts that "although comparatively little has been done to explicate the enforceable duties of the trustee, the trust relationship has played a pervasive role in serving as the philosophical basis for a number of important doctrinal advances. . . . Thus, in addition to the accountability of federal officials for trust violations, the trust has a diverse and continuing influence in the development of Indian law" (Wilkinson 1987, 85–86).

The "pro-trust" perspective does not deny that the federal government may wield extraordinarily broad power over tribal lands, resources, and rights. It does, however, adhere to a political and moral image of the United States exemplified by the 1787 Northwest Ordinance, where the federal government pledged that "the utmost good faith shall always be observed towards the Indians; their land and property shall never be taken from them without their consent; and in their property, rights and liberty, they never shall be invaded or disturbed, unless in just and lawful wars authorized by Congress; but laws founded in justice and humanity shall from time to time be made, for preventing wrongs being done to them, and for preserving peace and friendship with them" (1 St. 50, 52).

A few years later, the 1790 Trade and Intercourse Act also articulated federal responsibility toward tribes. The act stipulated that the federal government had to consent in order for tribal lands to be "alienated," or sold, to anyone other than the federal government—to private citizens, for example, or to a state. In the 1970s several eastern Indian tribes filed land claims based on their interpretation of the trust responsibility included in the Trade and Intercourse Act, and their case is an excellent example to examine here (Campisi 1985; O'Toole and Tureen 1971; Wallace 1982). The Passamaquoddy and Penobscot tribes of Massachusetts Colony had a long history of diplomatic relations with Great Britain and the American colonies. A 1794 Treaty with the Commonwealth of Massachusetts resulted in the loss of approximately 12 million acres of tribal land. The tribes would ultimately come under the political control of Maine when it became a state in 1820.

In the early 1970s the tribes hired an attorney, Thomas N. Tureen, who investigated the tribes' legal and proprietary (land-owning) history. Tureen's research validated the tribes' contention that the 1794 treaty violated the Trade and Intercourse Act, which contained provisions meant to protect tribal lands from private and state claims. The key point of the tribes' claim was that the federal government had not consented to the alienation of their lands to Massachusetts and other third parties; the 1790 act required that the federal government agree to the provisions of the 1794 Treaty with the Commonwealth. In negotiating with the tribes, the commonwealth had apparently simply ignored the 1790 Trade and Intercourse Act.

Consequently, in the 1970s, tribal leaders asked federal officials to sue the State of Maine on the tribes' behalf; because the 1794 treaty violated a federal law (the 1790 Trade and Intercourse Act), challenging the treaty was a federal responsibility. The Department of the Interior refused, on the grounds that there was no trust relationship with the Passamaquoddy and Penobscot tribes because they were not federally recognized in the 1970s. The Passamaquoddy Tribe then sued the federal government, challenging its refusal to recommend suit against Maine and claiming entitlement under the 1790 Trade and Intercourse Act. In 1974 the U.S. District Court in Maine issued a decision in the Passamaquoddy case, holding that the Trade and Intercourse Act did apply to the tribe, thus establishing a trust relationship with the federal government (*Passamaquoddy Tribe v. Morton*, 388 Supp. 649, 1975). This decision was upheld by the First Circuit Court of Appeals in *Passamaquoddy Tribe v. Morton* (528 F.2d 370, 1975), which held that federal restraints against alienation of Indian land applied to all tribally held lands, whether the tribe was "recognized" or not, and whether or not its lands were considered a part of Indian Country. The Passamaquoddy and Penobscot land claims litigation culminated in two major events: in 1978 the Department of the Interior established a process by which nonrecognized groups could petition to become federally recognized tribes, and in 1980 Congress passed the Maine Indian Claims Settlement Act (94 Stat. 1785; Brodeur 1985), settling the claims of the Penobscot, Passamaquoddy, and Maliseet Indians to up to 12.5 million acres in Maine.

Another example of the congressional expression of legally binding trust can be found in the American Indian Trust Fund Management Reform Act, enacted on October 25, 1994. The act states that the "Secretary's proper discharge of the trust responsibility of the United States shall include (but is not limited to) the following: 1) Providing adequate systems for accounting for and reporting trust fund balances . . . [and] appropriately managing the natural resources located within the boundaries of Indian reservations and trust lands" (108 St. 4239, 4240). In recent years the executive branch has expressed a similar sentiment. On April 29, 1994, President William Clinton issued a memorandum to the heads of executive departments and agencies, acknowledging that "the United States Government has a unique legal relationship with Native American tribal governments as set forth in the Constitution of the United States, treaties, statutes, and court decisions." He directed departments to handle activities affecting tribal rights or trust resources "in a knowledgeable, sensitive manner respectful of tribal sovereignty" (United States 1994, 936–37).

Beneficial and legally binding interpretations of trust, however, are not always operative in federal Indian policy. In 1995 Democratic senator Daniel Inouye (Hawaii), vice-chairman of the Senate Committee on Indian Affairs, expressed his concerns about federal-tribal relationships. In a February 22, 1995, speech to the United

South and Eastern Indian Tribes, Inouye questioned whether the Republicans' "Contract with America" intended to create a "change in the relationship between the U.S. and Indian Nations." Echoing the sentiment of many tribal people, Inouye said: "Long before the 1994 election, there was a contract with America. It was a contract with the first citizens of America. The terms of that contract were spelled out in treaties, and later in presidential executive orders and laws enacted by the Congress." He went on to observe that although "the responsibilities and obligations of the so-called 'Great White Father' were clearly delineated, few if any of these commitments have been fulfilled" (*News from Indian Country* 1995, 2).

A month later, Senator Inouye called an oversight hearing on the projected impact on indigenous peoples of congressional proposals to consolidate or "block grant" federal funds to the states. He invited testimony on the proposals (to rescind large amounts of federal funding) under study by the Congress and the president. Inouye articulated the trust doctrine in the course of those hearings: "Because the United States has assumed the trust responsibility for Indian lands and resources that arises out of the cession of millions of acres of Indian land to the United States, this trust responsibility is a shared responsibility. It extends not only to all agencies of the executive branch of our Government, but also to the Congress. And so we must each do our part to assure that the United States' trust relationship with Indian nations and Native Americans is generally honored" (U.S. Senate 1995, 3).

A variety of scholars have analyzed the trust doctrine's historical and legal evolution in order to argue either for or against the legal enforceability of trust (see "Rethinking the Trust Doctrine" 1984; and Newton 1982, 1984, and 1992). Nell Newton has suggested that "in modern-day Indian law, the trust relationship, although not constitutionally based and thus not enforceable against Congress, is a source of enforceable rights against the executive branch and has become a major weapon in the arsenal of Indian rights" (Newton 1984, 232–33). The issue of enforceability, however, depends on which of the "three kinds of trust" the federal courts may be considering: the general trust, a limited or bare trust, or a full-blown "fiduciary relationship" (Newton 1992, 801–2).

According to Newton, a *general trust* is simply an acknowledgment of the historic relationship between indigenous groups and the federal government. It is apparently not legally enforceable. The idea of a general trust usually is traced back to John Marshall's opinions in the Cherokee Nation cases of the early 1830s, *Cherokee Nation v. Georgia*, 30 U.S. (5 Pet.) 1 (1831), and *Worcester v. Georgia*, 31 U.S. (6 Pet.) 515 (1832). For example, in *Worcester*, Marshall said that the stipulations found generally in Indian treaties by which the Indians acknowledge themselves to be under the protection of the United States and of no other power "involved, practically, no claim to their lands, no dominion over their persons. It merely bound the nation to the British crown, as a dependent ally, claiming the protection of a powerful friend and neighbour, and receiving the advantages of that protection, without involving a surrender of their national character. . . . The same stipulation entered into with the United States, is undoubtedly to be construed in the same manner. . . . Protection does not imply the destruction of the protected" (552). The classic federal judicial expression of general trust is found in *Seminole v. United States*, 316 U.S. 286 (1942), in a decision written by Justice Frank Murphy:

> This Court has recognized the distinctive obligation of trust incumbent upon the Government in its dealings with these dependent and sometimes exploited people. . . . In carrying out its treaty obligations with the Indian tribes, the Government is something more than a mere contracting party. Under a humane and self-imposed policy which has found expression in many acts of Congress, and numerous decisions of this Court, it has charged itself with moral obligations of the highest responsibility and trust. Its conduct, as disclosed in the acts of those who represent it in dealings with the Indians, should therefore be judged by the most exacting fiduciary standards. (316 U.S. 286 [1942] 296–97)

The *bare or limited* variety of trust is construed as trust established for a narrow and limited purpose. A good example is the provision of the General Allotment Act of 1887 that spelled out the allotting process. Tribal lands held in common (i.e., reservations) were surveyed and divided into (typically) 160, 80, and 40 acre "allotments" assigned to individual Indian people. The subdivided lands were to be held in trust for twenty-five years, at which time the Indian "owner" received fee simple title to his/her allotment (citizenship was also granted at this time; nonallotted American Indian people were not considered U.S. citizens until the Indian Citizenship Act of 1924). The Allotment Act created a narrow trust, which was "limited to the original purpose for the statute, which is protecting Indian land from taxation and involuntary alienation because of failure to pay taxes or debts" (Newton 1992, 802).

The so-called fiduciary relationship is the most comprehensive type of trust. The term "fiduciary" is derived from Roman law and means "a person holding the character of a trustee, or a character analogous to that of a trustee, in respect to the trust and confidence involved in it and the scrupulous good faith and candor which it requires" (*Black's Law Dictionary* 1979, 563). Typically, a breach of fiduciary responsibility makes the trustee liable to the beneficiaries for any damages caused. In *Navajo Tribe of Indians v. United States*, a federal court held that the U.S. government's supervision of tribal monies or resources indicated that a fiduciary responsibility existed unless Congress specified otherwise, "even though nothing is said expressly in the authorizing or underlying statute or other fundamental document about a trust fund, or a trust or a fiduciary connection" (624 F.2d 981, 987). The 1997 class action lawsuit filed by the Native American Rights Fund (an Indian legal interest group) on behalf of thousands of Indians against the Bureau of Indian Affairs for its alleged mismanagement of Indian trust funds is another example of how Indians attempt to hold the federal government responsible for upholding its fiduciary responsibility. Newton asserts that in order to distinguish this kind of trust from the other two varieties, the term "full fiduciary relationship" is appropriate.

AN INDIGENOUS VISION OF THE TRUST DOCTRINE

Obviously, a sizable body of literature examines the contours of trust as it has been defined, expounded, or restricted by federal policymakers and commentators. What is missing from the debate is an authentic and coherent indigenous view of "trust." Frequently, previous articulations of indigenous trust have been found in loosely organized compilations of "famous Indian speeches" such as W. C. Vanderwerth's *Indian Oratory: Famous Speeches by Noted Indian Chieftains* (1971), in anthologies such as T. C. McLuhan's *Touch the Earth* (1971), and in a litany of New Age writings about "Indian spirituality." These publications contain eloquent, profound comments by indigenous speakers, but these "sound bites" are packaged in a way that mutes their oratorical power, intellectual clarity, and emotional impact. These collections "seem to remove experience from the trauma of human life and leave a residue of aphorisms that are unconnected with the emotions that call for the statement" (Deloria 1980, 111).

If we think about the internal logic of the term "trust relationship," the inadequate representation or omission of the indigenous vision of the trust doctrine is really quite remarkable. Whether one subscribes to the notion of a pervasive trust relationship or only to a more limited trust responsibility, either definition of trust requires two parties. "Relationship" implies reciprocity, whereas "responsibility" more usually means that one party (the tribe) is seen as a passive beneficiary of actions taken by the trustee (the United States). Regardless, both cases require two parties. Until now, scholars have focused almost exclusive attention on the meaning of "trust" from a federal perspective. We propose to expand that gaze by articulating the perspective of one tribe—the Cherokees—on trust, past and present. We presume that the over 550 indigenous groups in the United States have a clear sense of "trust" that they have articulated frequently over time.[2] Tribes have been finely attuned to pledges made by the federal government—whether spelled out in presidential annual messages to Congress or in congressional policy pronouncements such as the Northwest Ordinance of 1787, in bilateral ratified treaties, in unratified field treaties, in unilateral federal legislation enacted after the cessation of treaty-making in 1871, in mutual agreements post-1871, in secretary of interior rules and regulations, or in judicial decisions. For purposes of brevity, we use the Cherokee Nation and its distinctive trust perspective as our case study. Although we hesitate to generalize from the Cherokee people's trust perspective to all indigenous nations, we hope that this one case study will prompt others to articulate what trust means from other tribal perspectives. Broader comparative studies will no doubt lead to deeper insights into this crucial concept.

Defining trust from an indigenous viewpoint is crucially important as the Cherokees and other tribes enter the twenty-first century. Many indigenous nations, including the various Cherokee polities, are exercising higher degrees of retained sovereignty and are simultaneously being delegated certain elements of local authority through federal policies and laws. Increased revenues (including gaming dollars) and federal policy goals such as tribal self-governance (108 Stat., 4250) are assisting the resurgence of tribal sovereignty. Nevertheless, the majority of North America's First Nations, including the several Cherokee groups, continue to experience grinding, structurally embedded levels of poverty created and perpetuated by generations of colonialism.

The Cherokee Case

The Cherokee Nation, like other tribal nations, has a distinctive history, culture, and set of political institutions. In the 1700s and early 1800s the Cherokees drew on Euro-American models for particular governing and societal institutions typical of nation-states, such as a Constitution, separate branches of government, and the concept of an orthography to write their language (Strickland 1975). The forces of American colonization removed the Cherokees to lands west of the Mississippi in the 1830s and 1840s—the infamous Trail of Tears. Removal and contingent political, economic, and legal pressures spawned intratribal divisions that still affect the Cherokee Nation today.[3]

Ideological and political differences have resulted in an array of separate Cherokee political entities: the Eastern Band of Cherokees in North Carolina, the Cherokee Nation of Eastern Oklahoma, the United Keetowah Band of Eastern Oklahoma, and a host of non-recognized groups alleging to be Cherokee who are scattered throughout the United States (Champagne 1992; Finger 1991; King 1979; Mankiller and Wallis 1993; Wardell 1977). Tribal divisions have precipitated different types of political relations with the federal and state governments. Despite the significant geographic, cultural, and ideological diversity evident among the Cherokee people, their nation is well worth considering for its articulation of the trust doctrine. Despite the complexity of their history and the vagaries in their relationship with the federal government, we find in the documentary record a consistent sense of what the Cherokee people expect from the United States.

A Cherokee Vision of "Trust"

In 1817 six Cherokee leaders—Going Snake, Roman Nose, Richard Taylor, James Brown, George Harlin, and Richard Riley—met with Secretary of War John C. Calhoun in order to remind the government that their treaties recognized Cherokee self-government and land title. The Cherokee Nation had, by 1817, negotiated ten colonial treaties with southern colonies and the British between 1721 and 1783 and nine treaties with the United States, beginning in 1785 (Royce 1887). They were a diplomatically experienced and politically sophisticated nation, adept at pursuing their own political agendas in the complex international setting that had existed in eastern North America since the 1500s. They had dealt with European nations (Spain, France, and Great Britain) for over two centuries and with the United States since its inception as a nation in 1776; and of course they had negotiated with myriad other native nations for centuries before that. The Cherokee delegation's statement to the United States representatives reads in part: "And here we beg leave to ask of our father that, in future transactions of a public nature between the United States and our nation, the American Government will not require of our nation any thing which, as our protectors and guardians, they will not, after due deliberation, advise us to comply with" (U.S. Congress 1834, vol. 2, 147). This is not the language of simple, naive orators espousing blind faith in the "Great White Father." Rather, this is the language of a people fully aware of their treaty rights and responsibilities and equally attuned to the responsibilities their treaty allies had willingly assumed and were obligated to follow. By this statement, they were eloquently reminding Secretary of War Calhoun and President Monroe that the United States had a clear trust responsibility to the Cherokee Nation.

In this declaration the Cherokee chiefs expressed their clear expectations of the United States. The federal government had explicit legal obligations and had also voluntarily assumed the position of "protectors and guardians" of Cherokee interests and rights. As such, the United States should hold itself accountable—and would be held accountable by the Cherokees—to the highest standards of justice and humanity. Importantly, the United States, as the tribe's self-stated protector, was expected only to *advise* the Cherokees to make decisions that would serve the best interest of the Indians. The Cherokees, as a sovereign people, could accept or reject that advice depending on their own political proclivities. In other words, Cherokee consent was required before any actions were taken that might adversely affect their nation.

Going Snake and his brethren had an astute sense of "trust." They believed the federal government (1) would honor its legal obligations as they had been established in preexisting colonial and early federal treaties; (2) would feel legally and morally obligated as a Christian nation to follow its own laws; and (3) would voluntarily assume whatever additional duties were required to serve in the role as the tribes' "protectors and guardians." The Cherokees expected that this treble sense of trust would compel the United States to respect Cherokee sovereignty, rights, and territorial integrity.

The early 1800s posed tremendous challenges to the cultural and political integrity of the Cherokee Nation. As early as 1803, President Jefferson had raised the idea of removing American Indians from their homelands within and adjacent to the eastern states. He envisioned a process euphemistically referred to as "land exchange," where tribal lands in the East would be "exchanged" for lands west of the Mississippi over which the United States claimed federal jurisdiction subsequent to the Louisiana Purchase (Prucha 1962). A year earlier, federal authorities had already envisioned an end to Indian title to lands within the states. On April 24, 1802, the United States and Georgia had entered into an agreement whereby Georgia surrendered its claims to western lands.[4] The United States promised Georgia that the federal government would—at some unspecified time and in some unspecified fashion—"quiet" or extinguish all Indian title to lands within the state of Georgia.

Pressures mounted in the early decades of the century to assert Georgia state claims to Cherokee lands. Rising agricultural property values,[5] Cherokee gold mines, and growing white (and enslaved black) populations all fueled Georgia's desire for Cherokee lands. Despite constitutional assignment of jurisdiction over Indian affairs to the federal government, and the existence of several federal treaties with the Cherokee Nation, in 1829 the Georgia state legislature unilaterally "dissolved" the Cherokee National Government and "claimed" Cherokee lands. State laws were passed that claimed to nullify the Cherokee government, assert ownership of the gold mines and agricultural lands, and deny citizenship to Cherokee people. As violence and terrorism against Cherokee people escalated, Cherokees were denied due process by state law. No Cherokee, for instance, could testify in a court of law against a white person, so white depredations against Cherokee peoples and lands were legally unchecked. White citizens could assault, rob, or murder Cherokee people with impunity.

In the 1830s the Cherokee Nation, through its attorneys, William Wirt and John Sergeant, filed a motion in the Supreme Court for an injunction to prevent Georgia from executing its intrusive laws, which aimed to destroy Cherokee territorial and jurisdictional autonomy (*Cherokee Nation v. Georgia*, 30 U.S. [5 Pet.] 1 [1831]). The tribe lacked any trained Cherokee lawyers and was represented by Anglo-American attorneys, but there is no question that Cherokee leaders were in control. In fact, the Cherokee Nation's Council presented Wirt with a specific set of legal questions they wanted answered (Norgren 1996, 56). As part of the Cherokee Nation's brief to the High Court, the council delineated the tribe's comprehension of "trust":

> Can we under these circumstances deny that which they [Cherokees' numerous ratified treaties] necessarily import? Can we, consistently with any right rule of interpretation, or with the common obligations of good faith, call in question the character of the party, announced and admitted upon the face of the instrument itself, especially when by so doing we impair or take away from him the stipulated advantages of his compact? If it were morally or politically admissible, is it *judicially* possible, while the government acknowledges, as it continues to do, the existence and binding obligation of these treaties? (In a footnote Wirt wrote: "The act of the last session [of Congress] expressly declares, in a proviso, that they [Indian treaties] are not to be impaired or questioned.")[6] Can any court deny to them their natural construction? (Kurland and Casper 1978, 86–87)

As we have discussed in chapter 1, the majority decision in *Cherokee Nation v. Georgia*, written by Chief Justice John Marshall, a brilliant politician, never directly addressed the issue of whether Georgia had violated treaties or the U.S. Constitution. Instead, Marshall "extricated the court from the rough seas of politics with procedural sleight of hand. To shield the court from the Georgia-

Cherokee conflict and the larger maelstrom of Jacksonian politics, Marshall found that he needed only to pose—and answer—a single question: 'Is the Cherokee nation a foreign state in the sense in which that term is used in the Constitution?' " (Norgren 1996, 100–101). The Cherokee Nation, Marshall declared, was not a foreign nation or a constitutionally recognized state, but was instead declared to be a "domestic-dependent nation" existing in a relationship to the federal government that "resembled" that of a "guardian to his ward." A short time later, however, the Supreme Court received a legal dispute, in *Worcester vs. Georgia,* 31 U.S. (6 Pet.) 515 (1832), that allowed Marshall freer rein to explain the "actual state of things" between the Cherokee Nation and the states.

In *Worcester,* the chief justice acknowledged that Indian tribes had a significant degree of sovereignty; that sovereign rights were inherent; that tribes were independent and exempt from state law; and that Indian treaties had the same validity as treaties with foreign nations. This powerful ruling recognized the inherent—though diminished—sovereignty of the Cherokee Nation and substantiated tribal sovereignty, although, ironically, Indians were not parties in the suit. The Supreme Court regularly cites *Worcester* as a case affirming the dignity of tribal sovereignty.[7]

Two phrases used in *Worcester* by Marshall and Justice John McLean (in concurrence) deserve special attention. First, Marshall commented on what the phrase "under the protection of the United States" meant to the tribes and the United States. One contemporary argument held that the phrase weakened or belittled Cherokee sovereignty. Others interpreted it as a self-limiting idea used by the federal government to ensure the Cherokees that the United States would shield the Indians' rights from all forces, internal and external, intent on their destruction or diminishment. Marshall had this to say:

> The third article acknowledges the Cherokees to be under the protection of the United States of America, and of no other power. This stipulation is found in Indian treaties generally.

It was introduced into their treaties with Great Britain; and may probably be found in those with other European powers. Its origin may be traced to the nature of their connection with those powers; and its true meaning is discerned in their relative situation. . . . The Indians perceived in this protection only what was beneficial to themselves—an engagement to punish aggressions on them. It involved, practically, no claim to their lands, no dominion over their persons. It merely bound the nation to the British crown as a dependent ally, claiming the protection of a powerful friend and neighbor, and receiving the advantages of that protection, without involving a surrender of their national character. This is the true meaning of the stipulation, and is undoubtedly the sense in which it was made. Neither the British government nor the Cherokees ever understood it otherwise. The same stipulation entered into with the United States, is undoubtedly to be construed in the same manner. They receive the Cherokee Nation into their favor and protection. The Cherokees acknowledge themselves to be under the protection of the United States, and of no other power. Protection does not imply the destruction of the protected. The manner in which this stipulation was understood by the American government is explained by the language and acts of our first President. (*Worcester v. Georgia*, 31 U.S. [6 Pet.] 515 [1832], 551–52)

Equally important are Justice McLean's concurring comments on the sanctity and the scope of Indian treaties in comparison to federal treaties negotiated with other nations:

The question may be asked, is no distinction to be made between a civilized and savage people? Are our Indians to be placed upon a footing with the nations of Europe, with whom we have made treaties? The inquiry is not what station shall now be given to the Indian tribes in our country? [*sic*] but, what relation have they sustained to us, since the commencement of our government? We have made treaties with them; and are those treaties to be disregarded on our part because they were entered into with an uncivilized people? Does this lessen the obligation of such treaties? By entering into them, have we not admitted the power of this people to bind themselves, and to impose obligations on us? The President and Senate, except under the treaty-making power, cannot enter into compacts with the Indians, or with foreign nations. This power has been uniformly exercised in forming treaties with the Indians. Nations differ from each other in condition, and that of the same nation may change by the revolutions of time, but the principles of justice are the same. After a lapse of more than forty years since treaties with the Indians have been solemnly ratified by the general government, it is too late to deny their binding force. Have the numerous treaties which have been formed with them, and the ratifications by the President and Senate, been nothing more than an idle pageantry? By numerous treaties with the Indian tribes we have acquired accessions of territory of incalculable value to the Union. Except by compact, we have not even claimed a right of way through the Indian lands. We have recognized in them the right to make war. No one ever supposed that the Indians could commit treason against the United States. We have punished them for their violation of treaties; but we have inflicted the punishment on them as a nation, and not on individual offenders among them as traitors. (ibid., 582–83)

These statements on protection, on the genesis and timelessness of the trust relationship, and on the dignity of treaty rights vividly reflect the Cherokee Nation's opinion of its political relationship with the United States. Despite the rhetorical and judicial force of this important decision, however, the Cherokees and a majority of eastern Indian tribal communities were eventually forcibly removed to Indian Territory (later reduced in size and supplanted by the state of Oklahoma). The executive branch of the federal government, in the person of President Andrew Jackson, supported the position of the states and refused to enforce the judgment of the Supreme Court.

Removal was both an egregious abrogation of Cherokee (and other tribes') treaty provisions and an express disavowal of the federal trust responsibility to the Cherokee Nation. Nevertheless, the federal government negotiated new treaties with the tribes to be removed, to replace the abrogated provisions of the prior treaties. However ironic or unintentional from a federal perspective, the treaty process reinvigorated the sense of trust that the negotiating generation of relocated Cherokees believed in and acted upon. By simple virtue of being treaties, the "land exchange" or removal treaties reinforced the notion that Indian nations were in fact nations, with sovereign rights.

The majority of the Cherokee people were militarily relocated to present-day Oklahoma via the Indian Removal Act of 1830 (4 Stat., 411) and the Treaty of New Echota (7 Stat., 478–88), signed by only a small, nonrepresentative portion of the Cherokee tribe in 1835 (Prucha 1984). Some 4,000 Cherokees died en route to their new homeland, on a 900-mile journey chillingly mismanaged by the U.S. Army and known ever since as the Trail of Tears.[8] The Trail of Tears is in itself crushing proof that the federal government could and often did abrogate trust, both as tribes understood it and even as the federal government itself understood it (Foreman 1972). It is important to remember, however, that an abrogating act—even a series of acts—does not necessarily shatter the confidence of the beneficiary of the trust. A reborn sense of trust can still be constructed out of the ashes of the violated trust, or simply begun anew.

Governments are operated by individuals whose personalities, attitudes, beliefs, and values change over time. Indigenous peoples are keenly aware that flaws in one individual's, or one administration's, interpretations of laws and policies do not necessarily corrupt all subsequent generations of policymakers. Charles Wilkinson is correct when he notes that Indian policy and law are intimately connected to historical processes and events. While a tremendous

amount of legislation was enacted in the twentieth century, "many
of the basic rights of Indian tribes depend upon constructions of
treaties, statutes, and executive orders promulgated during the nineteenth or even the eighteenth century" (Wilkinson 1987, 13). However, we disagree with Wilkinson's idea that historically derived
tribal rights are "time-warped" or are compromised because they are
"old promises" (ibid., 4). While the federal courts do sometimes perceive tribal rights as "anachronistic, antiegalitarian, and unworkable"
(ibid., 5), that view is not shared by indigenous communities.

The tribal sense of trust holds that once a treaty or agreement
has been approved, the rights or lands guaranteed last in perpetuity (unless otherwise specified) or until such time as the two parties mutually agree to change the agreement's conditions. This is
especially true if lands were received or exchanged during the
negotiations, which was often the case during and after the 1830s.
Joel B. Mayes, principal chief of the Cherokee Nation, in a letter to
President Benjamin Harrison on February 24, 1890, expressed a
powerful view of trust. Chief Mayes's testimony had been prompted
when word came that Harrison had signed a proclamation—in
direct violation of the Cherokees' trust and treaties—forbidding the
Cherokees from running cattle in the Cherokee Outlet:

> I approach you, as you might say, an alien, subject, entirely,
> as it seems, only to your will as a ruler of a great nation, in
> this that you see fit to deprive the Cherokees of the use of a
> piece of property that they have been taught is rightfully
> theirs. They have been taught so from the fact of having been
> in peaceful and undisputed possession of it for the last half
> century. They have been taught so by a patent they have to
> this possession, signed by Martin Van Buren, President of the
> United States. They have always looked upon this as a very
> sacred document. It is a very beautiful document, engraved
> with the flag and coat-of-arms of your great government,
> with the proud eagle, the emblem of American liberty, at the
> head of it, under which stand the Indian and white man

shaking hands of friendship and giving their pledge and plighted faith. When they shook hands over this contract they used the word "forever." This beautiful patent embraces this tract of land upon which you say the cow shall graze no longer, and the Cherokees shall no longer derive $200,000 annually received for this grazing privilege.

They have also been taught by the Supreme Court, the highest tribunal of your Government, that this patent is good, and that the land is theirs. Now, is this all a mistake? Have they lived this long in this imaginary security? Is this a delusion? After coming to this country over fifty years ago, enduring all the privation and hardships that a people could possibly endure, and giving up for the white man their ancient home east of the Mississippi river, thereby doubly paying for this soil, are they now to be told by one who the Indian has been taught to call his "Great Father," that the Cherokees can no longer use their land, that this country must be turned into a waste, and that they can no longer receive a revenue from this source? Or will these lands be turned over by you to the despoiler just for the simple reason that the white man says he needs it, and all eyes and ears be turned away from the complaint of the Cherokees?

In the face of this proclamation, Mr. President, I, as chief of the Cherokee people, am compelled to ask these bitter questions. It seems the Indian has no place to go for protection, and I only ask what shall be their fate? What next? When will it be demanded that they depart from these lands? (1890, 1)[9]

In his statement, appropriately titled "A Manly Plea to the President for Justice," Mayes referred to the cultural, economic, and social sacrifices his ancestors had made in securing the tribe's Oklahoma lands. He was well aware that in the negotiation of their removal treaty in 1835 (7 Stat., 478–88) his ancestors had secured a permanent home in Indian Territory in fee-simple title. There is nothing "time-warped" or "anachronistic" in his assertion of Cherokee

claims to the outlet lands. Chief Mayes lucidly expressed his understanding of Cherokee treaty rights and the United States' legal and
moral obligations to enforce those rights. From an indigenous perspective, tribal treaty-based rights endure through time because
U.S. law has endured through time. They do not exist in law today
by virtue of a "time warp" any more than the Constitution does. If
anything is "warped" in this scenario, it is the federal government's
willingness coolly to abrogate ratified treaty provisions and to jet-
tison the trust relation, in the face of compelling constitutional and
pragmatic arguments.

Mayes's closing comment, that his people had no other place to
go for protection of their rights, is especially telling. Unlike other
groups and individuals in the United States whose rights are articulated through the Constitution (and its attendant Bill of Rights),
tribal nations understand that as separate sovereigns their collective rights have an extraconstitutional basis. As nations who pre-
existed the establishment of the United States and the drafting of
the constitutional document, they have a status outside, or prior
to, the Constitution. Hence, their rights can be called "extraconstitutional," in the sense that they predate and thus fall outside the
bounds of the Constitution. Tribal rights are dependent upon interpretation of treaty provisions. If the United States, technologically
and militarily superior to the Cherokees in the 1890s, chose to disavow its treaty and trust commitments, then that quite literally left
the Cherokees with no place to turn for enforcement of their rights.

We can turn to at least one other discussion of an indigenous
vision of trust that reinforces the Cherokee case study. The Cherokees' northern brethren, the Iroquois,[10] metaphorically described
the trust responsibility as a "Covenant Chain." In the Iroquois view
indigenous trust entailed an intergovernmental and intercultural
process—notwithstanding occasional lapses and violations in practice—that required constant maintenance, lest it "rust," "slip," or
"break." As Robert A. Williams, Jr.'s recent work on the Iroquois
and the Covenant Chain confirms, "as a Constitution, the Chain
was fundamentally a legal and political text, for both the English

and the Iroquois were guided in their relations by its underlying principle of a continually renewed reciprocity of rights and duties. The Chain's imagery and metaphor—of two once-alien groups connected in an interdependent relationship of peace, solidarity, and trust—became the governing legal and political language of English-Iroquois forest diplomacy for most of the Encounter era, and even into the Revolutionary era" (Williams 1994, 991). While the Covenant Chain metaphor may have fallen into disuse in the revolutionary period, the indigenous (and nonindigenous) under-standing of the trust doctrine persisted, even if its influence as a governing intergovernmental principle vacillated unpredictably throughout time.

The period from the late 1880s to the early 1920s—an era of allot-ment, assimilation, and plenary power—is arguably the bleakest period for tribes as they struggled to adapt to a radically changed political, demographic, and economic environment. Throughout these stark years, tribes persistently reminded the federal govern-ment of its multiple obligations, those retained by the tribes in treaties, those the United States was legally obligated to provide, and those "voluntarily assumed" by the federal government. An example can be found in the autobiography of James McLaughlin, a prominent U.S. Indian inspector, who had a hand in ten ratified treaties, a number of unratified treaties, and a sizable number of agreements from 1895 to the early 1900s. McLaughlin played a piv-otal role in the federal government's efforts to purchase tribal lands for the least amount of money or fewest guaranteed tribal entitle-ments. However, he also had a strong sense of justice and wanted tribes to secure what he considered adequate compensation for their ceded lands.

In 1888, for instance, McLaughlin was an ex-officio member of a federal commission negotiating to reduce the Standing Rock Sioux Nation's land base. Upon reading the agreement, he observed that it was "not the sort of proposition I would make to a friend of mine" (McLaughlin 1910, 274–75). "I know," he said, "that the concessions the Indians were asked to make were immensely more valuable than was indicated by the compensation proposed; that I was bound in good faith to the Indians at the agency to advise them for their good. Still, I was a member of the commission and could not counsel the Indians to reject the proposals" (ibid.). In light of this conflict of interest, he "asked to be released from service on the commission" (ibid.). As a federal employee McLaughlin was expected to be loyal to the United States and to negotiate in the best federal interests. As an Indian agent, he was charged with protecting and advising the Indians in a manner that did them no injury—in other words, with carrying out the government's trust responsibilities. His moral and ethical dilemma is regularly played out today.

The Cherokee groups, notwithstanding the sordid history of devastating federal policies and laws that violated their rights, still retain faith in the legal system to compel the federal government to fulfill its duties. Indian people generally maintain a sense that the United States government will one day fulfill its legislated, negotiated, and self-imposed duties toward native nations. McLaughlin also noted the Indian faith in the law in his autobiography. Describing the Indians' belief in "the rule of law" and in the "moral character" of the United States, he said:

> He [the Indian] is given much to the forms of law. The Indian is a natural litigant, and it is to be regretted that he is prone to this. He believes implicitly in the capacity of the white man's courts to remedy all wrongs, and is disposed to hire a lawyer whenever he gets a chance. There are bands and communities of Indians in this country who practically maintain the lobbies hired by law firms at Washington, and who often go hungry, when the fees they pay to lawyers would supply them with the material necessities of life. (McLaughlin 1910, 310)

McLaughlin's observation has lost no force in the last ninety years. Indian and non-Indian legal-interest groups might be termed a growth industry; and the number of Indian lawyers has grown from less than 25 in the 1960s to nearly 2,000 (Yellow Bird 2000).

Indigenous people continue to hope that the federal government will one day consistently respect both its own institutions and Indian nations.

Cherokee and other American Indian communities are prone to believe—to trust—what they have been told by the federal government's policymakers. The United States and preceding European nations have always maintained that they would exercise the "utmost good faith" in their political dealings with tribes and that they would be governed by laws of "justice and humanity" in their treatment of Indian peoples. The Cherokees will undoubtedly persist in their belief that they are entitled to dignity and respect, in no small part because they continue to display dignity and respect for the United States. Notwithstanding historical and ongoing debates with federal, state, and local governments over taxation, jurisdictions, gaming, water rights, and myriad other issues, the Cherokees retain a measure of confidence that the federal government—the preeminent sovereign the Cherokees are linked with via treaties and trust—will fulfill its duties.

TRUST IN THE CONTEMPORARY POLITICAL WORLD

The United States, despite its blemished treaty rights record, has shown through a substantial corpus of political and legal documentation an ongoing belief in the validity and sanctity of Indian treaties and agreements; federal policies that affirm a nation-to-nation relationship; federal laws that support Indian religious freedom, tribal self-governance, and tribal judicial systems; judicial decrees that recognize the inherent sovereignty of tribes; and presidential actions that carve out a path of positive intergovernmental relations. In short, the United States government has the capability of fulfilling its original and ongoing "Contracts with Native America."

Jim Wallis, in his powerful study *The Soul of Politics: A Practical and Prophetic Vision for Change* (1994), describes hope as "the most feared reality of any oppressive system. More powerful than any other weapon, hope is the great enemy of those who would control history" (236). Wallis continues: "The word hope is often used to refer to something mystical or rhetorical. Hope somehow lies outside the reality in which we have to live. Hope becomes a feeling or a mood or an inspired moment that is lived somehow above the painful and dull agonies of history" (ibid., 237). This description of hope is, we believe, comparable to the Cherokee vision of "trust." Wallis's explanation of the "nonsense of hope" closely parallels how Cherokee views of "trust" have been maintained through the "agonies of history":

> Hope unbelieved is always considered nonsense. But hope believed is history in the process of being changed. The nonsense of the Resurrection becomes the hope that shook the Roman Empire and established the Christian movement. The nonsense of slave songs in Egypt and Mississippi became the hope that let the oppressed go free. The nonsense of a bus boycott in Montgomery, Alabama, became the hope that transformed a nation. The nonsense of women's meetings became the hope that brought suffrage and a mighty movement that demands gender equality. The nonsense of the uneducated, the unsophisticated, "the rabble," became the hope that creates industrial unions, farmworker cooperatives, campesino collectives, and a myriad of popular organizations that challenge and sometimes defeat monopolies of wealth and power. (ibid., 238–39)

The Cherokees have found that while the notion of trust overarches and undergirds their political/legal relations with federal and state governments, the trust doctrine alone has been insufficient to safeguard their interests. They have also had to use other strategies when reliance on trust was not enough. Indigenous people share with peasant and other oppressed groups around the world the reality that sometimes the best they can do to survive is to work "the system . . . to their minimum disadvantage" (Scott 1985, xv). While the Cherokees may not be able to alter the federal system they live within, and cannot always expect "the law" to redress their needs, they have found ways throughout history to engage in what James Scott artfully terms "everyday forms of . . . resistance" (Scott 1985, xvi). Scott has "in mind the ordinary weapons of relatively powerless groups: foot dragging, dissimulation, desertion, false compliance, pilfering, feigned ignorance, slander, arson, sabotage, and so on" (ibid.). Scott, who lived in a small village in Malaysia for two years while he conducted his research, observed that in the Third World it is rare and often deadly for peasants to confront state authorities. They are more likely to "nibble away at such policies by noncompliance, foot dragging, deception" (ibid.). Ideological struggle underwrites resistance for many oppressed groups.

Profound differences separate North American Indian communities (with treaty and trust rights acknowledged, if not always fulfilled) and peasant communities in the Third World. Despite those differences in the late twentieth century, the historical experiences of these two sets of peoples contained many parallels. Most tribes, including the Cherokees, by the late 1800s could not effectively fend off federal assaults aimed at the absorption of Indians into the American body politic. Their disadvantages did not stop the Cherokees or other tribes from finding subtle ways to protect what rights and land they retained. Native people quietly resisted allotment of their lands (Mankiller and Wallis 1993), formed clandestine gangs within the rigidly regimented confines of boarding schools (Lomawaima 1994), disguised potlatches as Christmas gift-giving extravaganzas (Jonaitis 1991), and camouflaged ceremonial gatherings as Fourth of July celebrations (Biolsi 1992).

Indigenous groups have employed multiple cross-cutting strategies, suitable to the time and issue, in order to realize their vision of trust. One strategy has been a straightforward and active reliance on the trust doctrine (as they understand it) and concomitant faith in the rule of law, however ironic or naive that might seem to outside observers. Native people have also constructed or adopted new institutions of governance and acquired new economic skills to survive—the Cherokee Nation used both these strategies to resist removal in the early 1800s. Tribes have chosen paths of political participation (voting, memorializing Congress or the president) or nonparticipation (withholding their participation as an outward expression of their separate sovereign status) as they see fit. Sporadic outbursts of violence have punctuated U.S.-Indian relations, usually called "uprisings" or "revolts" in American history textbooks (if they are acknowledged at all).[11] Sometimes tribes or factions have colluded with federal authorities, as the "Pro-Treaty" party among the Cherokees did during the removal crisis. Sometimes people have found subtle ways (fleeing, footdragging, misdirecting Bureau of Indian Affairs officials, feigning ignorance) to blunt the effect of harmful policies or simply to survive.

History teaches us important lessons, but native people do not live only in the past. Like human beings everywhere, American Indians shape the present and plan for the future. The Cherokee vision of trust, for example, is not just historically based. It is constituted in the present and oriented toward the future. The indigenous vision of trust authorizes and allows both parties—the United States and the tribe—to do only what is diplomatically agreed or consented to. Any unilateral action that adversely affects either party violates the trust. One nation may voluntarily assume certain responsibilities, but these are acceptable only so long as the receiving party finds them in its best interest. The Cherokees will continue to hold the federal government accountable—legally, politically, socially, culturally, and economically—for activities that exceed negotiated positions; that do direct or indirect harm to Cherokee rights and resources; or that transgress the federal government's assumed role as the tribe's "protector." These three layers of trust represent an intertwining of moral, political, and legal obligations. Based on an indigenous, reciprocal vision of trust, tribes believe that tribal and federal rights, properties, and sovereignty are equally entitled to deep and profound respect.

The Cherokee Nation has evidenced this multidimensional layering of trust in January 31, 1994, testimony before the Senate Committee on Indian Affairs on the issue of health care reform in Indian

Country. The Cherokee Nation's position paper cogently summarized that tribe's position:

> Our paramount interest in ensuring the availability of optional health services for our people require [sic] that we work diligently to shape and challenge any plan for reform which promises to have an impact on health care services to Native Americans. *Rights guaranteed to our people through treaties and compacts with the federal government and our status as a sovereign government must be protected and honored as we consider changes within our nation's health care system.* (U.S. Senate 1994a, 171; emphasis added)

As Congress continues to vacillate in its commitment to provide social, health, and education programs to Indian peoples, the Cherokees and all federally recognized tribes anxiously await the results of these fiscal decisions, many of which are made without tribal involvement or with little substantive tribal consultation. It is presently unclear if Congress intends to diminish long-term treaty and trust entitlements. The federal courts would have to sanction such diminutions, and it is no comfort to tribes that the Supreme Court's recent decisions point toward a rise of antitrust sentiment in the law.[12]

Even if American Indian tribes suffer massive and unilateral cuts in federal services and dollars, and even if the federal courts constrict tribal sovereignty through opinions, tribes will not be convinced that the trust relationship is no longer viable. Tribes will regroup and continue their own campaign of quietly exercising sovereignty. This is the essence of an indigenous vision of trust.

CHAPTER THREE

"Such an Outrage": The Doctrine of Plenary Power

Suppose the Federal Government should send a survey company into the midst of some of your central counties of Kansas or Colorado or Connecticut and run off the surface of the earth into sections and quarter sections and quarter quarter sections and set apart to each one of the inhabitants of that country 60 acres, rescinding and annulling all title to every inch of the earth's surface which was not included in that 60 acres, would the State of Connecticut submit to it? Would Colorado submit to it? Would Kansas brook such an outrage? No!

DEWITT CLINTON DUNCAN (Cherokee), 1906

The political relationship between American Indian tribes and the United States has endured for more than two centuries. The relationship has been troubled, however, because of the conjuncture of geographical, historical, political, and constitutional issues and circumstances that influence tribal-federal affairs. A central paradox stems from the federal government itself. On the one hand, the

United States claims plenary power—that is, exclusive, preemptive, absolute, and unlimited power—over tribes, their resources, and the field of Indian affairs.[1] On the other hand, and often simultaneously, the United States acknowledges and sometimes supports the inherent sovereignty exercised by American Indian nations. Federal plenary power and tribal sovereignty are contrapuntal partners. Like children perched on opposite ends of the see-saw, or opponents straining at ends of the tug-of-war rope, one side gains perspective, or territory, at the expense of the other. This paradox or opposition is termed "irreconcilability" in Indian law and policy. Ball explains the term in this way: "[Americans] claim that the 'Constitution, and the laws of the United States which shall be made in pursuance thereof . . . shall be the supreme law of the land.' But we also claim to recognize the sovereignty of Native American Nations, the original occupants of the land. These claims—one to jurisdictional monopoly, the other to jurisdictional multiplicity—are irreconcilable" (Ball 1987, 3).

We propose that breaking down the definition of "plenary" into its component parts makes it possible to reconcile the seemingly contradictory impulses toward jurisdictional monopoly (by the federal government) and jurisdictional multiplicity (among the United States and tribes). Plenary power as an *exclusive* power of Congress is a constitutionally based and appropriate understanding of the term. This sense of exclusive does not impute any power to the executive or judicial branches of the federal government, nor to the states. *Preemptive* plenary power, where Congress preempts the action of states toward tribes, is also constitutionally based and appropriate. However, plenary power defined as *unlimited and absolute* power over tribes is insupportable. We present two arguments against an unlimited-absolute definition of plenary power. First, such a definition creates a constitutional impasse. The United States can not assert unlimited authority over tribal governments, their resources, and their peoples, because there is no constitutional justification for such power.[2] The second argument against an unlimited-absolute definition depends upon a paradox, the "irreconcilability" pointed out by

Ball—the fact that the United States frequently recognizes and supports the sovereign rights of tribes. Our discussion of plenary power here, accordingly, proceeds hand in hand with a discussion of tribal sovereignty. The federal government and tribes have been engaged in a tug-of-war since the federal government first asserted plenary power over tribes, and since tribes continued their assertions of inherent sovereignty, a process that began in the pre–United States colonial era.

Congressional exercise, or assertion, of unlimited plenary power has varied considerably over time, reaching its height roughly from the 1880s to the 1920s. It should be noted that the executive has on occasions acted as if plenary power were not an exclusively congressional prerogative; clearly, presidential opinions on their right to exercise plenary power over tribes have varied over time as well. Some who define plenary power as unlimited and absolute regard it as an aberrant and undemocratic doctrine that Congress arbitrarily uses to oppress or terminate tribal (or even individual) Indian rights (Ball 1987; Deloria 1985a; Newton 1984; Shattuck and Norgren 1991).[3]

From the late 1800s into the early 1900s, congressional plenary power, defined as unlimited-absolute, was exercised in its most malignant and extreme form. Treaties were unilaterally abrogated, land was confiscated, assimilation policies were forced on Indian people. Even during this period, however, on a number of occasions Congress, or sometimes the executive branch, did not employ plenary power to force tribes to comply with a particular treaty, agreement, or federal statute. Tribal leaders and their constituencies sometimes simply voted down pending agreements or laws perceived as potentially injurious or unfair to tribal interests.[4] These laws, treaties, or agreements were then returned to Washington for revision or, in some cases, were tabled indefinitely if Washington could not secure tribal consent.[5] For example, Congress enacted a statute in 1874 titled "An act authorizing the payment of annuities into the treasury of the Seminole Tribe of Indians" (18 Stat., L. 29). A proviso to the act read: "Provided, That said agreement shall provide that the sum of five thousand dollars shall be annually appropriated out of said annuity to the school fund of said tribe: And provided further, That the consent of said tribe to such expenditures and payment shall be first obtained." An attached note at the bottom of the page stated: "Indians withhold assent."

If Congress assumed it had unfettered plenary power over the tribes, why did it not simply use it all the time? In the 1903 decision *Lone Wolf v. Hitchcock* (187 U.S. 553), the Supreme Court went so far as to say that Congress had *always* had this power. "Why," as Vine Deloria has asked, "all the hoopla over treaties and agreements? Why, at that very moment, were a number of treaty and agreement commissions in the field on several reservations asking the tribes to make treaties and agreements with the United States?" (Deloria 1989, 221–22). In the following pages we explore how plenary power has been defined and what circumstances accounted for its radical transformation in Indian law and policy in the 1880s. We propose that plenary power, in its most problematic meaning as unlimited federal power, cannot be a viable political doctrine in a democratic country founded on the principles of limited government.

PLENARY POWER DEFINED

In its broadest commonsense use, "plenary" means complete, entire, perfect, possessing full power or authority. In law, the earliest use of "plenary" dates back to 1726: "the cause is hereby made a Plenary cause, and ought to be determin'd Plenarily" (Simpson and Weiner 1989, 1039). The term was first used by the U.S. Supreme Court in the seminal constitutional law case *Gibbons v. Ogden* (22 U.S. [9 Wheat.] 1 [1824]). Chief Justice John Marshall wrote: "[I]f, as has always been understood, the sovereignty of Congress, though limited to specified objects, is *plenary* as to those objects, the power over commerce with foreign nations, and among the several States, is vested in Congress as absolutely as it would be in a single government, having in its constitution the same restrictions on the exercise of the power as are found in the constitution of the United States" (ibid., 197). *Gibbons* was the first case to address the clause empowering Congress to regulate interstate and foreign commerce. Chief Justice Marshall, a strong federalist, made a classic statement in this opinion on the importance of nationalism. He showed his preference for the national government (not the states) to have exclusive authority over interstate commerce.

Plenary power has often been cited in cases dealing with the extent of federal powers vis-à-vis state governments. From very early in the American republic's history, when "plenary" was defined primarily as exclusive and preemptive power, the notion of plenary power has guided the federal government's relationship with Indian tribes and has been used to keep states at arm's length from tribes.

Plenary Power as Exclusive Power

The concept of plenary power, it is important to note, "merge[s] several analytically distinct questions" (Engdahl 1976, 363). First, there is the notion of *exclusivity*. The commerce clause (Article 1, sec. 8, cl. 3) of the Constitution recognizes the Congress, not the president or the courts, and certainly not the states, as the sole authority to "regulate commerce with foreign nations . . . states . . . and with the Indian tribes." The commerce clause is the only source of explicit authority over Indian affairs delegated to the Congress (nowhere does the Constitution explicitly grant Congress, or any other branch, authority over *tribes*). The commerce clause stipulated that the American trades were to be *exclusively* regulated by Congress and not the states, because the colonies/states had been terribly inconsistent and often unfair in their trade with tribal nations.

Although some commentators, most notably Felix S. Cohen, have suggested that Congress's commerce clause power is *over* tribes and that this power is "much broader" over tribes than is the Congress's power over interstate commerce, there is nothing in the

Constitution to support such an interpretation. In fact, a federal appellate court in *United States v. Doherty* (126 F.3d 769 [1997]) noted that there is no real distinction between the Indian commerce clause and the interstate commerce clause. *Doherty* raised an important issue given the recent redefinition of federalism taking place in Supreme Court jurisprudence: "Because neither party has raised the issue, we leave to another day the question of whether the newly re-affirmed limitations of the Interstate Commerce Clause . . . also impose limits on federal power under the Indian Commerce Clause" (ibid., 778, note 2).[6]

The commerce clause and the treaty clause (Article 2, sec. 2, cl. 2) are the bases for federal exclusive authority to deal with tribes. The authority to make treaties is implicit, because Indians are not expressly mentioned in the treaty clause, but treaties were the principal mechanism that linked tribes and the federal government from 1785 until 1871. States, under the Constitution, are expressly denied the power to enter into treaties (Article 1, sec. 10). In the commerce and treaty clauses, the federal government recognized that Indian affairs were an aspect of military and foreign policy, rather than subject to domestic law (Shattuck and Norgren 1991, 122). In early interpretations, the courts concurred with this interpretation of federal authority.

Plenary as *exclusive* power is the definition Congress uses most frequently in enacting Indian-specific legislation, such as the 1934 Indian Reorganization Act (48 Stat., 985), or when enacting Indian preference laws that withstand reverse discrimination lawsuits (*Morton v. Mancari*, 417 U.S. 535 [1974]). These are exclusively legislative powers—they are not executive or judicial powers. Congress may exercise exclusive plenary power in keeping with its policy of treating with tribes in a distinctively political manner, or to recognize specific rights, such as religious freedom, that Indians have been deprived of because of their extraconstitutional standing (e.g., the 1978 American Indian Religious Freedom Act, 92 Stat., 469). As Vine Deloria, Jr., has observed:

There may indeed be some kind of establishment of religious freedom for American Indians. If so, it is because Congress has dealt with the question of the practice of Indian religions and felt it to be necessary to extend the protection of federal laws further in the case of Indians than the Constitution allows it to extend to ordinary citizens. In this instance Indians are not to be regarded as "supercitizens"; rather, the practice of Indian religion is to be regarded as under the special protection of the federal government in the same way that Indian water rights, land titles, and self-government are protected. Congress has always dealt with Indians in a special manner; that is why Congress and the federal courts cherish and nourish the doctrine of plenary powers in the field of Indian affairs. (Deloria 1985b, 247)

Plenary Power as Preemptive Power

Plenary power is also often defined as *preemptive* power. In this definition, federal powers "preempt" or supersede state powers. In areas where federal powers are "preemptive," the states may not exercise any jurisdiction. Again, prime models for this interpretation are provided by the Congress's commerce power and the treaty-making process, both of which preclude involvement of the states. In *McClanahan v. Arizona State Tax Commission* (411 U.S. 164 [1973]), the Court rebuffed Arizona's attempt to tax income earned by a Navajo Indian within the reservation. The decision stated that "this Court has interpreted the Navajo treaty to preclude extension of State law—including state tax law—to Indians on the Navajo Reservation" (ibid., 164).[7]

Additional evidence for federal preemptive powers can be found in the constitutional disclaimers that eleven western territories were required to include in their organic documents before they were considered eligible for admission as states (North and South Dakota [1889], Montana [1889], Washington [1889], Wyoming [1890], Idaho [1890], Utah [1896], Oklahoma [1907], New Mexico

[1912], Arizona [1912], and Alaska [1959]).[8] These disclaimers declare that in order for a state to be able to tax Indian lands or property, the state must obtain both tribal and federal consent and must amend the state constitution. As Justice Thurgood Marshall put it in *McClanahan*: "Thus, when Arizona entered the Union, its entry was expressly conditioned on the promise that the State would 'forever disclaim all right and title to . . . all lands lying within said boundaries owned or held by any Indian . . . and that until the title of such Indian or Indian tribes shall have been extinguished the same shall be and remain subject to the disposition and under the absolute jurisdiction and control of the Congress of the United States' " (ibid., 175).

An important corollary doctrine to plenary power that needs to be interjected here is the political question rule (Coulter 1977; Kramer 1986; Shattuck and Norgren 1979). The Supreme Court invokes the political question rule when it refuses to hear a case, either because the case involves a question that is essentially "political" in nature or because the Court determines that it would be intruding on the powers of the legislative or executive branch. Because (under the commerce and treaty clauses) the federal government has exclusive and preemptive power in administering the field of Indian affairs, and because Indian affairs were seen as part of foreign policy, "the power of judicial review over the substantive content of federal Indian policy was limited to the same extent as judicial power to review foreign affairs decisions was limited" (Shattuck and Norgren 1991, 123). In other words, the U.S. power to make treaties with tribes was considered a political matter and was not subject to judicial scrutiny.

One could argue that so long as the treaty process continued (until 1871), the political question rule should also continue to be applied by the Supreme Court. Treaty-making, after all, very explicitly acknowledged tribal sovereignty. Treaty-making was by definition a process that occurred between governments; it was, therefore, undeniably a political process and not subject to Court review. Interestingly enough, however, the Supreme Court did not stop applying the political question rule to cases involving Indians after

1871. Even though the United States unilaterally and fundamentally altered the treaty process in 1871 and set about the task of domesticating Indians through forced assimilation—via land allotment, coercive Christian missionaries, and indoctrination of Indian children in boarding schools, among other policies—the Supreme Court still frequently refused to open its doors to aggrieved Indians.

The Court rationalized its reliance on the political question rule, and refused to hear many Indian complaints, until the late 1970s. Then, in two important decisions, *Delaware Tribal Business Committee v. Weeks* (430 U.S. 73 [1977]) and *United States v. Sioux Nation* (448 U.S. 371 [1980]), the Court ceased to disregard Indian litigants based solely on the so-called political nature of their cases. Discussion of the political question rule, particularly its post-1871 application, leads us directly to the third, and easily the most constitutionally problematic, definition of plenary power: unlimited or absolute political power.

Plenary Power as Unlimited and Absolute Power

By definition, no unlimited and absolute power should exist in the United States, since the Constitution limits the powers of both the federal and state governments to those powers expressly enumerated. In other words, governments possess only those powers that the Constitution very explicitly names. There is nothing in the U.S. Constitution granting the federal government "unlimited or absolute" authority over Indian nations or their citizens. In fact, there is nothing in the U.S. Constitution granting the federal government "unlimited or absolute" authority over anything or anyone. After all, our nation was founded in direct opposition to the unlimited and absolute powers claimed by Europe's royal crowns.[9] And yet the Supreme Court has ruled, more than once, that the Congress has unlimited and absolute power over tribes.

For example, in a number of contemporary decisions, the Court has described Congress's power vis-à-vis tribes in aggressive and graphic language:

- "The sovereignty that the Indian tribes retain is of a unique and limited character. It exists only at the sufferance of Congress and is subject to complete defeasance." (*United States v. Wheeler* 435 U.S. 313, 323 [1978])

- "As we have often noted, Indian tribes occupy a unique status under our law. At one time they exercised virtually unlimited power over their own members as well as those who were permitted to join their communities. Today, however, the power of the Federal Government over the Indian tribes is plenary." (*National Farmers Union Ins. Co's. v. Crow Tribe* 471 U.S. 845, 851 [1985])

- "Defendant correctly asserts that under Supreme Court doctrine, Congress holds virtually unlimited power over the Indian tribes." (*Red Lake Band of Chippewa Indians v. Swimmer* 740 F.Supp. 9, 11 [1990])

- "Indian tribes are separate sovereigns with the power to regulate their internal and social relations, including their form of government and tribal membership. . . . These powers of sovereignty are subject to the plenary authority of Congress." (*Fletcher v. United States* 116 F.3d 1315, 1326–27 [10th Cir. 1997])

- "The federal set-aside requirement also reflects the fact that because Congress has plenary power over Indian affairs . . . some explicit action by Congress (or the Executive, acting under delegated authority) must be taken to create or to recognize Indian country." (*Alaska v. Native Village of Venetie Tribal Government* 522 U.S. 520, 531, note 6 [1998])

- "Congress possesses plenary power over Indian affairs, including the power to modify or eliminate tribal rights." (*South Dakota v. Yankton Sioux Tribe* 522 U.S. 329, 343 [1998])

How and why did the Supreme Court redefine "plenary" from its constitutionally moored meanings of exclusive and preemptive to its highly problematic—even unconstitutional, in our view—definition as unlimited and absolute? We must return to the late 1800s to explain this remarkable development. From the 1880s to the early 1900s, the federal government directed all its policies, practices, and considerable powers to assimilate American Indians. The central weapon in the federal government's assimilative arsenal was the General Allotment Act (24 Stat., 388), inaugurated in 1887. The act authorized the president, at his discretion, to survey and break up the communal land holdings of tribes and to "allot" land holdings to individual Indians. Policymakers had such abiding faith in the deeply transformative powers of America's Protestant mercantile culture that they believed the mere prospect of private property ownership would magically transform tribal Indians into ruggedly individualistic, Christian, self-supporting yeoman farmers. The assimilative campaign did not, however, depend only on allotment to detribalize indigenous peoples. Other components of assimilation policy included (Prucha 1984; McDonnell 1991):

- Land loss via surplus land sales, specific allotment acts, amendments to the allotment policy, and fraudulent activities by land speculators and some state officials;
- Sponsorship of mission efforts to Christianize tribal members;
- Imposition of federal criminal jurisdiction over certain crimes in Indian Country;
- Eradication of Indian culture, facilitated by the establishment of Courts of Indian Offenses; and
- Mandatory enrollment of Indian children in federal and mission schools, especially the removal of children away from homes and communities, and their placement in boarding schools.

Most commentators agree that the era of the unlimited and absolute variety of plenary power exercised over Indian tribes was inaugurated with the Supreme Court's 1886 decision in *United States v. Kagama* (118 U.S. 375 [1886]; see Harring 1994). Although the term "plenary" is absent from *Kagama*, other language in the case strongly supports congressional efforts to diminish tribal sovereignty. At issue in *Kagama* was the constitutionality of the Major Crimes Act (23 Stat., 362, 385 [1885]). The act had authorized federal jurisdiction over several "major crimes" in Indian Country, such as murder, manslaughter, rape, assault with intent to kill, arson, burglary, and larceny. The Court exercised its vast interpretive power to rationalize and legitimate this unilateral assertion of plenary legislative power by Congress, despite the lack of tribal consent and the lack of any tribal surrender of their own jurisdiction, through treaty or some other agreement (Deloria 1988, 261).

Unable to locate a constitutional clause on which to base its ruling, the Court crafted an ingenious, even bizarre, two-pronged explanation that depended on ethnocentric (and untrue) assertions of Indian helplessness and on equally ethnocentric and flawed assertions of U.S. rights to land ownership based on European "discovery." First, Justice Samuel Miller transmuted John Marshall's mere analogy of Indians as "wards" to their federal "guardians" to a principle of law. Miller said: "These Indian tribes are wards of the nation. They are communities dependent on the United States" (118 U.S. 375, 383–84). The Court then said that federal power over these "weak" peoples was "necessary to their protection, as well as to the safety of those among whom they dwell." This power, the Court held, "must exist in that [United States] government, because it never has existed anywhere else" (ibid., 384). Regarding land ownership, Miller claimed that the federal government's "ownership" of land was based on the questionable doctrine of discovery and that with the inheritance of lands from prior European nations the United States had also secured virtually an unlimited power over tribes and their rights.

Critics of this case have pointed out several errors in the Court's analysis. First, how could Congress apply its laws to tribes when prior to 1886 tribes had not been subject to congressional jurisdiction, due to constraints imposed by the Constitution? The Constitution limits the authority of the government to enumerated powers, and nowhere does the Constitution enumerate federal powers to include jurisdiction over major crimes in Indian Country. The Court's inability to find any statement in the Constitution on which to base its decision clearly compromises this decision and leads to the second flaw in the argument. The Court was forced to search elsewhere in order to justify congressional passage of the Major Crimes Act, and so it cited extraconstitutional, or extralegal, reasons for holding the act to be constitutional (Deloria 1988, 261).[10] Finally, "consent of the governed" is a treasured democratic principle. The fact that most Indians at that time were not American citizens and were largely excluded from the American political arena because they had an extraconstitutional status rooted in treaties seemed irrelevant to the Court (Newton 1984, 215).

Coincidentally, on the same day *Kagama* was handed down the Court ruled unanimously in *Santa Clara v. Southern Pacific Railroad* (118 U.S. 394) that the Fourteenth Amendment's due process clause protected corporations as "legal persons." In effect, the Court was extending constitutional protection to corporate property rights, while declaring that tribal political and civil rights were vulnerable to congressional and judicial termination.

Lone Wolf v. Hitchcock (187 U.S. 553 [1903]) is most often cited as the supreme articulation of unfettered plenary power. *Lone Wolf* has received a tremendous amount of attention (see, e.g., Clark 1994; and Estin 1984) because of its ongoing legal implications and effects. Lone Wolf, a principal chief of the Kiowa Nation, sought a perpetual injunction against congressional ratification of a 1900 "agreement" that allotted tribal lands and led to a direct loss of more than 2 million acres of Indian territory. The tribes (Kiowa, Comanche, and Apache—hereafter KCA) contended that the forced allotment of their lands directly violated Article 12 of the 1867 Treaty of Medicine Lodge. The treaty article explicitly stated that no cession of tribal lands would be valid without the consent of "three-fourths of all the adult male Indians" (15 Stat., 581).

In 1892 the federally created Jerome Commission had concluded an agreement with certain representatives of the KCA tribes. Although the commissioners secured a number of Indian signatures, the three-fourths provision was unfulfilled. Nevertheless, the agreement was rushed to Washington, D.C., for congressional ratification. Almost immediately upon hearing about the allotment agreement, more than three hundred KCA tribal members urged the Senate to disapprove the 1892 agreement because "misrepresentations, threats, and fraudulent" means had been used to secure Indian signatures. Tribal consent had not been legitimately secured. In addition, as the 1892 agreement wound its way through the ratification process, Congress substantially revised the agreement. The revisions were never submitted to the KCA for their approval, as required under the treaty. Nevertheless, on June 6, 1900, Congress ratified the amended agreement, despite the vigorous protestations of the tribes.

Lone Wolf, supported by the Indian Rights Association (IRA), an influential reform organization based in Philadelphia, filed suit in the Supreme Court of the District of Columbia in 1901 to obtain an injunction against the act that confirmed the 1892 agreement. Lone Wolf and his associates lost their case. They next filed an appeal to the District Court of Appeals, where they lost as well. Despite mounting costs Lone Wolf and the IRA persisted, and they appealed to the U.S. Supreme Court. Justice Edward D. White wrote the opinion, which was, shortly after its pronouncement in 1903, called the "Dred Scott decision number two."[11] White proposed an interpretation that, since 1903, has become inculcated as a doctrine of Indian law. He declared that Congress could pass any federal law it wished and could disregard Indian property rights as defined by treaty—despite the fact that treaties, like the Constitution, are the supreme law of the land. White further stated that the 1867 treaty provision had been abrogated (overturned) by the 1900 agreement, even though the 1900 statute contradicted the treaty provision and lacked tribal consent. This, White said, was in keeping with "perfect good faith" toward the Indians. White inaccurately stated that Congress had exercised plenary authority over tribal lands "from the beginning" and that such power was "political" and therefore not subject to judicial review. These statements were legal rationalizations, yet they were in line with the reigning view that federal lawmakers held of Indians—Indians were dependent wards, subject to their sovereign guardian, the United States.

Lone Wolf was a devastating blow against tribal sovereignty. Congressional plenary power, understood as unlimited and absolute and unconstrained by the Constitution, was interwoven with the "political question" rule and judicial deference to the legislature to form an almost impregnable shield against any tribal interest. When federal interests and tribal interests clashed, the Supreme Court was ensuring that federal power would outweigh and virtually subsume tribal power. The Court's brazen refusal to examine congressional acts that abrogated treaty-recognized property rights was particularly oppressive because the majority of tribal sovereign, political, and property rights were defined by hundreds of ratified treaties and agreements. As a result of this decision, treaties as legal contracts/sacred covenants were no longer enforceable, if Congress decided to act in a manner that violated treaty provisions.

We believe it is important to note that even when plenary power was defined as unlimited/absolute, the federal government did not always wield the power as an absolute bludgeon. By the early 1900s the United States certainly was militarily capable of forcing itself on tribes. The fact that the federal government was unwilling consistently to force its laws and power over tribes is a testament to the government's adherence to the rule of law and support for treaty rights—at least sporadically. In a number of important cases during the late 1800s and early 1900s, the Supreme Court handed down rulings that explicitly and implicitly relied on the exclusive and preemptive definitions of plenary power (although the Court never denied that the United States could force itself upon the tribes if it so desired). In *Ex parte Crow Dog*, 109 U.S. 556 (1883), the Court recognized tribal sovereignty by denying that the federal courts had criminal jurisdiction over Indian-on-Indian crimes. In *Talton v. Mayes*, 163 U.S. 376 (1896), the Court confirmed that the U.S. Constitution's Fifth Amendment grand jury provision was inapplicable to tribal nations, since tribal rights predated the Constitution and derived from the sovereignty of the Cherokee people, not from the U.S. Constitution.[12]

The *Lone Wolf* precedent has never been overturned by the Supreme Court, although in two modern decisions discussed earlier, *Weeks* and *Sioux Nation*, the political question aspect of the case has been somewhat eroded. As the Court said in *Weeks*: "The statement in *Lone Wolf* that the power of Congress 'has always been deemed a political one, not subject to be controlled by the judicial department of the government,' however pertinent to the question then before the Court of congressional power to abrogate treaties . . . has not deterred this Court, particularly in this day, from scrutinizing Indian legislation to determine whether it violates the equal protection component of the Fifth Amendment" (430 U.S. 73, 84 [1977]). The Court in *Weeks* went on to say that while Congress's power over Indian affairs is of a plenary nature, it "is not absolute." However, the plenary nature of federal authority is still alive and well since "it remains true that no act of Congress concerning Indian affairs, with two minor exceptions, has ever been set aside or ruled unconstitutional by the Supreme Court. . . . The plenary power doctrine has extraconstitutional roots with only a limited accountability that has not been fully recognized or adequately addressed" (Pommersheim 1995, 47).[13]

Interestingly, as early as 1914 the Supreme Court in *Perrin v. United States* (232 U.S. 478) had suggested that congressional plenary authority did have some limitations: "As the power is incident only to the presence of the Indians and their status as wards of the Government, it must be conceded that it does not go beyond what is reasonably essential for their protection, and that, to be effective, its exercise must not be purely arbitrary but founded upon some reasonable basis" (ibid., 486). The *Perrin* Court, however, remained extremely deferential to Congress.[14] In fact, Justice Willis Van DeVanter conceded that Congress, because of its exclusive status as the branch named to deal with tribes, is "invested with a wide discretion and its action, unless purely arbitrary, must be accepted and given full effect by the Court" (*Perrin v. United States*, 232 U.S. 478). The Supreme Court has utilized the political question rule to avoid examining issues in Indian law that it deems suitable only for the legislative branches—this is called judicial deference. The Court is deferring to Congress. This type of judicial deference has been a critical problem for the tribal-federal relationship, because tribes inhabit a unique political and legal space as extraconstitutional entities. Judicial deference means there is no oversight, no judicial review, of congressional actions taken toward tribes. As long as tribes remain lodged in the commerce clause of the Constitution, there is little chance that the Court will exercise the degree of judicial scrutiny of congressional actions that tribal nations expect in fulfillment of their recognized status as sovereign entities.

The *Perrin* decision said that the federal government's actions toward Indians should not be "purely arbitrary but founded upon some reasonable basis" (ibid., 486). The notion of a "reasonable basis" is comparable to the "rational test" invoked in *Morton v. Mancari*, 417 U.S. 535 (1973). In *Mancari*, the Supreme Court upheld the Bureau of Indian Affairs' Indian preference hiring policy on the grounds of the unique political relationship between tribes and the United States. Justice Harry Blackmun stated: "As long as the special treatment can be tied rationally to the fulfillment of Congress' unique obligation toward the Indians, such legislative judgments will not be disturbed. Here, where the preference is reasonable and rationally designed to further Indian self-government, we cannot say that Congress' classification violates due process" (ibid., 555). Of course, determining what is "arbitrary" and what is "rational" is subject entirely to the interpretive power of the justices of the Court, who tend to defer to the political branches of the federal government. Evidence of this ongoing deference is found in a 1998 survey that showed that "no statute has been invalidated on such [rational] grounds" (Watson 1998, 456).

PLENARY POWER SUMMED UP

There is evidence in Indian law and policy of plenary power being applied by the legislative branches and the federal courts to tribes and individual Indians in three ways: as exclusive power, as pre-emptive power, and as unlimited/absolute power. We support the validity and appropriateness of the first two senses of plenary and absolutely deny the validity of the third. When Congress exercises *exclusive* plenary power as the voice of the federal government, ful-filling its treaty and trust-based relations with tribes, and acts with the consent of tribes, it is exercising plenary authority in a consti-tutionally legitimate way. When Congress acts in a plenary way to *preempt* state intrusion (without tribal consent) into Indian Coun-try, Congress is also properly exercising a power that is enumer-ated in the commerce and treaty clauses of the Constitution. As Vine Deloria astutely remarked: "Indians receive the protection of the federal government precisely because they are outside the pro-tections of the Constitution; they need and receive special consid-eration when the federal government interacts with them and han-dles their affairs. We have often called the government's power to accomplish this task 'plenary' because we supposed that it needed to be immune from arbitrary challenges which might otherwise hamper the wise administration of the affairs of Indians" (Deloria 1985b, 240).

However, when the Supreme Court recognizes Congress as having "full, entire, complete, absolute, perfect, and unqualified" authority over tribes and individual Indians (*Mashunkashey v. Mashunkashey*, 134 P.2d 976 [1943]), something is fundamentally wrong. Since "absolute" congressional power is not enumerated anywhere in the Constitution, the idea of "absolute" political power directly contradicts the very nature of democratic government. It also violates the treaty and trust relationship between the United States and Indian tribes. Congressional plenary power defined as absolute and unlimited is irreconcilable with tribal sovereignty. Tribal sovereignty, like any nation's sovereignty, is a dynamic and fluid process, not a rigid or totalitarian entity frozen in time. Ple-nary power, in contrast, is often considered static and absolutist, that is, as investing all political power in the federal sovereign. Nevertheless, as described earlier, even federal interpretations of plenary power have changed over time, as Congress and the courts have unilaterally transformed the bilateral relationship between tribes and the United States. The federal government, not the tribes, has said that it alone has the right to choose which definition of plenary power to apply. Tribes have not had the same luxury or privilege.

The Supreme Court, in particular, through decisions in *Kagama* and *Lone Wolf*, created an absolute and unlimited definition of plenary power that suited the late nineteenth century political agenda of forced assimilation of Indian people. As John Oberly, commissioner of Indian affairs, noted in his 1888 Annual Report, the Indian "must be imbued with the exalting egotism of American civilization, so that he will say 'I' instead of 'We,' and 'This is mine,' instead of 'This is ours' " (U.S. Department of the Interior 1889). In their zeal to support the assimilative policies and practices being forced on native peoples, the justices incorrectly asserted that the absolute and unlimited definition had always been in place, when in fact it was a fiction of their own creation—and a fiction they had a hard time justifying themselves, given the lack of constitutional basis.

In order to improve government-to-government relations between federal and tribal sovereigns in the nation we share today, a way must be found to address the irreconcilable nature of "plenary power" and "tribal sovereignty." The simplest way would be for the United States, in keeping with the Constitution and the treaty relationship, to resolve to use plenary power only in its *exclusive* and *preemptive* senses and explicitly to reject and renounce the unlimited/absolute definition as a violation of the democratic principles of enumerated powers, limited government, consent of the governed, and the rule of law.

CHAPTER FOUR

"TREATIES AS COVENANTS": THE DOCTRINE OF RESERVED RIGHTS

The Indian nations viewed treaties as covenants, as moral statements which could not be broken unless by mutual consent. . . . The purpose of these intergovernmental contracts was not to give rights to the Indians— rights which as sovereign nations they already possessed—but to remove *from them certain rights which they already had. In treaty making, tribes were the grantors and the United States the recipient, and rights were granted to the U.S. by or from Indian nations. . . . rights to land, water, hunting, government, etc., which were not expressly granted away by the tribes in a treaty, or taken away by later federal statute, were reserved by that tribe.*

STAN WEBSTER (Oneida),
Wisconsin Indian Resource Council
(emphasis in the original)

Contemporary debates over reserved rights are a good illustration of the apparent schizophrenia that the American public and many lawmakers exhibit toward tribal nations. On the one hand, reserved lands—reservations—are taken for granted as a "fact" of Indian-U.S. relations. On the other hand, reserved rights are seen as "special rights" that set Indians apart from non-Indian citizens in ways that many Americans feel are inappropriate, even unconstitutional. States, local governments, and non-native citizens have reacted strongly—indeed violently—against assertions of tribally reserved rights. In the 1970s and 1980s, the Pacific Northwest was in an uproar over Indian tribes' treaty-based rights to fish in their "usual and accustomed places," both on- and off-reservation. Confrontations among native and non-native fishers and State Game and Fish officers escalated from tense standoffs to violent clashes, and native fishers lost their gear and boats to state confiscation (American Friends Service Committee 1975; Cohen 1986). Slade Gorton, then state attorney general, accused native people of trying to create a new status for themselves as "supercitizens" (Cohen 1986, 90) and encouraged non-native fishers to break federal laws. Attorney General Gorton stood by while Federal Court Judge George Boldt, who had decided in favor of the tribes in *U.S. v. Washington* in 1974 (384 F.Supp. 343), was burned in effigy on the steps of the state capitol (American Friends Service Committee 1975; Cohen 1986).

In the Great Lakes area, native fishing rights have also been the flash point for conflict among tribes, non-natives, and states. In the 1980s non-native citizens in Wisconsin protested the treaty-guaranteed rights of Chippewa tribal members to spear-fish for walleye on ceded lands (that is, on lands that the tribes had ceded, or sold, through treaty; these are nonreservation lands today). Bumper stickers epitomized how ugly the protest over reserved native rights can be: "Save a Walleye, Spear a Pregnant Squaw" (Metz 1990; Whaley and Bressette 1994). In the 1990s in western Washington, the Makah decision to revive their cultural tradition (and treaty right) of whale hunting has raised a firestorm of media interest, protests by animal rights organizations such as Sea Shepherd, and vitriolic public protest.[1]

Treaty-stipulated fishing, hunting, or gathering rights are not the only kinds of reserved rights that have provoked protests.[2] As we begin a new century, states continue their efforts to block or regulate gaming on Indian lands, despite appalling poverty and unemployment on many reservations, and occasionally despite public support for the tribes. The state of Arizona, for example, has opposed Indian gaming despite opinion polls and state referenda indicating widespread non-native support for tribally controlled gaming enterprises (Editorial 1995; Feldman 1993; Rubio 1995; Tuttle 1992).

Why do Americans generally recognize tribal rights to reserved lands, but frequently refuse to recognize other reserved rights such as rights to hunt, fish, or gather, even when rights are expressly spelled out in treaties? What are the differences, real or perceived, between reserved lands (reservations) and reserved rights? Many Americans have at least a vague notion of the existence of reservations.[3] The word "reserve" is the root of "reservations," the lands that constitute a fundamental aspect of the Indian/U.S. relationship. Many Americans will accept, if reluctantly, that Indian tribes may have "lost," "surrendered," or "sold" most of America to the United States (or to the railroads, or to states, or to enterprising whites), but that tribes have rightfully retained smaller regions through sheer determination or through liberal federal policies. Those smaller or remnant areas of once vast homelands are designated as Indian reservations. Many Americans annually trek to reservations during the summer months in search of "authentic" tribal culture and identity. Interestingly, these same Americans are sometimes surprised, even outraged, when tribal nations assert reserved rights. Reserved rights can include a property right, such as the right to hunt, or gather, or fish; or a political right, such as the power to regulate domestic relations, tax, administer justice, or exercise civil and criminal jurisdiction.

Non-native citizens' confusion or disquiet over Indian reserved rights might stem from the lack of a definitive answer to the question: what, exactly, are the parameters of tribal powers and rights? Uncertainty over the scope of tribal powers can be summed up in the following, more legally precise question: do Indian tribes reserve all those powers and rights that they have not expressly surrendered, or do they exercise only those rights that have been expressly delegated to them by act of Congress? "Expressly" means "explicitly," and it usually means "in writing." Tribes might expressly surrender certain rights in a treaty or some other agreement; Congress might expressly grant certain rights to tribes in legislation or other action. Do tribes reserve all rights not expressly surrendered? May tribes *only* exercise rights expressly granted to them by Congress? Unfortunately, these crucial questions have no definitive answers, since the history of federal-tribal affairs has left us with a contradictory record on the status of reserved rights. Sometimes reserved rights have been defined one way, sometimes another, apparently on the whim of individual justices, congresspersons, or Bureau of Indian Affairs officials.

Following the precedents set by two prominent scholars of Indian law and policy, Vine Deloria, Jr. (1996), and Charles Wilkinson (1987), we propose a vision of the reserved rights doctrine that we feel is judicially supported and historically accurate. Deloria and Wilkinson compare the reserved rights clause contained in the U.S. Constitution's Tenth Amendment with similar expressions lodged both explicitly and implicitly in Indian treaties (and agreements). These statements—some express, some implied—reserved to tribes sovereign powers not expressly surrendered to the federal government. In our interpretation, reserved rights are those rights that a tribe never expressly surrendered or gave up. Importantly, *all rights* are reserved except those specifically given up in a treaty or similar agreement. Tribes do not exercise rights because Congress granted them rights. Tribes exercise rights based on their original and indigenous sovereignty. Tribal sovereignty has undeniably eroded over the last few centuries, but we assert that it should erode no further than what tribes have expressly allowed. Congressional and state claims to the contrary, tribal sovereignty and tribal rights do not arise from congressional action.

Our definition of the doctrine of reserved rights rests on two foundations: the Tenth Amendment to the Constitution and judicial decisions. We consider each in turn and end with a discussion of the importance of the reserved rights doctrine in the contemporary period. We conclude that tribal reserved rights will be vulnerable to state and federal attack until, or unless, tribally reserved rights attain a status comparable to the Tenth Amendment.

CONSTITUTIONAL ORIGINS OF RESERVED RIGHTS

The Constitution (generally) and the Tenth Amendment (specifically) embody the principle we know today as federalism. Federalism refers to a system of governance in which a national, overarching government shares powers—shares sovereignty, really—with subnational or state governments. In the late 1700s supporters of the powers of the newly created federal government, people such as Alexander Hamilton, James Madison, and James Wilson, were known as Federalists. Anti-Federalists feared possible political abuses by a powerful, centralized government, citing the example of the British Crown. The anti-Federalists lobbied for an express guarantee that the states would retain control over, that is, reserve powers over, their internal affairs. Many Federalists felt the states' fears were exaggerated, but could not resist popular support for a reserved powers amendment. Of all the amendments demanded by the anti-Federalists in the state conventions that ratified the Constitution, "the one calling for a reserved powers clause was most common" (McDonald 1992, 861). Accordingly, the "reserved powers" or Tenth Amendment was ratified in 1791 as part of the Bill of Rights, declaring: "The powers not delegated to the United States by the Constitution, nor prohibited by it [the Constitution] to the States, *are reserved to the States respectively, or to the people"* (emphasis added). This means that the United States only exercises those powers expressly granted to it by the Constitution.

The Tenth Amendment speaks eloquently to the delicate balance of powers between federal and state governments in the nation. Through the Tenth Amendment, supporters of states' rights aimed to preserve sovereignty of the states and sovereignty of the people. The amendment was a way to ensure that neither the federal nor the state government was the ultimate sovereign. They were meant to share. In reality, the balance between federal and state has tipped to one side and the other in the course of history. State powers eroded, for example, during the Civil War and the Depression and were embellished preceding the Civil War and in the 1990s through many Supreme Court rulings.[4] Despite these fluctuations, states may generally rest assured that at any given time at least some of their inherent sovereign powers are respected, that their existence as polities is constitutionally established and protected, and that they need not fear being terminated as polities. Tribes have none of these assurances.

What are some of the logical implications of federalism, and of powers reserved by the states, for Indian/U.S. relations and for powers reserved by the tribes? In ways similar to the Tenth Amendment, Indian treaties reserve to Indian tribes all those powers specifically stated *and* all those not expressly ceded. Treaties have a status in law similar to the Tenth Amendment, because the Constitution declares that the Constitution and treaties are the supreme law of the land. In its interpretation of a key provision of the 1855 Makah Treaty (12 Stat. 939), a federal district court said in *Makah Indian Tribe v. McCauly*, 39 F.Supp. 75 (1941), that "this court is of the opinion that as contended by plaintiffs [the Makah Tribe] the answer to this question as to the treaty's validity turns upon the sounder theory that the treaty granted nothing to the Indians, but that the treaty in truth and in fact merely *reserved and preserved inviolate to the Indians the fishing rights which from time immemorial they had always had and enjoyed*" (emphasis added). The doctrine of reserved powers has been important to both states and tribes. Each of these governments has "sought to preserve as much of their original sovereignty, powers and rights as could be done in the face of grasping federal ambitions. As the commerce and welfare clauses became vehicles for federal intrusion on state government, so the trust doctrine became the means of radical federal intrusion on Indian political rights. Nevertheless, the treaty performs the same function for Indian nations as does the Tenth Amendment for States" (Deloria 1996, 972).

One critical difference between the states and tribes in respect to reserved powers is that state powers have more permanence because they are constitutionally enshrined, while Indian treaty rights, according to the Supreme Court, "can be altered without recourse to the constitutional amendment process" (Wilkinson 1987, 102–3). The fragility and tenuousness of Indian reserved rights, despite their treaty pronunciation, results from Court interpretations. This exercise of power by the Court is very disturbing, since tribes were not created by the U.S. Constitution and theoretically are not subject to constitutional limitations. How can the federal government justify its abridgments of Indian reserved rights, given the extraconstitutional nature of tribes and the fact that treaties are constitutionally recognized as the supreme law of the land? The doctrine of reserved rights raises important questions of fairness, justice, and intergroup relations in the United States.

In our view, tribal sovereignty is akin to a bundle of inherent powers. Accordingly, "the Indian nation arrives at the treaty-making process with every power possessed by any other nation in the world" (Deloria 1996, 972). To determine what powers and rights inhere in tribes today, our task is simply to identify what specific attributes of sovereignty tribes have ceded, recognizing that they reserve all other powers, both external and internal, to themselves. Over the last century and a half, however, judicial interpretations of reserved rights have ranged far and wide, and we turn to judicial questions next.

JUDICIAL ORIGINS OF RESERVED RIGHTS

The doctrine of tribal reserved rights has been tested most prominently in legal arenas involving conflicts among tribes, and states, and the federal government. The problematic and shifting balance of powers among these diverse, yet independent, sovereigns makes tribal-state conflicts particularly difficult for the federal government and federal courts. They must determine what factors should motivate federal involvement, what that involvement should entail, and which of the conflicting parties best warrant federal support and alliance. States are, of course, an integral part of the constitutionally established federal system; tribes, however, often have explicit treaty-based rights guaranteeing them lands and access to and use of natural resources. A clear-cut line can not always be drawn between federal obligations to states and federal responsibilities to tribes.

Land and natural resources have occupied a central role in tribal, federal, and state relations because of their cultural and economic importance. Land claims, natural resource allocation and management of water, timber, game, fish, and minerals, and environmental regulation, including pollution control and hazardous materials transportation and disposal, have frequently resulted in contention among the three sovereigns. The conflicting interests of tribes and states arise from the realities of shared boundaries, shared resources, and shared citizens (as Indians are citizens of their tribe, and of the state, and of the United States). When the federal government enters the arena to assert its own position, to support states, or to support tribes because of its legal obligations as trustee of tribal property, the situation becomes even more entangled.

We began this chapter by mentioning the volatile situation in the Pacific Northwest over tribal reserved rights, especially fishing and shell-fishing rights. The Pacific Northwest is an ideal case to consider more closely here because it is home to many tribal nations, has abundant natural resources, and experienced the early establishment of treaty-based political relations. Reserved rights debates are engaged with passion and vigor by all participants, who manifest diverse, and equally sincere, emotional attachments to lands and resources. The intense conflict between the many tribes and bands and the states of Washington and Oregon dates back to the 1850s, when the United States entered into treaties with the tribes.[5] Through these bilateral treaty agreements, the tribes ceded vast portions of their aboriginal lands, retained all other rights, and established diplomatic relations with the United States government.

One of the most important retained rights was the Indians' right to fish at their customary places, most of which were located off their newly established, and typically quite small, reservations.[6] The pertinent treaty provision is found, in identical boilerplate language, in each of the so-called Stevens Treaties. Isaac Stevens was the designated negotiator for the federal government; he also happened to be the governor of Washington Territory and surveyor for the railroads. Article 3 of the 1855 Yakama treaty identifies the important rights reserved by the tribes:

> The exclusive right of taking fish in all the streams, where running through or bordering said reservation, is further secured to said confederated tribes and bands of Indians, as *also* the right of taking fish *at all usual and accustomed places, in common with the citizens of the Territory*, and of erecting temporary buildings for curing them; together with the privilege of hunting, gathering roots and berries, and pasturing their horses and cattle upon open and unclaimed land. (Kappler 1904, 524–28; emphasis added)

The first case to arrive at the Supreme Court that called upon the judiciary to interpret the treaty provision reserving tribal rights to hunt, fish, and gather was *United States v. Winans*, 198 U.S. 371 (1905), and the reserved rights doctrine was first articulated in this case.

In the late 1800s, Lineas and Audubon Winans established a private fishing company at the treaty-recognized fishing grounds of the Yakama Indians on the Columbia River.[7] The Winans brothers claimed an exclusive right to fish there because they had purchased a Washington state license. They erected fish wheels that were extremely efficient in snaring fish, and the Yakamas complained to federal officials about their depleted fish supply. The United States, "together with certain Indian plaintiffs," filed a suit in federal circuit court for an injunction to stop the Winans from interfering with "fishing rights guaranteed to the Indians of the Yakama Nation, by the terms of the treaty made and concluded between the United States and said Indians" (73 Fed. 72 [1896]).

District Judge Cornelius H. Hanford reviewed the appropriate provisions of the 1855 Treaty (which was ratified in 1859) and found that the document acknowledged two kinds of rights held by the Indians: exclusive rights and rights to be enjoyed in common with non-Indians. Judge Hanford supported the arguments of the federal government and the Yakamas that the Indians retained exclusive rights to fish within the reservation border and that the Winans' company could not prevent the Yakamas from fishing at off-reservation sites. "But," said Hanford, "the right of the Indians to erect temporary buildings on any particular spot of ground, according to the terms of the treaty, as I construe it, ceased when the title to that land was transferred from the government, and became vested as private property" (ibid., 75). This partial tribal victory proved unsatisfactory, and the United States appealed to the Supreme Court on behalf of the Yakama Nation.

The solicitor general, in his brief before the justices, noted the importance of the fishery to the Indians. It had, he said, "always . . . been a famous one [and is] one of the best, if not the best place, on the Columbia River. The Yakama Indians have resorted to it above all others and depended on it for the supply of fish which was their steady subsistence. *The treaty was negotiated with distinct recognition of this right*" (198 U.S. 371 [1905]; emphasis added). He went on to say that the Yakamas' "claim is not merely meritorious and equitable; it is an *immemorial right like a ripened prescription*" (ibid., 374; emphasis added).

The Winans brothers' attorneys used two principal arguments, both enunciated in the 1896 Supreme Court case *Ward v. Race Horse*, 183 U.S. 504. First, the *Race Horse* court held that tribal treaty rights were nothing more than temporary and precarious "privileges"; they were not firm entitlements. Second, the justices employed the "equal footing doctrine" to override the Indians' treaty claims. "Equal footing" refers to the circumstances of admitting territories to statehood on a legal footing equal to that enjoyed by the thirteen English colonies that first confederated as the "United States." In the *Race Horse* case, Justice Edward White had maintained that

Wyoming's admitting act had repealed the Indians' treaty rights to hunt since the admission act and the treaty provision were, in his words, "irreconcilable." Both could not apply: Indians could not have treaty rights to hunt, unregulated by the state, while the state had rights to regulate hunting within its borders. White privileged the admissions act over federal treaties based on his interpretation of the equal footing doctrine.[8] The Court held that on admission to the Union, a state "at once became entitled to and possessed of all the rights of dominion and sovereignty which belonged to the original States. She was admitted and could be admitted, only on the same footing as them" (ibid., 512–13). Relying on this doctrine, the Winans' lawyers asserted that when Washington became a state, it became sovereign, as had the original states. As a sovereign it had the right to regulate fishing—including the right to grant exclusive fishing rights to non-Indians—notwithstanding the Yakamas' treaty agreement with the federal government, reserving to tribal members the right to fish.

Supreme Court Justice Joseph McKenna wrote a powerful opinion in *Winans* in strong support of tribal rights reserved through treaty. First, Justice McKenna recited one of the more popular treaty rights doctrines, that treaties should be interpreted the way Indians would interpret them. A treaty must be construed as "that unlettered people" would have understood it, since it was written in a foreign (to native peoples) language and was drafted by a military power that was greater than tribes (a power that is nonetheless charged with caring for and protecting Indians).

Second, the court dramatically reaffirmed federal supremacy over the states in certain areas and weakened the "equal footing" argument. The justices declared that it was within the power of the United States to "secure to the Indians such a remnant of the great rights they possessed," such as fishing at their usual places, and that this was not an unreasonable demand on the state.

Third, and most importantly, McKenna announced the reserved rights doctrine. He took some pains to establish the context for this doctrine:

The right to resort to the fishing places in controversy was a part of larger rights possessed by the Indians, upon the exercise of which there was not a shadow of impediment, and which were not much less necessary to the existence of the Indians than the atmosphere they breathed. New conditions came into existence, to which those rights had to be accommodated. Only a limitation of them, however, was necessary and intended, not a taking away. *In other words, the treaty was not a grant of rights to the Indians, but a grant of rights from them, a reservation of those not granted. And the form of the instrument and its language was adapted to that purpose.* Reservations were not of particular parcels of land, and could not be expressed in deeds, as dealings between private individuals. The reservations were in large areas of territory, and the negotiations were with the tribe. *They reserved rights, however to every individual Indian, as though named therein.* (ibid., 381; emphasis added)

Interestingly, this emphatic ruling came a mere two years after the repressive *Lone Wolf* decision that clearly deprived tribes of their reserved treaty rights. A probable explanation for these two radically disparate judicial views and interpretations of treaty rights involves the roles played by Congress and the executive branch (as interpreted by the Court), as well as the Court's own perception of what was in the best interest of the Indians. For instance, in one enlightening passage in *Lone Wolf,* the Court stated that treaty abrogation would only be exercised "when circumstances arise which will not only justify the government in disregarding the stipulation of the treaty, but may demand, in the interest of the country and the Indians themselves, that it should be so" (183 U.S. 553, 566 [1903]). The Court did not attempt to explain how it would be in the Indians' interest to have their treaty rights abrogated; after all, the Kiowas, Comanches, and Apaches had filed the *Lone Wolf* suit to protect their treaty rights, not to have them terminated.

A pragmatic reading of the *Lone Wolf* case is that the Court was implicitly acknowledging that many whites had already established homesteads on the tribes' former lands. Relocating the non-native squatters, although it might have been the proper legal action, would have created massive political problems for the state, the squatters, and the American president, who had already authorized their illegal settlement. In addition, the Court, in justifying this congressional confiscation of tribal reserved treaty lands, asserted that Indians simply did not need all the land they had originally reserved to themselves. As Indians became "civilized" and "individualized," supposedly they would not require large, communal land bases and could get by on much smaller, individually apportioned allotments.

Winans, by contrast, was less threatening and involved no major national political issues. In other words, no white "settlers" needed to be removed from "their" lands; and the power of the president, and of Congress, was not at stake. What was at stake was the supremacy of a federally sanctioned treaty over state rights to regulate. The Court understood that fishing represented far more than a simple commercial economic enterprise for the Yakamas. It represented, in a physical sense, their life; without the ability to fish the Indians would surely have faced grave difficulties. In addition, allowing state regulatory exercise over treaty-guaranteed activities would have seriously injured the status of treaties as the supreme law of the land; it might have set a dangerous precedent privileging state sovereign powers over federal powers. *Winans*, therefore, was a crucial and timely acknowledgment that a tribe's sovereign rights, recognized and specifically reserved in treaties, warranted respect and were to be enforced by the federal government (as treaty signatories). In a sense, it did not contradict *Lone Wolf* at all. Both decisions underscored national, federal powers. *Lone Wolf* reinforced federal powers to decide what was "best" for Indians; and *Winans* reinforced the supremacy of federal (and treaty) law over state law.

Winans recognized that the United States had not given anything to the tribes. The only rights lost by the Indians, the Court said, were those that were specifically granted away by the Indians: tribes reserved all other rights to themselves. This case offers compelling judicial evidence that, despite the continuing twin federal policy goals of Indian individualization and allotment, there was a growing consciousness among federal justices that tribes as sovereign entities (in certain cases) had substantive property rights that were enforceable against states and private citizens. Three years later, in *Winters v. United States*, 207 U.S. 564 (1908), the reserved rights doctrine was applied—in an implied fashion—to the water rights attached to Indian lands. At issue in *Winters* was whether a landowner could construct a dam on his property that prevented water from reaching a downstream Indian reservation. In this case, a Montana landowner had constructed a dam across the Milk River that completely blocked any flow to the Fort Belknap Reservation downstream. Congress had established the Fort Belknap Reservation in 1888, several years before the white landowner had bought his property, but the agreement establishing the reservation did not mention water rights. Because specific water rights language was absent, the landowner argued that the reservation was not entitled to a specific amount of water (in fact, that it was not entitled to any water at all).

The Supreme Court ruled otherwise, supporting the tribe and, by extension, the federal government as the Indians' water trustee. The court, led by Justice McKenna, fashioned a creative four-point rationale in its ruling for the United States and the Indians: (1) the reservation had been culled from a "much larger tract," which was necessary for a "nomadic and uncivilized peoples"; (2) the government's policy and the "desire of the Indian" was to be transformed and to elevate tribal culture from a "nomadic" to an "agrarian" lifestyle; (3) this transformation could only occur if the tribal lands were severely reduced in size, making them more amenable to agricultural pursuits; and finally, the capstone argument completing the package, (4) since the lands were judged "arid," they would remain "practically valueless" without an adequate supply of water for irrigation (ibid., 576). While these four points were not a part of the law at the time, they recognized the reality of history and indicate the Court's ability sometimes to generate plausible arguments to protect tribal reserved rights.

The Court then, in rapid succession, added two more concrete pieces to its already formidable effort to enforce federal supremacy over states on water rights and to maintain federal "guardianship" of Indian resources. First, Justice McKenna cited the Indian treaty/ agreement rule of interpretation, asserting that ambiguities in the document would be "resolved from the standpoint of the Indians." Second, Winters's "equal footing" argument was disallowed. "The power of the Government," said McKenna, "to reserve the water and exempt them [the Indians' water rights] from appropriation under the state laws is not denied, and could not be" (ibid., 577). In conclusion, the Court noted that it "would be extreme to believe that within a year Congress destroyed the reservation [by admitting Montana to statehood in 1889] and took from the Indians the consideration of their grant, leaving them a barren waste—took from them the means of continuing their old habits, yet did not leave them the power to change to new ones" (ibid.). In short, when the United States entered into diplomatic relations with the tribes, or when it unilaterally created reservations, there was an implicit reservation of as much water as was warranted by the tribes' potential for managing their own needs and for future uses (Nelson 1977).

Winters, on the one hand, must be viewed as a landmark case that supported a tribe's implied right to water and that reinforced the doctrine that treaties must be understood as Indians would understand them. On the other hand, the case raises an important question regarding who actually owns the reserved water: the tribe or the United States? Furthermore, *Winters* is an interesting case because the Court acted in a dual capacity. First, the Court legitimated existing federal Indian policy because it supported the federal government's goals of transforming Indians from hunter/ gatherers to agriculturalists. Second, the Court *initiated* policy because it established, for the first time, Indian reserved water rights.

The Court apparently felt compelled to articulate federal and Indian reserved water rights because Congress had failed specifically to act on this important matter.

The *implied reservation* of Indian property rights in treaties, which the *Winters* decision articulated for water rights, has also been extended to hunting and fishing rights. Such reserved rights are free from state law or state regulation, and even survive congressional termination of the federal trust relationship. Termination was a federal policy of the 1950s, when Congress exercised what it believed at the time were its unilateral powers to void the federally recognized political existence of tribes. The Bureau of Indian Affairs was directed by Congress to draw up a list of tribes deemed most capable of handling their own affairs, and with significant economic resources, with the intent of abrogating all federal government-to-tribal government relations and all federal trust responsibilities. "Termination" meant the cessation of federal supervision over the property, and members, of the tribe, and that meant that thereafter state law—not federal law—would be applied to the Indians. The termination act, in effect, rescinded the federal authority over "Indian affairs" established in the commerce clause of the Constitution and passed that authority over the states. The Menominee Tribe of Wisconsin was the first tribe to lose its status, effective in 1961, under the Menominee Termination Act of 1954.[9]

Two months after the termination act became law, Congress amended Public Law 280—which granted certain states jurisdiction over offenses committed by or against Indians—to include Wisconsin. However, P.L. 280 said that "nothing in this section shall authorize the alienation, encumbrance, or taxation of any real or personal property, including water rights, belonging to any Indian or any Indian tribe, band, or community that is held in trust by the United States . . . or shall deprive any Indian or any Indian tribe, band, or community of any right, privilege, or immunity afforded under Federal treaty, agreement, or statute *with respect to hunting, trapping, or fishing or the control, licensing, or regulation thereof*" (67 Stat. 588; emphasis added). Despite this explicit statement that reserved rights such as rights to hunt, fish, or trap as reserved in treaty language should not be impaired by the states who gained jurisdiction over tribes, the state of Wisconsin moved to regulate Menominee hunting and fishing. The state denied that the tribe retained any reserved rights after being terminated.

In response, the Menominee Tribe of Wisconsin tribe brought suit in the Court of Claims to recover compensation for the loss of hunting and fishing rights. The Wisconsin Supreme Court held that Menominee hunting and fishing rights had been abrogated by the Menominee Termination Act of 1954, but the U.S. Supreme Court overturned the state court's decision. In *Menominee Tribe v. United States*, 391 U.S. 404 (1968), the Court ruled that implied hunting and fishing rights are *not* ended unless there is a clear indication that Congress intended to sever them. In the *Menominee* case, Justice William O. Douglas, in a fit of judicial activism, determined that the tribe's hunting and fishing rights "survived" the termination. His interpretation stemmed from his insistence that the two acts—termination and P.L. 280—must be read together. "We decline," said Douglas, "to construe the Termination Act as a backhanded way of abrogating the hunting and fishing rights of these Indians. While the power to abrogate those rights exists . . . 'the intention to abrogate or modify a treaty is not to be lightly imputed to the Congress'" (391 U.S. 404, 412–13).[10]

THE RELATION BETWEEN THE RESERVED RIGHTS DOCTRINE AND THE TRUST DOCTRINE

The issue of Indian reserved rights, and the conditions under which these rights will be respected, is intimately connected to the trust relationship between the federal government and Indian tribes. Respect for tribes' reserved rights often depends on whether or not there has been some explicit federal recognition of the reserved rights in question. In other words, the courts have generally held that rights explicitly named in treaty or statutes (i.e., rights that are "expressly" stated, usually in writing) enjoy a higher (though not unassailable) level of legal protection than implied rights. Expressly recognized rights have certainly been privileged over aboriginal rights, that is, rights arising from Indian use and occupancy of territory since time immemorial, but lacking formal federal recognition. Judicial disregard for aboriginal rights was most clearly expressed in the case *Tee-Hit-Ton v. United States*, 348 U.S. 273 (1955).[11] In *Tee-Hit-Ton*, the Supreme Court made the troubling claim that aboriginal land title of a federally unrecognized character is, in effect, no title whatsoever. The Tee-Hit-Tons, a Tlingit clan residing in Alaska, had sued the federal government for compensation because the government harvested timber without permission on lands claimed by the Tee-Hit-Tons under aboriginal title. The Court had to decide whether the government's assumption of title, and the consequent timber harvest, was a "taking of title" compensable under the Fifth Amendment's just compensation clause. The Court's decision held that aboriginal title did not constitute a property right, but merely a right of occupancy that the United States could terminate at any time. Justice Stanley Reed wrote: "This was true not because an Indian or an Indian tribe has no standing to sue or because the United States has not consented to be sued . . . but because Indian occupation of land without government recognition of ownership creates no rights against taking or extinction by the United States protected by the Fifth Amendment or any other principle of law" (348 U.S. 273 [1955], 285).

Congress could take the lands in question and did not have to compensate the Tee-Hit-Tons because Congress had never explicitly "recognized" the Tee-Hit-Tons' legal ownership of their aboriginal lands. The federal government had never had reason to "notice" the Tee-Hit-Tons in treaty or statute, and therefore it was as if the Tee-Hit-Tons had never existed. Their mere presence in Alaska did not, in the Court's view, establish their rights to territory they had inhabited for millennia. In this judicial interpretation, tribes possess *nothing* that the federal government has not created or imagined into existence.

We have seen, however, in the *Winters* and the *Menominee* decisions, that implied reserved rights are *sometimes* given just as much judicial weight as expressly stated reserved rights. Why then are implied reserved rights sometimes *not* respected by the courts? What operating principle are the justices using to differentiate among cases? What is the important difference between expressly stated, federally recognized reserved rights and "unexpressed" rights that are part of aboriginal rights arising from immemorial use and occupancy? Why do the courts make so much of this distinction? We would argue that the courts, the Supreme Court in particular, are not very concerned with preserving, respecting, or even articulating aboriginal rights. In fact, many decisions, such as *Tee-Hit-Ton*, ignore or disallow the possible existence of aboriginal rights. What the courts and justices do respect, however, is the power of the federal government.

Federal power over Indian affairs, after all, means that the government acts as trustee of Indian lands and resources, whether one interprets trustee as legal owner or as legal agent asserting the preexisting rights of the Indians. The courts tend to respect those reserved rights that are expressly federally recognized because impositions on those rights, by states or private citizens, are affronts to the trustee, the federal government. Affronts to aboriginal rights are "only" affronts to tribes, in this scenario, and thus much less interesting to the courts. In this view, *Tee-Hit-Ton* makes perfect sense; the Court privileged federal power to define or "recognize" tribes, and tribes' titles, over the sovereign power of tribes to define themselves or to assert their title. Simply privileging federal powers, however, does not explain all judicial interpretation of reserved rights. The parameters of federal powers and responsibilities still have to be determined (usually case by case), and here is where the issue of federal government as *trustee* of tribal interests comes to the fore. The position of the federal government as trustee of Indian lands and resources has not been well defined, as previous chapters have outlined, and thus we come to another critical unanswered question that muddies the waters around tribal reserved rights.

Is the federal government the legal owner of the reserved rights in question, or is the federal government the designated legal agent acting in the interests of the legal owners, the tribal nations? The Supreme Court has expressed great ambivalence on this important issue. For example, in *Leavenworth Railroad Co. v. United States*, 92 U.S. 733 (1876), the Court was called upon to interpret the meaning of the phrase "reserved to the United States," which applied to lands designated as reservation lands in the Osage Treaty of 1825. The Court said "the treaty reserved them [the lands] as much to one as to the other of the contracting parties. Both were interested therein, and had title thereto. *In one sense, they were reserved to the Indians; but, in another and broader sense, to the United States, for the use of the Indians*" (92 U.S. 733 [1876], 747).

Winans, Winters, and *Menominee* can be read as judicial endorsements of reserved rights, but, we argue, they were not merely intended as endorsements of the reserved rights *of tribes*. In other words, these are not solely judicial endorsements of powers or rights that inhere in tribes because of aboriginal sovereignty; they are also judicial endorsements of the rights and powers of the federal government. The Court was protecting the rights of the federal government over land and resources, but it was also protecting the inherent reserved rights of tribes (whether expressly or implicitly retained). In *Winans, Winters,* and *Menominee,* the Supreme Court asserted federal supremacy over private and states' rights. In each case, the Court was particularly attentive to the treaty and property clauses of the U.S. Constitution, which in the Court's consciousness elevated the federal government above states, corporations, and private parties. The Court acknowledged that since the federal government signed treaties and established reservations it either explicitly or implicitly reserved or, in some cases, created certain rights for tribes to aid in their subsistence and transformation to a civilized status. Any challenges by states or other interests were deemed a direct challenge to federal supremacy, and the inherent and retained rights of tribes, acts that, in these cases, would not be sanctioned by the federal courts.

The political independence of the Court, vacillations in federal Indian policy between forcible assimilation of Indians and limited measures of independence, and conflicts between the federal and state governments over jurisdiction regarding Indian affairs allow the Court to exercise a wide discretionary authority when it comes to handling Indian issues. In other words, the Supreme Court in *Winans, Winters,* and especially *Menominee* could easily have denied the existence of reserved rights and thus ruled in favor of the non-Indians, had it been so inclined. After all, while the Court was concerned with recognizing tribal reserved rights, it was equally, if not more, concerned to defend the powers of the federal government. This indeterminacy of judicial construction concerning the exact status of tribes and tribal rights exasperates Indians:

> One of the frustrating circumstances surrounding Indian law is, not infrequently, the existence of one set of rules that apply specifically to Indian issues and a different set of rules that apply to the law in general. One judge may apply the Indian law precedent and rules of construction, while another judge may ignore these and incorporate the traditional rules of construction, and a third judge may cite the developed rules of construction traditionally used in Indian cases and then announce that the facts of the situation or other circumstances taken together make it necessary to depart from these rules in this particular case. The decisions emanating from the use of different rules may be in marked contrast—one might favor Indian claimants while the other could destroy their chance of prevailing. (Deloria and Lytle 1983, 50)

The Supreme Court's ability, and willingness, to use judicial rules arbitrarily to yield contrary decisions is wonderfully exemplified by two 1999 rulings: *Minnesota v. Mille Lacs Band of Chippewa Indians,* 526 U.S. 172, and *Amoco Production Co. v. Southern Ute Indian Tribe,* 526 U.S. 865. The Supreme Court handed down two very different rulings in these cases involving Indian natural resources and the reserved rights doctrine. In *Minnesota v. Mille Lacs Band of Chippewa Indians* the Court ruled that the Chippewas *did* retain the right to hunt, fish, and gather on lands that had been ceded to the United States in an 1837 treaty. In *Amoco Production Co. v. Southern Ute Indian Tribe* the Court ruled that the tribe did not retain or reserve rights to the methane gas that is found within the coal formations lying under reservation lands (even though rights to the coal were reserved). We first examine the facts of the two cases and then try to discern the Court's reasoning in arriving at its disparate determinations re reserved rights.

First, the history of the *Mille Lacs* decision: the Mille Lacs band of Chippewas ceded millions of acres of land in the current states of Minnesota and Wisconsin to the United States in 1837, but specified in the treaty their continuing rights to hunt, fish, and gather on ceded lands. During the Removal era of the mid-1800s, pressure was brought to bear to force the Chippewa bands to remove to western lands, and a presidential executive order was even issued that required the tribe to remove. The Chippewas, however, mounted successful resistance, with the help of some non-native neighbors who recognized, among other things, how critical Chippewa labor was to local mining, fishing, and lumbering industries. The presidential order for Chippewa removal was never enforced. In the 1980s, various Chippewa bands, including the Mille Lac, battled in the courts to assert their reserved rights, especially to fish, on ceded lands (which include federal, state, and privately owned lands). The state of Minnesota argued that the rights reserved in the Treaty of 1837 had been abrogated by the subsequent 1850 Presidential Order directing Chippewa removal.

The Supreme Court's decision in *Mille Lacs* to uphold the Indians' off-reservation treaty rights was important for several reasons. First, the Court reaffirmed a long-standing (if not always supported) doctrine that Indian treaty rights cannot be *implicitly* terminated. That is, treaty rights may only be abrogated by Congress, and only when Congress unequivocally expresses its intent to terminate the rights. Second, the Court explicitly reaffirmed two canons of treaty construction: that Indian treaties are to be interpreted liberally in favor of the Indians and that any ambiguities in language are to be resolved in the tribes' favor. Third, the Court forcefully reminded the states that they were without inherent power over Indian rights or resources and denied the power of the "equal footing" doctrine to extend state jurisdiction over Indians. The fact that territories were admitted to statehood on an "equal footing" with existing states did not give the states any constitutional or statutory powers over Indians, and certainly not powers over Indians exercising treaty-specified rights. The Court held that the equal footing doctrine, which had been recently revived in federal court discourse,[12] did not interfere with the federal government's authority to control the nation's Indian affairs under the commerce clause, the property clause, the supremacy clause, and the treaty-making authority stipulated in the Constitution.

Finally, the majority implicitly overruled *Ward v. Race Horse*, the 1896 ruling that had upheld states' rights over Indian treaty rights. Justice Sandra Day O'Connor wrote:

> But *Race Horse* rested on a false premise. As this Court's subsequent cases have made clear, an Indian tribe's treaty rights to hunt, fish, and gather on state land are not irreconcilable with a State's sovereignty over the natural resources in the state. Rather, Indian treaty rights can coexist with State management of natural resources. Although States have important interests in regulating wildlife and natural resources within their borders, this authority is shared with the Federal Government when the Federal Government exercises one of its enumerated constitutional powers, such as treaty making. (526 U.S. 172 [1999])

Three months later, the Supreme Court handed down a remarkably different decision in *Amoco Production Co. v. Southern Ute Indian Tribe*. The Southern Ute Tribe had ceded much of its aboriginal territory to the federal government in 1880, but in 1938 regained trust title to the ceded lands, which in 1938 were still owned by the United States (the lands had not passed into state or private ownership). Coal deposits underlying the ceded lands had been patented by the United States under the 1909 and 1910 Coal Lands Acts.

When the Southern Ute Tribe regained trust title to the ceded lands, the coal patents also transferred to the tribe. More recently, ownership of the significant methane gas deposits associated with the coal reserves had come into dispute. In the *Amoco* case, the tribe and the United States argued, unsuccessfully, that the Coal Acts reserved rights to both the coal and the methane gas. Supreme Court Justice Anthony Kennedy disagreed, based on his interpretation of congressional intent. He argued that Congress could not have intended to reserve rights to the methane gas because, at the time of the Coal Lands Acts, methane was considered a dangerous waste product of coal mining, not a valuable energy resource. Even with the federal government acting as trustee of the tribe, the Court ruled against the Indians' reserved rights. In this case, unlike *Mille Lacs*, the Court ignored the canons of construction that direct it to read ambiguities in treaties or laws in favor of the tribe.

What are the relevant circumstances or facts that might have prompted these apparently incompatible decisions? *Mille Lacs* concerned reserved rights that had been explicitly spelled out in treaty language. Treaties are constitutionally privileged as the law of the land and are legally binding statements of federal intent and responsibilities. When Minnesota challenged treaty-reserved rights, it challenged federal authority to control the nation's Indian affairs (to repeat, authority established under the Constitution's commerce clause, property clause, supremacy clause, and treaty-making authority). As we have seen, the Court does not usually countenance this type of challenge to federal and constitutional authority. *Amoco*, on the other hand, contained no such challenge. The Court was defining a right to economic profit from a "resource" that had not been specifically named because it was not until recently even recognized as a "resource." Why go to all the trouble of applying canons of construction to a case that only involved competing claims to income between a tribe and a large corporation? Most native people would certainly not be surprised that the Court privileged the claims of the corporation over the tribe, given that no "higher order" issues, such as threats to federal sovereignty, were involved.[13]

CONCLUSION

The reserved rights doctrine is often listed with three other canons of construction as evidence that the federal government supports Indian treaties and the trust doctrine. The three canons of construction direct the courts to: (1) resolve ambiguities expressed in treaties in favor of Indians; (2) interpret treaties as the Indians themselves would have understood them; and (3) liberally construe treaties in favor of the tribe.[14] Each of these "canons" theoretically stands for a system of fundamental rules and maxims that the Court agrees to recognize and use in its interpretation of written instruments. This sense of "canon" as an authoritative rule does not always hold up in the area of Indian law. As we have seen with other doctrines of federal Indian policy and law, each canon has an opposite corollary that may be cited by the courts when it suits the justices' purposes. For example, while the canon of liberal construction for tribes is supported in cases such as *Worcester v. Georgia* (1832), *The Kansas Indians* (1866), and *United States v. Winans* (1905), it has been ignored or shunted aside in cases such as *The Cherokee Tobacco* (1871) and *Race Horse* (1896). Similarly, the courts have held in other cases that the canon of interpreting ambiguous phrases in favor of tribes does not permit the Court to disregard the expressed intent of Congress.[15] The doctrine of reserved rights has clearly been subject to similar processes of indeterminacy and ambiguity. A close reading of the cases and decisions we have surveyed in this chapter leads, we believe, to a clearer understanding of *why* the courts and the justices have swung one way and then another on reserved rights decisions. Justices tend to privilege explicit rights over implied rights; but much more importantly, justices often highly privilege federal power over tribal powers, questions of federal authority over questions of tribal authority, federal "grants" of recognition to tribes over tribal assertions of identity arising from aboriginal sovereignty, and the production of profits over efforts spent carefully delineating tribal rights.

The fact that Indian treaties may be expressly abrogated by Congress reveals the tenuous nature of Indian legal rights. History shows that treaties—including Indian reserved rights—have been "honored more in the breach than the fulfillment," with the treaty process itself being dramatically and problematically transformed in 1871. In that year Congress informed the president, via an Appropriation Act rider, that he could no longer recognize Indian nations through treaties, although theoretically all preexisting treaties were to remain the law of the land (Deloria 1996). Notwithstanding their treaty basis, Indian reserved rights have historically and contemporarily—from a federal perspective—been equated with other canons of construction. As a canon of law, the doctrine of reserved rights has therefore been thought of—from a federal perspective—as being subject to judicial interpretation, or as being subject to unilateral congressional termination. As a result, Indian rights based on the reserved rights doctrine have been inconsistently recognized, and federal enforcement and protection of reserved rights has been spotty at best. Until tribal reserved rights attain a status comparable to the U.S. Constitution's Tenth Amendment, tribes will not be able to rest assured that their land (and other) cessions to the federal government, made in exchange for reserved lands and all other reserved rights, will be supported by federal and state lawmakers.

CHAPTER FIVE

"Justices Who Bent the Law": The Doctrine of Implied Repeals

The Indian treaty has achieved a status just short of folkloric in the American consciousness. "Breaking the treaty," as invoked in motion pictures and on television, is generally the lawless act of frontier settlers rather than a deliberate act of the federal government. But more treaties were "broken" by judges and justices who bent the law to accomplish certain political ends than were ever broken by boomers and sooners.

DELORIA AND DEMALLIE
(1999, vol. 1, 6)

As we have discussed in earlier chapters, treaties are critically important political and legal instruments that bind tribes and the federal government. The central question of this chapter has to do with the power to change or terminate treaties. Termination of treaties, legally, is termed "abrogation." Treaties are, by definition, bilateral or multilateral agreements; it takes at least two to engage in this form of diplomacy. Two or more nations enter into the treaty-negotiation process, and that is how treaties begin. How treaties might end, however, has been a critical issue in tribal-federal relations. Who has the power to abrogate treaties or change their provisions? Does the federal power to abrogate or modify Indian treaties and agreements rest solely with the political branches—that is, with Congress or the president[1]—or does the Supreme Court have the constitutional right to abrogate Indian treaties? The Supreme Court has never asserted that it has the express power to abrogate treaty rights. The Court has instead consistently recognized that only the political branches may modify or abrogate treaty rights, since the political branches—specifically the president and the Senate—have the right to negotiate and ratify treaties.

In several cases, however, the U.S. Supreme Court has quashed or dramatically modified Indian treaty rights without congressional authorization or tribal consent. The Supreme Court has justified its actions in these cases on the basis of what is called the doctrine of "implied repeal." What does this term mean? The Court occasionally must decide cases where treaty language disagrees with, or contradicts, the language of later congressional or state statutes. In other words, there are cases where treaty stipulations conflict with later statutory law. The Court may decide to abrogate a treaty because a later law contains provisions perceived to be so irreconcilable with those of the earlier treaty that only one of the two can stand in force. This is known as "repeal" of the earlier treaty. In effect, the force of the later law is understood to repeal the force or intent of the earlier treaty. "Implied" refers to a situation where congressional intent in the later law is not made clear by explicit and direct words, but is gathered by implication or deduction from the circumstances, the general language, or the conduct of one or both of the parties. The use of "implied" in this chapter refers to cases where the Court must decide what the intention of Congress was, relevant to a particular treaty. The Court has to figure out if Congress intended to repeal the provisions of a particular treaty when it passed a conflicting law, especially when that law made no explicit reference to the earlier treaty.

The conjunction of the two terms in "implied repeal" means that the Court acts to supersede an existing law, rule, or treaty provision *without* an express congressional directive to do so. The Court, in essence, assumes the power to act in a political arena—Congress's arena of authority over Indian affairs—without a directive from Congress to do so. The Court, when it implements the doctrine of implied repeals, assumes that a later law repeals, by implication, an earlier treaty, if the two appear to be in conflict. When the Court rules that a treaty right—the right to hunt, fish, or gather off-reservation, for example—is unconstitutional on the basis of "implied repeals," the Court is "by implication severing" those rights because it has read some later statute—state law, for example—as contradicting the treaty right. The Court, by such an action, effectively abrogates a treaty without any expression of congressional intent to abrogate.

We argue, and the evidence bears out, that the power to abrogate or modify Indian treaties (or agreements) or provisions of these documents may *only* be exercised by the Congress, and then only after the legislative branch has expressly and unequivocally stated its intent to alter or annul the diplomatic arrangement between the United States and a particular tribal nation. When the Supreme Court hands down opinions that by implication sever specific Indian treaty rights, and does so without a specific legislative mandate directing the termination of the treaty right, the Court has vastly overstepped its juridical power. In such instances, the Court violates the Constitution and acts contrary to the acknowledged trust relationship to tribes, which holds that the United States has both a legal and a moral duty to assist tribes by protecting their lands, resources, sovereignty, and cultural heritage.[2] In what ways does the Court overstep its juridical powers when it "by implication" repeals or modifies treaty provisions?

Treaties are politically created instruments. They are the results of negotiations between authorized agents: representative agent(s) of the president, on the federal side, and representative agent(s) of the tribe(s) on the other. Any sovereign nation retains the power to abrogate its treaty commitments unilaterally, although since treaties are diplomatic arrangements between two or more nations, formal unilateral abrogations might result in a declaration of war by the other treaty signatories or international embarrassment before the family of nations. In the case of the United States, the congressional power to abrogate, as Charles Wilkinson and John Volkman noted, "is based on the notion that a treaty represents the political policy of the nation at the time it was made. If there is a change of circumstances and the national interest accordingly 'demands' a modification of its terms, then Congress may abrogate a treaty in whole or in part" (Wilkinson and Volkman 1975, 604). We do not dispute any sovereign nation's right to abrogate any treaty unilaterally; we do wish to point out the potential consequences and the fallacy of overestimating the legal and moral standing of unilateral abrogation.

While agreeing that treaties are political arrangements that may be abrogated by either treaty party, and that from the federal government's perspective it specifically falls to Congress to be the nullifying agent, we disagree with Wilkinson and Volkman's later contention that "[t]here are so many tests for determining whether an abrogation has been effected, and most of them are so vague, that a court has little recourse but to arrive at an ad hoc, almost arbitrary decision when faced with the question of whether a particular treaty guarantee has been abrogated by Congress" (ibid., 608). With this statement, Wilkinson and Volkman vest in the Supreme Court an amount of political power and policy-making leeway not authorized by Article 3 of the U.S. Constitution. The authors' statement on the Court's judicial discretion contradicts prior judicial precedent as well as the doctrine of tribal sovereignty and directly opposes federal Indian policy, which recognizes that Congress has the exclusive authority to regulate the federal government's affairs with tribes. Exclusive federal authority includes the power to alter the nation's will—as evidenced in treaties—toward tribes. Since Congress is the principal agent responsible for overseeing the United States' exercise of its trust obligations toward tribes, it falls to the legislative branch, not the judicial branch, to terminate or modify the trust.

The judicial doctrine of implied repeals of treaties is an invalid and unwarranted exercise of power by the Court. Judicial repeal of politically created instruments is not sanctioned by the Constitution; nor does it reflect the distinctive political relationship between tribes and the federal government. When there is a conflict between a preexisting treaty right and a later congressional or state statute, the courts must uphold the federal government's treaty obligations to tribes, based on the trust doctrine and the good faith test. The only exception to this rule would be in a case where Congress has passed a specific repealing or terminating statute. The principal task of the Supreme Court in sorting out alleged irreconcilable differences between treaty provisions and statutory provisions, then, should be to uphold the treaty and to interpret the statute in conformity with the context in which the treaty was negotiated.

We believe this position is defensible throughout the history of treaty relations between the United States and tribes, but that it was made more compelling after 1871 when Congress unilaterally stopped negotiating treaties with tribes (16 Stat., 544, 566). Indian nations, who remained outside the U.S. Constitution's pale, were thereby unilaterally excluded from this important form of negotiation. It seems especially incumbent on the courts, then, to uphold treaty provisions agreed upon before 1871, when Congress—without tribal consent or agreement—ended tribes' rights to negotiate treaties. Other factors that should motivate the courts to uphold treaties, unless Congress explicitly directs otherwise, or the United States and tribes agree otherwise, are (1) that tribes, as tribes, lack congressional representation, and (2) that tribal rights are based largely on inherent sovereignty and treaties/agreements and are not grounded in the U.S. Constitution.

Finally, as American Indian individuals gradually became naturalized as American citizens, state citizenship and federal citizenship were "layered" onto their tribal citizenship via treaty provisions, land allotments, and specific statutory measures. This layering of multiple citizenships, in conjunction with the ongoing federal trust doctrine, means that a congressional decision unilaterally to abrogate Indian treaty rights would normally occur only in the event of compelling national reasons (such as Indian land

cessions for the expanding Euro-American presence), and sometimes with the direct concurrence of a tribe. The Supreme Court,
charged with upholding the Constitution, the laws, and "all treaties
made" as the supreme law of the land, is required to examine any
conflicts closely and when it finds *no direct congressional intent* to
abrogate an Indian treaty should not presume the Court has the
authority to repeal the treaty by implication.

The doctrine of implied repeal is critically important for tribal
nations whose collective sovereign rights, and some individual
Indian rights, hinge on treaties. The doctrine is also significant for
American democracy, because it raises questions of nondiscrimi-
nation, consent, and self-determination, as well as justice, fairness,
and respect for the rule of law.

DOCTRINES THAT SHAPE CONGRESSIONAL INTENT: TRUST AND "GOOD FAITH"

Any discussion of implied repeals requires us to consider how the
courts ascertain congressional intent. This is an important process
because the commerce clause of the Constitution, as we have discussed in earlier chapters, gives Congress exclusive authority to
regulate the federal government's affairs with tribes. Strictly speaking, the Court cannot create Indian policy itself; it can only act as
interpreter of congressional intention. In order to interpret or
understand intentions, then, the Court looks to the doctrines that
guide Congress in its relations with tribes. One of the critically
important doctrines that has influenced Court decision-making
concerning implied repeals is the "good faith" doctrine. The polit-
ical/legal doctrine of good faith is a close corollary to the trust doctrine and was first articulated by the Congress in the 1787 Northwest Ordinance. The ordinance succinctly states that the federal
government would always observe "the utmost good faith towards
the Indians, their lands and property shall never be taken from
them without their consent; and in their property, rights and liberty, they never shall be invaded or disturbed, unless in just and

lawful wars authorised [*sic*] by Congress; but laws founded in justice and humanity shall from time to time be made for preventing wrongs being done to them, and for preserving peace and friendship with them" (1 Stat., 50).

As we see in a number of the cases discussed in this chapter, the courts often turn to the good faith doctrine as a guide for appropriate federal action and for appropriate judicial decision-making. As the Northwest Ordinance quite specifically articulates in its first exemplar of acting in good faith, Indian "lands and property shall never be taken from them without their consent." Tribal consent is critically important to any federal actions that impinge upon lands, property, rights, and liberty. Tribal consent is at the core of any discussion of implied repeals, because tribal consent was at the core of treaty agreements (in theory, at least, if unfortunately not always in fact). The Constitution invested Congress with authority over Indian affairs; therefore only Congress has the authority expressly to abrogate or modify Indian treaties. We vigorously argue against the Supreme Court's authority to repeal tribal or treaty rights based on Court interpretations of what might be implied by contradictions between treaties and statutes. If such Court authority is allowed, then there is no room for either congressional authority or tribal consent. When Congress has modified or abrogated treaties, it has acted by virtue of its constitutionally granted authority—it has acted unilaterally on occasion, but has frequently taken care to seek out tribal consent or has clearly expressed its intentions to proceed without that consent.

In the course of this chapter, we first consider the role—sometimes acknowledged, sometimes not—the Supreme Court has played in the "political" (as opposed to judicial) realm of policy-making. Clearly the Court has taken on policy formulation in Indian affairs. The actions of the Rehnquist Court to reinvigorate the doctrine of implied repeals in its privileging of states over tribes is evidence of how the Court can, and does, directly affect the political lives of tribes. We next investigate how the Court has used the "political question" rule to bolster congressional plenary power over tribes, to restrict or disavow Indian rights, and even to deny Indians a legal venue to have their grievances heard. We argue that the Supreme Court has the constitutional authority to interpret Indian treaty rights and should be available as a forum to which aggrieved Indian tribes or tribal members can take their treaty rights complaints. The Supreme Court does not, however, have the constitutional authority to abrogate those rights either explicitly or by implication. The power of abrogation does remain a political question.

We examine a number of cases to illustrate how the Court has defined and exercised its judicial power of implied repeals; the most important of these cases is undoubtedly *Lone Wolf v. Hitchcock*, 187 U.S. 553 (1903), which we consider in some detail. After outlining arguments and examples used in support of judicial exercise of the implied repeals doctrine, we present arguments and examples of precedent against implied repeal. Examples of official, express treaty abrogation—express repeals of foreign treaties, express congressional repeals of Indian treaties, and express congressional modification of Indian treaties—clearly delineate a federal intention to abrogate or repeal primarily *through express language*, and not through implication or indirection.

POLICY-MAKING BY THE SUPREME COURT: CRITERIA FOR POLITICAL ACTION

In a classic article written nearly forty years ago, Robert Dahl (1957), a political scientist and leading student of democratic theory and practice, analyzed the Supreme Court's political policy-making role in its judicial decisions. In determining the extent to which the Supreme Court makes policy decisions, Dahl underscored the importance of distinguishing if the Court goes outside established "legal" criteria found in past precedent, statutes, and the Constitution. On occasion members of the Supreme Court are required to render decisions "where legal criteria are not in any realistic sense adequate to the task" (ibid., 280). In other words, cases sometimes come before the Court involving profound disagreements in society, such as cases about abortion, desegregation, drug use and regulation, criminal and victims' rights, or religious issues. The setting of the case is clearly "political," and the justices must look beyond so-called legal criteria or precedents in their decisions.

Historically, this has certainly been true of Indian issues. The Court has occasionally acted contrary to congressional policy, administrative direction, and public sentiment in rendering Indian law decisions. In *Worcester v. Georgia*, 31 U.S. 515 (1832), for example, the Court ruled that state law is inferior to Indian treaty law, despite intense state lobbying and presidential support for state powers over tribes. In *Ex parte Crow Dog*, 109 U.S. 556 (1883), the Court ruled that tribes have criminal jurisdiction over their own members, despite a congressional proclivity to deny such jurisdictional rights to tribes. In *Matter of Heff*, 197 U.S. 48 (1905), the Court ruled that Indians who become naturalized as American citizens have the right to drink liquor, despite a political climate of extreme surveillance and control over Indian individuals' rights, property, and behavior. In *Choate v. Trapp*, 224 U.S. 665 (1912), the Court ruled that Indian allottees are exempt from state taxation, despite public and state pressure to the contrary. In each of these actions in a clearly "political" arena, the Court upheld the rights of tribes or Indian individuals. Despite this record of support for Indian rights in certain contexts, we would argue that the Supreme Court exceeds its constitutional authority when it relies on the doctrine of implied repeal explicitly to abrogate Indian treaty rights. The important difference is that a treaty is a formal political arrangement between two or more sovereign entities. Treaties are negotiated by designated individuals and ratified by the nations of the participatory powers. Hence, as political agreements, it follows that the power to abrogate them should be wielded solely by the branch constitutionally empowered to act.

Robert Dahl argued that the Court has used two conflicting criteria in cases involving political questions: the *majority criterion* and the *criterion of right or justice*.[3] Subsequent legal scholars have critiqued Dahl's arguments and data, especially his analysis of the majority criterion, but a reexamination of Dahl's larger thesis with an emphasis on his second criterion, the justice criterion, still has merit. The criterion of right or justice, according to Dahl, assumes that the Supreme Court's most important policy function is to protect basic or fundamental rights. The Constitution, in other words, assumes an underlying body of fundamental rights and liberties, which the Court guarantees by its decisions. Dahl found that—except for short-lived transitional periods—the Supreme Court was inevitably a part of the dominant national political scene and generally supported contemporary major policies. The main task of the Court, Dahl said, was to confer legitimacy on the fundamental policies of the political branches and also, more broadly, on the basic patterns of behavior required for the operation of democracy. Dahl recognized, however, and the evidence vividly shows, that the Court is not simply or only an agent of the dominant ruling alliance. In fact, the Supreme Court has real power bases of its own, the most important of which is the distinctive legitimacy extended to the Court's interpretations of the Constitution. The evidence in Indian law bears out this claim. There are more than a few cases like those mentioned above, which Dahl would categorize as justice cases, in which the Supreme Court has rendered powerful rulings supporting tribal rights and sovereignty, even when the exercise of that sovereignty clashes with majority sentiment.[4] However, when analyzing the entire history of the Court, one finds that on balance the bulk of the law pronounced by the Court, as Petra Shattuck and Jill Norgren put it, "has not been 'a better way' for Indians" (Shattuck and Norgren 1991, 197). While noting Indian legal gains, they found that those gains "are never final nor are they secure from political manipulation" (ibid.).

The Rehnquist Court is openly supportive of the major policies of the dominant national alliance, policies that generally do not reflect positively on the distinctive extraconstitutional role of tribes in the American polity. The Court, at least as tribes are concerned, has adopted the majority criterion as its central policy perspective and relies much less on the justice criterion when it decides to hear

Indian-related cases. The Rehnquist's Court's reinvigoration of the doctrine of implied repeal is one compelling piece of evidence of the Court's regressive view of tribes.

THE SUPREME COURT AND THE POLITICAL QUESTION DOCTRINE

Under Article 3, section 2, of the U.S. Constitution, the Supreme Court's power is said to extend to "all cases, in law and equity, arising under this constitution, the laws of the United States, and treaties made, or which shall be made, under their authority." Despite this seemingly clear authority to hear cases involving treaties, the Supreme Court has frequently declined to rule on matters involving treaties by claiming that those agreements were "political questions" that should be resolved by the political branches. The so-called political question doctrine is used by the Court to defer certain questions to the political branches (legislative or executive) of the federal government and to decline to give a judicial opinion or decision. The doctrine originated in *Marbury v. Madison*, 5 U.S. 137 (1803), when Chief Justice John Marshall said that "the province of the Court is, solely, to decide on the rights of individuals. . . . Questions in their nature political, or which are, by the Constitution and laws, submitted to the executive can never be made in this Court."[5] For example, in *The Chinese Exclusion Cases*, 130 U.S. 581 (1889), the Court held that "the question whether our government is justified in disregarding its engagements with another nation is not one of determination of the courts" (602). Additional rulings have elaborated other reasons, besides deference to the political branches, for implementing the political question doctrine. The Court sometimes lacks information and resources needed to make an informed decision. In some areas, especially foreign policy and international relations, the Court lacks appropriate standards for resolving disputes or the means to enforce its decision (O'Brien 1995, 115).

In federal Indian affairs, the Supreme Court has frequently used the political question doctrine (often in conjunction with the doctrine of congressional plenary power) to restrict or disavow Indian rights, or even to deny Indians a legal venue to have their grievances heard.[6] The political question doctrine, first used expressly in Indian law in *U.S. v. Rogers*, 45 U.S. 567 (1846), was used frequently during the allotment and assimilation years from the 1880s to the early 1920s, when the Court was extremely deferential to the legislature, and when the federal government mounted a frontal and unabashed assault to "Americanize" native peoples.

During the treaty-making period, 1778 to 1871, Indian affairs, like foreign affairs, were clearly constitutionally delegated to Congress. Accordingly, the power of judicial review of Indian affairs was constrained, just as judicial power to review foreign affairs decisions was constrained, so that "the federal government's power to make treaties with the Indians was considered a political question, beyond judicial examination" (Shattuck and Norgren 1991, 123).[7] So long as tribes remained largely independent and were dealt with as sovereigns via treaty-making, the federal government's largely unreviewable power to deal with tribes was justified.

However, the Court should have altered its stance when Congress radically transformed treaty-making with tribes in 1871. Thereafter, Indian nations were generally treated as domestic national entities. The federal government was dedicated to the allotment of tribal lands, as well as to the assimilation and the Christianization of tribal persons. In 1924, after some decades of official reluctance and piecemeal extension of citizenship, all individual Indians were naturalized as American citizens. At that point, the Court should have altered its stance toward tribes and individual Indians and strictly scrutinized congressional activities regarding Indians. When Congress altered treaty-making, it should by extension also have lost the associated privilege of exclusion from judicial review, especially when congressional actions violated Indian treaty rights. The Court, on the contrary, continued its extreme deference to the political branches and frequently cited the political question doctrine as justification when it chose to ignore what—for tribes—were substantive federal violations of Indian rights.[8]

Examples of judicial deference to Congress in Indian affairs abound. In *Thomas v. Gay*, 169 U.S. 264 (1897), the Court said that "it is well settled that an act of Congress may supersede a prior treaty and that any questions that may arise are beyond the sphere of judicial cognizance, and must be met by the political department of the Government" (271). In the most famous case of judicial deference (discussed in more detail later), *Lone Wolf v. Hitchcock*, 187 U.S. 553 (1903), the Court spliced the political question doctrine with the plenary power doctrine. The Court declared that Congress's plenary power vis-à-vis tribes "has always been deemed a political one, not subject to be controlled by the judicial department of the government"; regardless of the manner in which Congress dealt with tribes, "as Congress possessed full power in the matter, the judiciary cannot question or inquire into the motives which prompted the enactment of this legislation" (ibid., 568).[9]

The political question doctrine remained a viable and largely unrestricted legal doctrine until it was disavowed in two late twentieth century cases: *Delaware Tribal Business Committee v. Weeks*, 430 U.S. 73, 83–85 (1977), and *United States v. Sioux Nation*, 448 U.S. 371 (1980). In *Weeks* the Court rejected the claim that congressional power over Indian property was all-encompassing enough to render legislative acts not subject to judicial review. In *Sioux Nation*, a case with important repercussions for Indian land rights, the political question doctrine was swept away as a legal mechanism the Court could rely upon to deny Indians a legal forum. As Justice Harry Blackmun said, "the doctrine was expressly laid to rest in *Delaware*" and "the presumption of Congressional good faith has little to commend it as an enduring principle for deciding questions of the kind presented here" (414–15). The Supreme Court, then, has the constitutional authority to interpret Indian treaty rights and should be available as a forum to which aggrieved Indian tribes or tribal members can take their treaty rights complaints. The Supreme Court does not, however, have the constitutional authority to abrogate those rights either explicitly or by implication. The power of abrogation remains a political question.

EXERCISING THE JUDICIAL POWER OF IMPLIED REPEALS

The irony of implied repeals is that the Court asserts its rights to repeal treaty provisions by implication, while denying its rights to repeal treaty rights expressly. In other words, the Court does by indirection what it recognizes it cannot do directly. The Supreme Court has never asserted that it has the power expressly to abrogate treaty rights. The Court has instead consistently recognized that only the political branches may modify or abrogate treaty rights, as it ruled in *U.S. v. Old Settlers,* 148 U.S. 427 (1893): "unquestionably a treaty may be modified or abrogated by an Act of Congress, but the power to make and unmake is essentially political and not judicial" (468). If the Court lacks this greater, overt power, which it has recognized as belonging solely to Congress, on what legitimate basis can it assert that it has the lesser power to abrogate treaty rights by implication? The Court has the power to interpret treaties, to exercise the art of deciding the meaning of language; treaty abrogation is a wholly different matter.

A good example of the Supreme Court exercise of implied repeals in order to abrogate expressed Indian treaty rights without specific authorization by the Congress can be found in the 1871 case *The Cherokee Tobacco,* 11 Wall. 616. In this case, Justice Noah Swayne pitted Article 10 of the 1866 Cherokee Treaty with the United States against a section of the 1868 General Revenue law. Article 10 stated that Cherokee citizens had the right to sell any product or merchandise without having to pay "any tax thereon which is now or may be levied by the United States on the quantity sold outside of the Indian Territory" (14 Stat., 799). The provision of the General Revenue law, by contrast, imposed taxes on liquor and tobacco products "produced anywhere within the exterior boundaries of the United States" (15 Stat., 167). While there was no language in the revenue law or in the accompanying documentary record expressly or by implication stating that this law would apply to Indian Country, Justice Swayne, speaking for a deeply divided Court (three justices concurred, two dissented, and three did not participate), said that the case came down to which of the two laws was superior. Swayne maintained that "undoubtedly one or the other must yield" since "the repugnancy is clear and they cannot stand together" (*The Cherokee Tobacco* 1871, 620).

Swayne went on to enunciate the infamous "last-in-time" principle, which has troubled tribes ever since. He observed that although the Constitution lacks language that might settle an alleged conflict between a treaty and a statute, it was clear to the Court that "the question is not involved in any doubt as to its proper selection. A treaty may supersede a prior act of Congress and an act of Congress may supersede a prior treaty" (ibid., 621). This statement has proven to be a most disastrous legal rule. Two months earlier, in March 1871, Congress had attached a rider to an Indian Appropriation Act that squelched the Indian treaty process (16 St. 544, 566). With treaty-making terminated, although agreements continued to be made through the early 1900s, any act of Congress passed subsequent to March 1871 could be interpreted as overriding a preexisting Indian treaty right. Tribes were frozen in political limbo. They were no longer recognized as nations capable of formally treating with the federal government, yet they remained separate nonconstitutional political entities.

Justices Joseph Bradley and David Davis noted, however, in a spirited dissent to *The Cherokee Tobacco* that Indian populations were to be treated as "autonomies" and, that being the case, "all laws of a general character passed by Congress will be considered as not applying to the Indian territory, unless expressly mentioned" (622). The dissenting justices maintained that "an expressed law [like a treaty right to be exempt from taxation] creating certain rights and privileges is held never to be repealed by implication by any subsequent law couched in general terms nor by any expressed repeal of all laws inconsistent with such general law, *unless the language be such as clearly to indicate intention of the legislature to reflect such a repeal*" (ibid.; emphasis added).

Another decision that drew upon the implied repeal doctrine was *Lone Wolf v. Hitchcock*, 187 U.S. 553. The *Lone Wolf* opinion holds tremendous significance for federal Indian law because, among its precedents, it held (1) that congressional plenary power had always been present and that Congress's power over tribal property was unlimited; (2) that the federal government could unilaterally abrogate Indian treaties; and (3) that congressional plenary power was not subject to judicial review, because of the political question doctrine. *Lone Wolf* warrants more detailed analysis because it is so important to our discussion and because it continues to be used as precedent.

THE LONE WOLF DECISION: IMPLICATIONS FOR IMPLIED REPEALS

The *Lone Wolf* case arose out of conditions in the Indian Territory (which would become the state of Oklahoma in 1906) in the late 1800s. The Kiowas, Comanches, Apaches, and several other southern plains tribes had negotiated a treaty with the federally sponsored Indian Peace Commission in southern Kansas in 1867 (15 Stat., 581).[10] The Kansas treaty, like many during that era, contained a specific clause, Article 12, regarding future Indian land cessions: "No treaty for the cession of any portion or part of the reservation herein described, which may be held in common, shall be of any validity or force as against the said Indians, unless executed and signed by at least three-fourths of all the adult male Indians occupying the same" (15 Stat., 581). The provision for three-quarter adult male approval addressed the Indians' concern that federal representatives might, in the future, gain control of Indian lands by manipulating a minority of the tribal membership.

As more non-natives settled in Indian Territory, the pressure mounted to allot tribal lands, since the process of breaking up communally held lands and allotting 80 to 160 acres to individuals invariably left "surplus" lands of great value to land speculators and white homesteaders. In 1892 the three-member Cherokee Commission (also known as the Jerome Commission), despite resistance by many Indians, concluded an allotment and land cession agreement with certain representatives of the Kiowa, Comanche, and Apache (KCA) tribes. The commissioners secured a number of Indian signatures, but not enough to meet the "three-fourths of adult males" provision. Nevertheless, the controversial agreement was rushed to Washington, D.C., for congressional ratification. Almost immediately, over 300 KCA tribal members memorialized the Senate, urging that body to disapprove the 1892 agreement because the negotiating sessions had not been conducted in open council or with the knowledge of tribal leaders, and because many signatures had been obtained through misrepresentations, threats, and fraud. Tribal consent of three-quarters of the adult men had never been legitimately secured. In addition to these flaws, Congress substantially revised the agreement as it wound its way through the ratification process, a journey that took eight years. The revisions were never submitted to the KCA tribes for their approval, as required by the 1867 treaty. Despite all the legal and procedural irregularities, Congress ratified the amended agreement on June 6, 1900.

Lone Wolf, also known as A-Kei-Quodle, a principal chief of the Kiowa Nation, and several Comanche and Apache leaders brought suit against the United States challenging the legality of Congress's actions. Lone Wolf sought a permanent injunction against ratification of the 1900 agreement that allotted the KCA tribes' lands, resulting in a loss of over 2 million acres. The tribes contended that the federal government had directly violated Article 12 of the 1867 treaty. Lone Wolf, supported and represented by the Philadelphia-based Indian Rights Association, filed suit in the District of Columbia's Supreme Court in 1901. He lost, and his appeal was rejected by the District Court of Appeals. The KCA tribes then turned to the U.S. Supreme Court for justice.

The KCA tribes' hopes, and by implication the hopes of all tribes with treaty-based property rights, were crushed by the Court's unanimous ruling in 1903. Justice Edward D. White issued the *Lone Wolf* opinion, a crippling synthesis of the plenary power concept and the political question doctrine. The Court refused even to consider the tribes' core argument, of "fraudulent misrepresentation" by government officials in securing Indian signatures. The justices also refused to consider the issue of the Senate's unilateral alteration of the 1892 agreement's provisions. The only question the Court considered was whether the act of June 6, 1900, was constitutional. Despite *Lone Wolf's* arguments, Justice White accepted the government attorneys' view that since Indians were "wards" their treaty-defined property rights had not vested. The Indians' claim, said White, "in effect ignores the status of the contracting Indians and the relation of dependency they bore and continue to bear toward the government of the United States" (187 U.S. 553, 564). White, in effect, retroactively bestowed wardship status on the tribes to make the abrogation of their treaty rights appear legal. The Court's decision, shortly after its pronouncement, was labeled by one startled U.S. senator, Matthew Quey (R, Pennsylvania), the "*Dred Scott* decision No. 2 except that in this case the victim is red instead of black. It practically inculcates the doctrine that the red man has no rights which the white man is bound to respect, and, that no treaty or contract made with him is binding" (*Congressional Record* 1903, 2028).

Justice White created a reading of congressional plenary power in this case that unabashedly supported the colonial and assimilationist programs of the federal government. In his view, no legal or political constraints ought to be placed on the exercise of absolute power over Indians. White wrote: "To uphold the claim [of the Indians] would be to adjudge that the indirect operation of the treaty was to materially limit and qualify the *controlling authority* of Congress in respect to the care and protection of the Indians, and to deprive Congress, in a possible emergency, when the necessity might be urgent for a partition and disposal of the tribal lands, of *all power to act*, if the assent of the Indians could not be obtained" (187 U.S. 553, 564; emphasis added). However, clearly no "emergency" existed to justify White's position. The ratification process of the 1892 agreement had taken a full eight years to complete.

The Court's discussion of Congress's allegedly implied power over tribal rights and resources is of special importance for our discussion. White first cited previous cases in which the Court had equated Indian title with fee-simple title, the kind of legally binding title firmly entrenched in Euro-American law and the kind of title the Court was bound to uphold. While the precedents of these cases clearly supported KCA claims to their lands, White then set up a situation in which he was able to circumvent prior opinions. He claimed the *Lone Wolf* controversy was not at heart about land title, but about power: "But in none of these cases was there involved a controversy between Indians and the government respecting the power of Congress to administer the property of the Indians" (ibid., 565; emphasis added). He was correct, to a point. Prior to *Lone Wolf,* Congress had acknowledged that it had no right to challenge treaty-recognized Indian property rights. One of the cases cited by White, however, *Beecher v. Wetherby,* 95 U.S. 517 (1877), had stated that the United States had a superior authority over Indians based on guardianship and that such authority "might be *implied,* even though opposed to the strict letter of a treaty with the Indians" (187 U.S. 565; emphasis added). White built an argument that first posited federal superior and complete authority over Indian tribes and followed that assertion with the assumption that superior, complete authority (plenary power) could be *implied,* even if it was not explicitly stated in "the strict letter of a treaty." White's "abrogation by implication" argument led him to revise history and falsely assert that "plenary power over the tribal relations of the Indians has been exercised by Congress from the beginning, and the power has always been deemed a political one, not subject to the control of the judicial department of the government" (ibid.).

What circumstances led White to rule that Congress had "always" had plenary authority, not subject to judicial review? At the turn of the last century, the Court was intent on legitimating the federally directed breakdown of communally held tribal lands. Federal policymakers, citizens intent on reforming federal Indian policy, and justices of the Court all agreed on one thing—allotment was essential for Indians to approximate Euro-American civilization. If treaties needed to be broken in the process, it was judged to be done for the ultimate good of Indians. The Court set out to sanction the abrogation of treaty rights, notwithstanding the KCA tribes' well-articulated concerns about lost land, lost rights, and denied sovereignty. White's intent, and his patronizing view of Indians, is evident in the following passage, where he calmly describes the traumatic breakup of Indian communal lands into individualized allotted parcels as "a mere change in the form of investment of Indian tribal property, the property of those who, as we have held, were in substantial effect the wards of the government" (ibid., 568).

The Court did make some attempt to ameliorate the damage it had done to treaties in the *Lone Wolf* decision. The amelioration was phrased, once again, in terms demeaning to Indian people. The Court characterized the government's actions toward Indians as those of a "Christian people in their treatment of an ignorant and dependent race." The Congress, the Court presumed, was acting "in perfect good faith" with the Indians and was using its "best judgment in the premises" (ibid.). The Court had to "presume" that Congress had acted in good faith in dealing with the tribes, because subsequent to the treaties' ratification the Court could find no historical or legal assurance to show that Congress had "in reality" acted in good faith.

The Court's use of the implied repeal doctrine has increased since the mid-1970s in federal court cases.[11] The increased use of the implied repeals doctrine may be attributed to the Supreme Court's ideological turn toward a radical brand of conservatism, combined with a resurgence of states' rights. Recently, the Court has frequently favored states' rights as superior to Indian treaty rights.[12]

PRECEDENT AGAINST IMPLIED REPEALS

In the prior section, we outlined arguments for use of the doctrine of implied appeals and examples of how the Court has implemented the doctrine. What are the countervailing arguments and examples? Let us now turn to arguments and precedents that illustrate the invalidity of the doctrine of implied repeals. In 1880 a federal district court in *United States v. Berry*, 4 Fed. 779 (D.C. Colo. 1880), held that an Indian treaty "by its terms was to be permanent, and the rights conferred thereby were not to be taken away without the consent of the Indian." While conceding that Congress had the power of repeal, the judge said: "[I]t is clear to my mind that such repeal can only be enacted in expressed terms, or by such language as imports a clear purpose on the part of congress to effect that end" (788).

In 1883 the Supreme Court turned its attention to the doctrine of implied repeals in the important Indian criminal law case *Ex parte Crow Dog*, 109 U.S. 556 (1883). In *Crow Dog* the Supreme Court unanimously held that one of a tribe's remaining sovereign powers was exclusive criminal jurisdiction over its own members. The government, in seeking to execute Crow Dog for killing another Sioux, Spotted Tail, had argued that it had criminal jurisdiction based on Articles 1, 2, and 5 of the 1868 Sioux Treaty with the United States. The 1868 treaty dealt with the establishment of peace, the creation of the reservation, and the agent's appointment and with Article 8 of the federal government's 1877 agreement with the Sioux Nation, which said: "And Congress shall, by appropriate legislation, secure to them an orderly government; they shall be subject to the laws of the U.S., and each individual shall be protected in his rights of property, person, and life" (109 U.S. 556, 568). The federal attorneys argued that the wording of the 1877 treaty, which termed the Sioux "subject to the laws of the U.S.," constituted an effective extension of federal jurisdiction over criminal offenses. The Supreme Court disagreed, citing the fact that section 2146 of the Revised Statutes had never been expressly repealed. Section 2146 excluded criminal cases in Indian Country involving offenses by one Indian against another from U.S. jurisdiction. The Sioux Nation's right of self-government, the Court insisted, necessarily entailed "the regulation by themselves of their own domestic affairs, [including] the maintenance of order and peace among their own members by the administration of their own laws and customs" (ibid.).

The Court's detailed discussion of the implied repeal doctrine is entirely relevant to our discussion here. Justice Thomas Matthews and a unanimous court emphatically rebuffed the doctrine:

> It must be remembered that the question before us is whether the express letter of [section] 2146 of the Revised Statutes, which excludes from the jurisdiction of the United States the case of a crime committed in the Indian country by one Indian against the person or property of another Indian, has been repealed. If not, it is in force and applies to the present case. The treaty of 1868 and the agreement and act of Congress of 1877, it is admitted, do not repeal it by any express words. What we have said is sufficient at least to show that they do not work a repeal by necessary implication.... *Implied repeals are not favored*. The implication must be necessary. There must be a positive repugnancy between the provisions of the new laws and those of the old. (ibid., 570; emphasis added)

Justice Matthews then elaborated on the important principle that specific and express rights are not to be interpreted as being overruled by general acts unless there is explicit reference to them:

> The language of the exception is special and express; the words relied on as a repeal are general and inconclusive. The rule is *generalia specialibus non derogant*. "The general principle to be applied ... to the construction of acts of Parliament is that a general act is not to be construed to repeal a previous particular act, unless there is some express reference to the previous legislation on the subject, or unless there is a necessary inconsistency in the two acts standing together." And the reason is ... that the legislature having had its attention directed to a special subject, and having observed all the circumstances of the case and provided for them, does not intend by a general enactment afterwards to derogate from its own act when it makes no special mention of its intention so to do. (ibid., 571; emphasis in the original)

More recently, the Supreme Court has insisted in several important cases, *Menominee Tribe v. U.S.*, 391 U.S. 404 (1968), *Washington v. Fishing Vessel Association*, 443 U.S. 658 (1979), and *Minnesota v. Mille Lacs Band of Chippewa* 119 S.Ct. 1187 (1999), that the government's intent to abrogate Indian treaty provisions must be clear and unequivocal. This "clear and plain" standard also applies to non-treaty situations if the federal action threatens tribal rights created via statute, aboriginal title, or executive orders.[13] There have been very few cases where the U.S. Congress or the president *officially* exercised the power to abrogate Indian or international treaties (although many treaties or treaty provisions have been "unofficially" violated).[14] The procedure, either an act of Congress or some form of direct presidential action, like a proclamation, must be quite explicit. Let us consider several examples in detail, to illustrate just how explicit an intentional repeal (or change) can be.

Express Repeals of Foreign Treaties

On July 7, 1798, Congress enacted a law that abrogated treaties between the United States and France. The law was entitled "An act to declare the treaties heretofore concluded with France, no longer obligatory on the U.S." Congress declared that "whereas the treaties concluded between the United States and France have been repeatedly violated on the part of the French government . . . [a]nd whereas, under authority of the French government, there is yet pursued against the United States, a system of predatory violence, infracting the said treaties, and hostile to the rights of a free and independent nation," it was held that "the United States are of right freed and exonerated from the stipulations of the treaties, and of the consular convention . . . and that the same shall not henceforth be regarded as legally obligatory on the government or citizens of the United States" (2 St. 578).

In our second example, in 1978 President Jimmy Carter terminated a mutual defense treaty with Taiwan. The Senate considered a resolution that would have required the approval of the Senate, or both houses of Congress, before the president could terminate any defense treaty, but final action was never taken on the measure. A federal district court in 1979 in *Goldwater v. Carter* (481 F.Supp. 949, 963–64) held that some form of congressional concurrence was required before the abrogation of a treaty, but the district court decision was overturned by an appellate court (617 F.2d 697 [1979]) and the Supreme Court (444 U.S. 996 [1979]) because of Congress's failure to confront the president directly. The Supreme Court, in fact, split along several lines, providing no clear consensus on future treaty terminations by the chief executive. Moreover, Congress has not yet enacted legislation defining appropriate rules for the executive and legislature on this matter (Fisher 1990, 309). While such rules are lacking, the fact remains that treaty termination is a political decision.

Express Congressional Repeal of Indian Treaties

No American president has had a significant role in Indian treaty (or agreement) negotiation or interpretation since 1871, when Congress usurped the presidential treaty-making power with Indian tribes by unilaterally terminating the federal government's negotiation of any additional Indian treaties.[15] The House of Representatives led the movement to stifle treaty-making because members were concerned over treaty expenses, and they wanted more control over treaty-related appropriations. As a result of the recent Supreme Court ruling *Minnesota v. Mille Lacs Band of Chippewa*, 119 S.Ct. 1187 (1999), it is clear that the president lacks the power via executive order to revoke preexisting Indian treaty rights. Thus our primary focus on explicit Indian treaty abrogation is on the process used by Congress expressly to terminate Indian treaties.

The most vivid and direct congressional action to abrogate an Indian treaty resulted from the outbreak of war between Santee Sioux and white citizens in Minnesota in 1862. Several hundred whites were killed by Sioux who rose up in arms after being deprived of their lifestyle and some of their treaty entitlements by government agents (Lazarus 1991, 27–28). The U.S. Army responded quickly and soon pacified the Santees. General Henry Sibley, the militia commander in Minnesota and a prominent political figure in the state, ordered a court martial of several hundred Sioux. Three hundred Santees were sentenced to hang, regardless of their level of involvement in the violence. President Abraham Lincoln, however, commuted the death sentences of all but forty of the Indians. Eventually, thirty-eight were hanged—the largest mass execution in U.S. history. Congress responded to the "eruption" by enacting a law on July 5, 1862: "whenever the tribal organization of any Indian tribe is in actual hostility to the United States, the President is authorized, by proclamation, to declare all treaties with such tribe abrogated by such tribe, if in his opinion the same can be done consistently with good faith and legal and national obligations" (12 St. 528). In what Prucha calls "an unprecedented move" (Prucha 1994, 289), Congress canceled certain provisions of earlier treaties with the Sioux and the following year, on February 16, 1863, enacted a law declaring that "all treaties with the Sisseton," and several other bands of Sioux, were "abrogated and annulled, so far as said treaties or any of them purport to impose any future obligation on the United States" (12 St. 652–54).

In a second example, Congress explicitly abrogated an Indian treaty right with an act passed on February 28, 1877 (19 St. 254), which also involved the Sioux. In this act, which ratified an agreement with some Sioux bands and the Northern Arapahoes and Cheyennes, Congress clearly and unequivocally abrogated Article 16 of the 1868 Sioux treaty. Article 16 had guaranteed the integrity of Sioux unceded territory, permitting no whites within their borders without tribal consent and requiring the United States to abandon all military posts and to close roads. In 1877 Congress succinctly said: "And Article 16 of the said treaty is hereby abrogated" (ibid., 255).

Finally, in 1895 Congress acted to "annul" and "disapprove" a November 13, 1888, treaty (the legislation referred to this agreement as a treaty, even though all bilateral negotiations between tribes and the United States after 1871 were technically known as "agree-ments"). The 1888 treaty/agreement between the United States and the Southern Utes of Colorado superseded an earlier, June 15, 1880, treaty, which called for the allotment of Ute lands (28 St. 677). The 1895 act contained a consent provision in which Congress declared that the act would be inoperative until it was accepted by a major-ity of the adult male Indians on the reservation.

In short, when the federal government officially decides to abro-gate an Indian treaty or specific treaty provisions, it always acts through the Congress, which is authorized to oversee federal Indian affairs. The legislature exercises this power openly and unam-biguously, and sometimes after the legislature has decided that the tribe in question has done something to warrant abrogation. We can understand the Santee example cited above in this light. The Santee violence against encroaching whites was deemed a viola-tion of their treaty agreement to live in peace with their white neighbors. There is no reason for the Supreme Court, or any other judicial body, to have to imagine scenarios when Congress *meant to* "imply" a repeal of Indian treaties or treaty provisions, but did not bother to say so. Ample evidence shows us that when Congress means to repeal, it does so explicitly. Imputing an intent to Congress in order to abrogate treaties, we say again, oversteps the bounds of judicial authority.

Express Congressional Modification of Prior Treaties/Agreements

On other occasions when Congress wished to modify existing Indian treaties or agreements, it enacted specific laws. Several examples of this kind of congressional action can be found by the late 1860s, when the United States began to add provisions to many Indian treaties that guaranteed that reservation land could not be ceded (sold) without the express written consent of a majority (usually three-fourths) of adult males.[16] As the devastating *Lone Wolf* case well illustrates, this consent provision was sometimes brushed aside or abused by federal officials. Notwithstanding the bleak precedent of the *Lone Wolf* case, Congress has, in some instances, secured tribal consent before acquiring Indian lands or terminating treaty rights. In some cases, Congress acted only after passing an express act to amend a prior treaty/agreement. For example, on June 30, 1864 (13 Stat. 324), Congress authorized the president to negotiate with the Confederated Tribes of Oregon, urging the tribes to relinquish certain off-reservation hunting, fishing, and gathering rights that were retained in an 1859 treaty. Congress authorized the expenses of the treaty negotiations and an offer to the tribes of $5,000 for cession of those rights.

In 1872 Congress passed an act (17 Stat., 98) to implement certain provisions of the 1866 Cherokee Treaty having to do with the so-called Cherokee Strip lands owned by the Cherokee Nation in Kansas. Strip lands were to be surveyed and sold, but only after the sale had been approved by the Cherokee National Council or by a duly authorized Cherokee delegation. In yet another example of explicit repeal, Congress passed a measure in 1874 (18 Stat., 29) pertaining to the eighth article of the 1856 treaty with the Creek and Seminole Indians. Article 8 authorized the federal government to expend $5,000 annually for the "comfort, civilization, and improvement" of the Indians. In a proviso, Congress stated that "the consent of said tribe to such expenditures and payment shall be first obtained." The Osage Tribe also received congressional assurances (21 Stat., 509) that its consent would be obtained before its Kansas lands, known as the Osage Indian trust and diminished reserved lands, were sold at public auction to the highest bidder. These sales were not to occur "until at least two-thirds of the adult males" agreed to the provisions outlined by Congress.

In yet another example, on July 1, 1902, Congress passed an act to accept, ratify, and confirm the allotment agreement and memorial that had been proposed by the Kansas or Kaw Tribe of Oklahoma Territory (32 Stat., 636). Article 13 contained the consent provision: "The said Kansas or Kaw Indians hereby memorialize Congress to ratify and confirm this agreement and to make provision for carrying it into effect: Provided, That if any material amendments are made in this agreement by Congress the same shall not become effective until such amendments are approved by a majority of the adult members of the . . . tribe." The Kaws, like most tribes, were under enormous pressure to have their lands allotted. As Commissioner of Indian Affairs (CIA) William A. Jones stated in his report accompanying the Kaw agreement: "The agreement is in entire harmony with the views of this [CIA] office . . . The Indian must ultimately be thrown upon his own resources, and this agreement proposes to do this for the Kaw tribe" (U.S. House 1903, 3). The consent provision, however, was designed to provide the Indians with some assurance that their rights would not be *unilaterally* altered by Congress, though it was clear that their rights were going to be altered, like it or not.

The 1903 *Lone Wolf* decision established an ominous precedent in Indian affairs: that Congress could unilaterally abrogate Indian treaty rights over the protests of Indians by exercising an unreviewable plenary power over Indian property. As Prucha states in *American Indian Treaties*, "after the *Lone Wolf* decision the idea of requiring Indian consent for the disposition of their lands was largely discarded in regard to statutes as well as to agreements, and Congress unilaterally provided for the sale of surplus lands remaining after allotments had been completed" (Prucha 1994, 356–57). Prucha cites as evidence a 1901 agreement with the Rosebud Sioux for the sale of their unallotted lands. The government's Indian inspector, James McLaughlin, properly secured the signatures of three-fourths of the adult Sioux males for the land cession. This agreement, however, was later amended and ratified by Congress in 1904 in a way that eliminated the requirement to secure Indian consent. The House Committee on Indian Affairs that made the changes in the agreement, calling for the elimination of the need to get Indian consent, justified this action largely on the basis of the *Lone Wolf* opinion (ibid., 357).

Prucha (1994, 328) also claims that "Indian consent . . . gradually disappeared as a major element" of federal Indian policy after the 1880s as a result of the force of the February 8, 1887, General Allotment Act (24 Stat., 388), the policy directive issued by Congress to hasten the individualization of Indian communal land through the allotment of individual shares to Indian families and members. On a broad level Prucha is correct; there is significant evidence that many tribes fought valiantly against allotment—and never gave their consent freely—only to have the federal government push ahead. Nevertheless, while federal pursuit of American Indian assimilation was a powerful force that tribes could not completely resist, there are still clear examples of congressional persistence in obtaining tribal consent and/or examples of explicit legislative action before modifying treaties/agreements. Congress has acted less frequently to gain Indian consent before allotting Indian reservations or selling surplus lands after allotment, but the fact remains that the legislature, not the judiciary, had to modify prior Indian treaties/agreements explicitly. One final example makes this point quite clearly. On June 11, 1934, Congress passed an act (48 Stat., 927) "to modify the effect of certain Chippewa Indian treaties" and expressly amended Article 7 of two Chippewa treaties (February 22, 1853, and September 30, 1854), which defined "Indian Country" for jurisdictional purposes. Again, the important point is that this modification of treaty rights required an express and unequivocal statement by the Congress that had negotiated and ratified the original treaties.

The evidence shows that when the Congress has officially and expressly abrogated or modified Indian treaties it has formally acted through the legislative process and has sometimes sought tribal consent. Most commentators and ample litigation confirm that when it is deemed vital to the national interest, Congress may enact a precise law abrogating (or amending) a prior treaty/agreement. Officially, the power to abrogate Indian treaties unilaterally has not been wielded often. Treaties are viewed as solemn and binding pacts, and breaking them can have serious consequences, as Attorney General Caleb Cushing noted in 1854, in an opinion on the land rights of several Kansas Territory tribes:

Let me not be understood as acceding to the doctrine, that all stipulations of treaties are subject to be repealed or modified at any time by act of Congress. Without going into that question here, it suffices to remark that every treaty is an express compact, in the most solemn form in which the United States can make a compact. Not to observe a treaty, is to violate a deliberate and express engagement. To violate such engagements of a treaty with any foreign power affords, of course, good cause of war. (United States 1854, 663–64)

Cushing went on to note, however, some important distinctions between Indian treaties and treaties with foreign nations: "[E]xamples may be cited of acts of Congress, which operate so as to modify or amend treaties with Indians. As their sovereign and their guardian, we have occasionally assumed to do this, acting in their interest and our own, and not, in such cases, violating engagements with them, but seeking to give a more beneficial effect to such engagements. For though they be weak, and we strong,—they subjects and we masters,—yet they are not the less entitled to the exercise towards them of the most scrupulous good faith on the part of the United States" (ibid., 664). In Cushing's words, the federal government was legally and morally bound to uphold Indian treaties not only because treaties were important political covenants, but also because of the added trust/moral dimension. The federal government, in asserting its physical superiority, assumed an additional set of responsibilities to protect the lands and interests of Indians.

The treaty power, as Attorney General Amos T. Akerman stated in 1870, "binding the will of the nation, must, within its constitutional limits, be paramount to the legislative power which is that will" (United States 1873, 358). Tribes, of course, after a time, declined and in some cases surrendered their right to wage war by negotiating treaties. Through treaties, tribes reluctantly agreed to reduced lands, peace, and amity with the United States in exchange for continued recognition of tribal sovereignty and all reserved rights. Hence, it must not be assumed that differences between U.S. treaties with foreign powers and U.S. treaties with indigenous powers outweigh the legal comparability of the documents (pertinent differences include tribes' geographic locations, the trust and plenary doctrines, and tribal military disadvantages). As a federal court held in *Turner v. American Baptist Missionary Union*, 24 Fed.Cas. 344 (1852), "it is contended that a treaty with Indian tribes, has not the same dignity or effect, as a treaty with a foreign and independent nation. This distinction is not authorized by the Constitution. . . . They are treaties, within the meaning of the constitution, and, as such, are the supreme laws of the land" (346).

CONCLUSION

The Supreme Court lacks constitutional authority to abrogate specific treaty rights or to divest Indian tribes of their rights by implication; such power is constitutionally vested in, and on a few occasions has been expressly wielded by, the U.S. Congress. From an indigenous perspective, corroborated by a plethora of federal policy, judicial opinions, and some historical practice, the Supreme Court's decision in *The Kansas Indians* (72 U.S. 737 [1866]) contains the most reasonable articulation of how Indian treaties/agreements may be changed. The Court held that Indian treaties and the rights affirmed or created by treaty provisions may be modified, amended, or terminated only through bilateral treaty stipulations, by purchase, or by voluntary abandonment by the tribal organization.

The evidence shows that the United States and tribes have, on a number of occasions, mutually agreed to amend treaties; and that the federal government has sought, on some occasions, to purchase Indian treaty rights. While federal power over tribal lands and rights was far more oppressive after the *Lone Wolf* decision, because Congress regularly acted as if tribal consent was no longer required, it was still federal policy that changes in treaties/agreements required Congress to enact statutes with exact language specifying modification or elimination of treaty provisions. We can look to the important water rights case, *Winters v. United States*, 143 F. 740 (1906), for a clearly articulated process for changing treaty rights that allows both parties to act in good faith. Judge Thomas Hawley wrote in the federal district court ruling: "We must presume that the government and the Indian, in agreeing to the terms of the treaty, acted in the utmost good faith toward each other; that they both understood its meaning, purpose, and object" (745).

The political and moral principle of "utmost good faith," combined with the trust doctrine, requires that both parties work to fulfill not only the letter but especially the spirit of the treaties. Any modification or abrogation of a treaty should be carried out mutually, consensually, and voluntarily through the same political/diplomatic channels that led to the treaty's creation in the first case. On those few occasions when the federal government has formally abrogated treaties or provisions of treaties, Congress has wielded the abrogating power, but only through express wording in a statute. In the more numerous cases where Congress negotiated agreements and then sought to amend them, it also passed specific legislation identifying its intention, and frequently sought Indian consent as well.

It is not the province of the Supreme Court to generate a congressional intent and then, by implication, repeal specific treaty rights that have been negotiated and ratified through political channels by tribal nations and by the federal government. Indian treaties, like all treaties, are vital diplomatic arrangements between nations. While treaties may be abrogated by the Congress (or by the tribes, for that matter), depending on the confluence of particular if ill-defined circumstances, a clear and specific intent to abrogate must exist, and it must be carried out by those political branches that oversee the United States' relationship with tribes. This directive stems from the distinctive trust and good faith doctrines, and from the exclusive authority of Congress with regards to Indian affairs. When conflicts erupt between Indian treaty provisions and later statutes, the Supreme Court's principal task is to uphold the honor and will of the nation, as outlined in the treaty, and to interpret the conflicting statute in a way that conforms to the national will and to the federal government's trust obligations to tribes.

CHAPTER SIX

"No Reasonable Plea":
Disclaimers in
Tribal-State Relations

The Cherokee nation have never promised to surrender, at any future period, to the United States, for Georgia, their title to lands; but, on the contrary, the United States have, by treaties, solemnly guarantied [sic] to secure to the Cherokees forever their title to lands which have been reserved to them: therefore, the State of Georgia can have no reasonable plea against the Cherokees for refusing to yield their little all to the United States, so that her own aggrandizement may be raised upon their ruins.

JOHN ROSS, GEORGE LOWREY,
MAJOR RIDGE, AND ELIJAH HICKS
in a letter to Secretary of War John C. Calhoun,
February 11, 1824, responding to his entreaty to surrender
to the inevitability of Cherokee removal westward

Tribes and states, from their first encounters, have struggled with one another because of notions of race, conflict over resources, cultural differences, and contending political agendas. As a result, when the U.S. Constitution was ratified (replacing the Articles of Confederation), relations with tribes were firmly situated as a federal responsibility, specifically the responsibility of Congress; in other words, official political relations with tribes were federalized. As new states entered the Union, especially in the West, they were required in their organic acts and constitutions to disclaim jurisdiction over Indian property and persons forever. In this chapter we examine these "disclaimer clauses," explain the factors that have enabled states to assume some jurisdictional presence in Indian Country, examine the key issues in which disclaimers continue to carry significant weight, and explain the vacillating role of the federal government, which has sometimes protected tribes from states and sometimes fostered state intrusions into tribal life. We argue that the federal government should reclaim its role as the lone constitutional authority to deal with indigenous nations. Disclaimer clauses are an important but often overlooked tool in the arsenal available to tribes to assert their own sovereignty against state threats and to privilege the tribal government-to-federal government relationship over any inappropriate intrusion by the states.

Tribes and states have been contentious political sparring partners since the beginning of the American Republic, and tribes and colonies were often at odds before that as well. British taxation and lack of political representation in British government were not the only discontents that led to the American Revolution. The colonies also resented and ignored royal regulation of affairs with Indian nations. The British colonies had for some time objected to royal injunctions against English settlement west of the Royal Proclamation line of 1763—basically, west of the Appalachians—injunctions that were intended to prevent illegal encroachment on Indian lands and thus help preserve the peace. English colonists also objected to strict royal controls over the Indian trade and traders.

When the formerly British colonies confederated as the first states of the new Union, they wanted to retain jurisdiction over Indians in their borders and only reluctantly agreed to federal (specifically congressional) control over Indian affairs in the federal territories to the west. At least one state, Georgia, very reluctantly surrendered its claims to western lands. In return for Georgia's

agreement to a western boundary, the federal government promised in 1802 that it would, at some unspecified time, "quiet" (that
is, eradicate) all Indian title to lands within the state. Georgia called
on the federal government to make good its 1802 promise and
forced the issues with its own legislative actions. Beginning in 1827,
the state attacked the original jurisdiction of the Cherokee court,
unilaterally dissolved the Cherokee tribal government, took over
Cherokee national assets (gold mines), harassed and terrorized
Cherokee citizens, destroyed the Cherokee free press, denied Cherokee citizens rights to testify in courts against white people, and confiscated Cherokee lands to distribute to whites through state lot-
tery. The federal government ultimately refused to move against
the state and protect the Cherokees under the terms of existing
U.S.-Cherokee treaties.

The federal Union was still fragile and precarious, and President Andrew Jackson ardently supported states' rights. In the end,
despite a Supreme Court ruling in *Worcester v. Georgia* that declared
Georgia's actions unconstitutional and that upheld the rights of the
Cherokee Nation to its own government and lands, the Cherokees
and other eastern tribes were forcibly removed to so-called Indian
Territory west of the Mississippi. In the case of removal, the states
successfully implemented their agenda of removing Indians from
within their borders, and the federal government backed away from
its treaty-based legal and moral responsibilities to protect tribes. The
1830s were certainly not the last time that tribes, states, and the federal government tangled over issues of jurisdictions and powers.

In the late 1800s and throughout the 1900s, Wisconsin, Arizona,
and other states asserted alleged jurisdictional rights to regulate
Indian hunting, fishing, and gathering or to impose state taxes,
despite explicit statements in federal treaties, state constitutions,
enabling acts, and congressional laws reserving and protecting those
rights (Reed and Zelio 1995; U.S. Commission on Civil Rights 1981).
Social workers in many states removed Indian children from Indian
homes and placed them in non-native homes without tribal consent
or tribal input into the adoptive process (Byler 1977; U.S. House

1978). By the 1950s and 1960s, in Washington and Wisconsin, as many as one-third of all Indian children had been removed from Indian homes by state social welfare agencies. State abuses against tribes led to a plethora of federal legislation, such as the Indian Child Welfare Act (1978) and the 1988 Indian Gaming Regulatory Act; and Supreme Court cases, such as *U.S. v. Washington*, designed to articulate, assert, and enforce tribal rights and privileges against aggressive and illegal actions taken by the states. Despite the reassertion of tribal rights and sovereignty, tribal-state relations continued to deteriorate through the 1990s, as some states doggedly contested the right of tribes to run gaming enterprises, to manage on- and off-reservation resources such as fish and game, to exercise jurisdiction over adoptive placement of Indian children pursuant to the Indian Child Welfare Act, or to regulate and tax on-reservation businesses.

State assertions of jurisdictional supremacy in Indian Country—unless tribal and federal consent have been obtained—are without constitutional merit.[1] In *Native American Church v. Navajo Tribal Council*, 272 F.2d 131 (1959), a federal district court stated that "Indian tribes are not states. They have a status higher than that of states." Despite such court pronouncements throughout the 1900s, states often acted as if they were the political superiors of tribal nations.[2] State assertions of superiority over tribes violate the doctrine of inherent tribal sovereignty, are contrary to judicial precedent, run afoul of the treaty relationship, damage the federally recognized trust doctrine, and breach the doctrine of federal supremacy in the field of Indian affairs outlined expressly in the commerce clause, and implicitly in the treaty clause, of the Constitution.[3] These two clauses, the Supreme Court has held, provide Congress with "all that is required" for complete control over Indian affairs (*Worcester v. Georgia*, 559). Furthermore, and most important for our purposes, state efforts to interfere with the internal affairs of tribal nations violate the disclaimer clauses that the federal government required most western states (plus Wisconsin) to include in their territorial acts, enabling acts, and constitutions.

Disclaimer clauses expressly preclude the states from extending authority inside Indian Country. The eleven western states included in tables 1, 2, and 3 are home to more than eighty percent of the United States' indigenous population and nearly all of the country's 278 Indian reservations. Disclaimer clauses, dating from Wisconsin's territorial disclaimer of 1836 to Alaska's constitutional disclaimer of 1959, expressly declare that these territories or states cannot extend their authority inside Indian Country. Tables 1, 2, and 3 illustrate the variable language found in the clauses, but generally each contains specific language designed to assure both tribes and the federal government that the territory/state will never, without federal consent and/or a treaty modification, interfere with tribal nations' internal affairs. Alaska's disclaimer clause is a clear example:

> The State of Alaska and its people forever disclaim all right and title in or to any property belonging to the United States or subject to its disposition, and not granted or confirmed to the State or its political subdivisions, by or under the act admitting Alaska to the Union. *The State and its people further disclaim all right or title in or to any property, including fishing rights, the right or title to which may be held by or for any Indian, Eskimo, or Aleut, or community thereof,* as that right or title is defined in the act of admission. The State and its people agree that, unless otherwise provided by Congress, the property, as described in this section, shall remain subject to the absolute jurisdiction of the United States. *They further agree that no taxes will be imposed upon any such property, until otherwise provided by the Congress.* This tax exemption shall not apply to property held by individuals in fee without restrictions on alienation. (Columbia University 1995, 27–28; emphasis added)

This passage explicitly declares that the state will not interfere with the property rights of Alaskan natives, nor attempt to tax native lands, unless such lands have been individualized and trust restrictions lifted. This type of powerful constitutional disclaimer of jurisdiction, we argue, should serve, along with preexisting treaty and trust protections, to form an impenetrable shield protecting indigenous rights and resources from state designs.

States, particularly the western states that are home to most Indian nations, have tended to disregard disclaimer clauses. Congress holds the responsibility to remind all states (those with and without disclaimer clauses) that under the Constitution the political branches of the federal government exercise and administer

TABLE 1.

Territories with Indian Disclaimer Clauses

DATE	TERRITORY	KEY LANGUAGE
1836	Wisconsin	Indian rights not to be impaired until extinguished by treaty
1838	Iowa	Same as above
1848	Oregon	Same as above
1853	Washington	Federal government retains power to make Indian policy by treaty or by law
1854	Kansas	Indian rights not to be impaired until extinguished by treaty; Indian lands not to be included in territory without tribal consent
1854	Nebraska	Same as above
1861	Colorado	Same as above
1861	North Dakota	Indian rights not to be impaired
1863	Idaho	Same as above
1864	Montana	Indian rights not to be impaired until extinguished by treaty; Indian lands not to be included in territory without tribal consent
1868	Wyoming	Indian rights not to be impaired
1890	Oklahoma	Indian rights not to be impaired until extinguished by treaty

TABLE 2.

State Enabling Acts with Indian Disclaimer Clauses

Date	State	Key Language
1861	Kansas	Indian rights not to be impaired unless extinguished by treaty; Indian lands not to be included in state without tribal consent; tribes must signify their assent to the president to be included within state
1889	North Dakota	The people and the state forever disclaim all rights to Indian lands; those lands remain under absolute federal jurisdiction; state may only tax land of individual Indians who have severed tribal relations, but not if that land was granted by Congress with an express tax exemption
1889	South Dakota	Same as above
1889	Montana	Same as above
1889	Washington	Same as above
1894	Utah	Same as above
1906	Oklahoma	Indian rights are not to be impaired so long as they have not been extinguished; federal government retains exclusive authority to make Indian policy by treaty, agreement, or law
1910	New Mexico	Same as Utah
1910	Arizona	Same as above
1958	Alaska	The people and the state forever disclaim all right to Indian land and to any land or other property (e.g., fishing rights) held in trust by the U.S.; all lands and property under absolute federal jurisdiction, except when held in fee-simple title

TABLE 3.
State Constitutions with Indian Disclaimer Clauses

DATE	STATE	KEY LANGUAGE
1889	North Dakota	The people forever disclaim all right and title to Indian held lands; they remain subject to U.S. disposition and under absolute federal jurisdiction; state may only tax individual Indian land if person has severed tribal relations and has title to land; lands granted by Congress containing tax exemption, however, are not taxable by state
1889	South Dakota	Same as above
1889	Montana	All lands owned by or held by Indians remain under absolute jurisdiction and control of Congress until revoked by consent of the U.S. and people of Montana
1889	Washington	Same as North Dakota
1890	Wyoming	People forever disclaim all right and title to Indian lands; those lands subject to absolute federal jurisdiction
1890	Idaho	People and state forever disclaim all right and title to Indian lands; those lands subject to absolute federal jurisdiction
1896	Utah	Same as North Dakota
1907	Oklahoma	The people forever disclaim all right and title to Indian lands; they remain subject to U.S. jurisdiction
1912	New Mexico	Same as North Dakota
1912	Arizona	Same as North Dakota
1959	Alaska	State and people disclaim all right and title to any property, including fishing rights; such property subject to absolute federal jurisdiction; state will not impose taxes on Indian property unless directed by Congress, except for lands held in fee-simple title

this nation's Indian policy.[4] Congress must also let states know that they cannot cavalierly disregard their fundamental laws absent a modification of the treaty or trust relationship or without tribal and federal consent. This chapter analyzes the historical, legal, and political import of state disclaimer clauses and argues that the federal government must reclaim its role as the government vested with constitutional authority to treat with indigenous nations. We begin by examining and redefining the notion of federalism, the political model of the relationship between federal and state governments.

REDEFINING FEDERALISM

Federalism is a system of governance in which a national, overarching government shares power with subnational or state governments. This model, or theory, of governmental relations is not static. Since the 1980s, we have seen a political, legal, and economic growth spurt in the relative powers of states, spearheaded by the states and sanctioned by the Supreme Court (and to a lesser, though still impressive extent, by the Congress and the presidency). Fluctuations in the definition and character of governmental relations are not unusual in U.S. history. Woodrow Wilson characterized federalism in 1911 as something that could not be settled "by the opinion of any one generation" (quoted in Scheiber 1992, 278). Wilson observed that changes in the social and economic condition of society, in the public's perception of issues needing to be addressed by government, and in the dominant political values require each successive generation to deal with federal-state relationships as a "new question," subject to comprehensive and searching analysis (ibid.). Ongoing and reevaluative analysis is indeed called for in issues such as welfare policy, religious issues, or economic regulation. We argue, however, that U.S. dealings with Indian nations are not constitutionally open as a "new question" for each generation because the Congress was given exclusive jurisdiction over Indian affairs in the commerce clause (and by practical application, in the treaty, supremacy, and property clauses) of the Constitution.

Exclusive federal jurisdiction over Indian Country affairs was most powerfully expressed in the landmark case *Worcester v. Georgia*, 31 U.S. (6 Pet.) 515 (1832), when the Supreme Court ruled that tribes were distinct, independent political bodies in which the laws of the states can have no force "but with the assent of the Cherokees themselves, or in conformity with treaties, and with the acts of Congress. The whole intercourse between the United States and this nation is by our Constitution and laws vested in the Government of the United States" (561). Tribal nations stand as pre- and extraconstitutional polities alongside, but not constitutionally subject to, the federal government.[5] For example, in *United States v. Rickert*, 188 U.S. 432 (1903), the Supreme Court held that the federal government's constitutional power to control property belonging to the United States, combined with the South Dakota's constitutional disclaimer clause, prohibited the state from taxing Indian land. "No authority exists," said the Court, "for the State to tax lands which are held in trust by the United States for the purpose of carrying out its policy in reference to these Indians" (ibid., 441). In *Dick v. United States*, 208 U.S. 340 (1907), the Supreme Court sustained federal authority to prohibit the introduction of liquor onto lands ceded by the Nez Percé Indians.[6] The Court held that while a state is admitted on an equal footing with other states, congressional power to regulate commerce with Indian tribes is a power "superior and paramount to the authority of any State within whose limits are Indian tribes." Similarly, in *United States v. Chavez*, 290 U.S. 357 (1993), the Supreme Court held that the State of New Mexico had no authority to prosecute non-Indian defendants charged with larceny committed within the Isleta Pueblo, because the United States Constitution vested exclusive authority over such crimes in the federal government. Despite admission of New Mexico into the Union "on an equal footing" with the original states, "the principle of equality is not disturbed by a legitimate exertion by the United States of its constitutional power in respect of its Indian wards and their property" (365).

Federal courts are not alone in confirming the primacy of the tribal-federal relationship; some state case law argues the same

point. In *State v. Arthur*, 261 P.2d 135 (1953), the Idaho Supreme
Court declared that the admission of Idaho into the Union did not
repeal hunting rights reserved by treaty to the Nez Percé Indians.
Although Idaho's Admission Act was silent regarding Indian rights,
both the Organic Act and the state's constitution "recognize their
[Indian] rights which arise under the Treaty of 1855 and subsequent
agreements and treaties prior to statehood" (138). In *Chino v. Chino*,
90 N.M. 203 (1977), the New Mexico Supreme Court held that the
state had not assumed jurisdiction over the Indian reservations in
the state because it failed to take "affirmative steps under Public
Law 280" or under more recent congressional acts. Thus, "the treaties
and statutes applicable in this case preclude the state from exercising
jurisdiction over property lying within the reservation boundaries"
(206).

The New Mexico court constructed its decision around many of
the arguments we discuss in this chapter. Tribes have a special government-to-government relationship with the federal government,
based on inherent tribal sovereignty, treaties, and various clauses
within the Constitution. States are constrained from exercising jurisdiction over tribes, unless federal or tribal governments affirma-
tively authorize states to act. States may have a right to act when
tribal relations are not involved and when the rights of Indians will
not be jeopardized, but states may not act where the United States
has preempted the field by treaties or relevant statutes, and where
disclaimers expressly deny states the power to assume jurisdiction.

Tribes are connected to the federal government by treaties, agreements, the trust doctrine, and clauses of the Constitution. Tribes are
also heavily impacted by, and major players in, the latest reshap-
ings and reimaginings of the doctrine of federalism. For example,
in 1996 the Supreme Court in *Seminole Tribe v. Florida*, 116 S.Ct. 1114,
struck down important provisions of the 1988 Indian Gaming Regulatory Act (IGRA, 102 Stat. 2475), which had authorized federal
courts to resolve disputes between tribes and the states. IGRA had
been formulated in line with the long-standing, and constitutionally sanctioned, federalization of Indian affairs. In the case of Indian

gaming, Congress had granted the states the privilege of negotiating contracts with gaming tribes. The contracts gave states an entry into the regulatory process erected around Indian gaming, an entry they would not have had without specific congressional legislation. The states were enjoined by IGRA to negotiate compacts "in good faith" with the tribes, but in cases where tribal-state disagreements could not be resolved, authority to resolve reverted back to the federal government (specifically, the secretary of the interior). When the Rehnquist Court, in *Seminole Tribe*, disallowed that federal dispute resolution, the justices shifted the balance of power between the states and federal government toward the states. Since the historic nation-to-nation relation for nearly all tribes has been at the federal level, this redefinition of federalism does not bode well for the retention of indigenous rights. Through its ruling in *Seminole Tribe*, the Supreme Court has effectively stated its intention to disregard or sever the tribes' constitutional linkage to the federal government via the commerce clause.

The current reshaping of federalism to strengthen the states, and weaken the federal government and tribes, is occurring despite the fact that tribal sovereignty does not derive from state or federal constitutions, and despite the fact that tribal sovereignty is inherent and originates from within the collective will of each indigenous community. The privileging of states in the federalist model is occurring in spite of the fact that the trust doctrine, treaties, and the supremacy, property, and commerce clauses of the U.S. Constitution vest exclusive jurisdiction to protect and assist tribes in the federal government. The reimagination of federalism is ongoing in the courts, although one can find very few recent actions where the federal government has consciously and expressly authorized state supremacy over Indian affairs or tribal lands.[7] Federalism is changing, even though tribes have not significantly modified any treaty or trust arrangements with the federal government. Finally, federalism is metamorphosing despite explicit disclaimer provisions in territorial acts, enabling acts, and constitutional arrangements that specifically deny states the power to exercise jurisdictional or taxing authority over Indians within reservations or within Indian Country.

We build our argument against the current reconfiguration of federalism on the Constitution, the trust doctrine, inherent tribal sovereignty, and state disclaimer clauses. Disclaimers are important legal and political building blocks, and their import should not be overlooked. The federal government, when it required states to include disclaimer clauses, assumed the double duty of *"preserving* to the Indians the quiet possession of the reservation as their future home and *protecting* their persons and property therein, and this duty and obligation still exists, never having been released by the actions of the Indians or by treaty or agreement with them" (*U.S. v. Ewing*, 47 Fed. 809, 813 [1891]; emphasis added). Of course, in a few instances Congress has acted to delegate its constitutionally vested authority over Indian affairs to states. We argue that Congress cannot legitimately make such a delegation to a state without attaching the existing treaty and trust protections that tribes legally and morally expect from the United States.[8] If the states, the subnational governments, are indeed constitutionally intertwined with the national government, then the treaty and trust commitments of the United States—as a nation—toward tribes cannot be unilaterally terminated simply by delegating those commitments to the states (termination of such commitments would require a mutually agreed upon treaty modification with the tribes' informed consent).

WHAT DISCLAIMER ACTS SAY

Disclaimer clauses can be found within the organic acts that created territories, within the enabling acts that incorporated states into the Union, and within state constitutions. All these laws taken together outline the steps a territory's citizenry must take to become a state. The inclusion of disclaimer clauses in these core political documents explicitly recognizes the supremacy of the federal government in the field of Indian affairs. Although we have seen states chafe at federal supremacy, claiming that it infringed on their rights, as a federal court noted in *United States v. Board of Commissioners* of Osage County, 26 F.Supp. 270 (1939), "there cannot be an invasion of State rights because a condition of statehood was the reserving by the Federal Government of power and authority over Indians, their lands and property" (275).

Territorial Disclaimers

The American territorial system was distinctively transitional and progressive, looking toward statehood. Under the Constitution, Congress retained supreme power over the territories, which makes the insertion of disclaimer clauses in the territorial acts all the more interesting, since the Constitution already vested Congress and the president with plenary exclusive authority over Indian affairs. Twelve territorial acts contain express Indian disclaimer clauses (see table 1).[9] One example of an explicit disclaimer clause is found in section 1 of Wisconsin's statute (5 Stat. 11):

> That nothing in this act contained shall be construed to impair the rights of person or property now appertaining to any Indians within the said Territory so long as such rights shall remain unextinguished by treaty between the United States and such Indians, or to impair the obligations of any treaty now existing between the United States and such Indians, or to impair or anywise to affect the authority of the Government of the United States to make any regulations respecting such Indians, their lands, property, or other rights, by treaty, or law, or otherwise, which it would have been competent to the Government to make if this act had never been passed.

Federal lawmakers were warning territorial residents and leaders not to interfere with the treaty-based political relationship between the tribes and the federal government. The United States' exclusive and constitutionally grounded authority to enact regulations dealing with tribes and their property or rights, whether

derived from treaties or laws, was not to be intruded upon. Interestingly, the territorial acts for New Mexico (1850), Arizona (1863),
Michigan (1805), Alaska (1854), and Minnesota (1844)—all home
to many indigenous groups—contained no express disclaimers.
The only references to Indians in those territorial acts are the statement that Indians cannot be counted for purposes of determining
the number of congressional representatives and a declaration that
the governor of the territory was also the superintendent of Indian
affairs.

A major exception to the process discussed so far is the unique
development of the Indian Territory into the state of Oklahoma
(Debo 1972; Foreman 1972). A majority of the Indian nations now
inhabiting Oklahoma either migrated there or were forcibly relocated there during the Indian Removal period of the 1830s–60s. In
1834 Congress passed an act for the government of the Indian
Country, which recognized that the land belonged solely to the
Indians, and established regulations for trade and intercourse with
the tribes (4 Stat. 729). Years later, in 1890, despite treaty assurances
reserving the Indian Territory to Indians, the rapidly expanding
white population wanted to establish its own governing mechanisms. By the Act of May 2, 1890, a sizable portion of the Indian
Territory was transformed into the new Territory of Oklahoma.
The territorial act contained an express disclaimer, designed to
assure tribes in the area that their remaining lands, resources, and
rights would be respected. This disclaimer clause reads like many
of those described above, although the words have a hollow ring
coming in the wake of direct treaty violations, the failure of the
government to protect Indian lands, and the establishment of a foreign territorial government out of tribal lands:

> That nothing in this act shall be construed to impair any right
> now pertaining to any Indians or Indian tribe in said Territory
> under the laws, agreements, and treaties of the United States,
> or to impair the rights of person or property pertaining to said
> Indians, or to affect the authority of the Government of the

United States to make any regulation or to make any law
respecting said Indians, their lands, property, or other rights
which it would have been competent to make or enact if this
act had not been passed. (Thorpe 1909, vol. 5, 2940)

Enabling Act Disclaimers

Congress passed the first enabling act on April 30, 1802, authorizing the inhabitants of the eastern district of the Northwest Territories to elect representatives to a convention and to draft a constitution (Gates 1968, 289). While Congress easily created territories,
it was far more reluctant to create states. From 1860 to 1880, only
four western states entered the union: Kansas, 1861; Nevada, 1864;
Nebraska, 1867; and Colorado, 1876 (Milner et al. 1994, 184). Six
territories finally gained statehood in 1889 and 1890, and all of them
had disclaimer clauses in their constitutions. Ten of the eighteen
western states had disclaimer clauses in their enabling acts (see
table 2). However, Wyoming and Idaho were admitted to statehood without enabling acts because their territorial governments
launched statehood and proposed constitutions that were largely
in compliance with federal policies (Cohen 1982, 268). Both states
included disclaimers in their constitutions.

The enabling act admitting Kansas to the Union in 1861 was the
first to contain an explicit disclaimer clause. Like Kansas's 1854 territorial disclaimer, the 1861 measure declared that nothing in the
act should be read to impair any preexisting Indian rights or "to
affect the authority of the government of the United States to make
regulations respecting such Indians, their lands, property, or other
rights" (12 Stat. 126–27). Congress was stating its intent to abide by
preexisting treaties with Kansas tribes and reminding states of federal supremacy in the field of Indian policy. The other three states
admitted between 1861 and 1889 (Nevada, Nebraska, or Colorado)
were not required to insert similar disclaimers in their enabling acts,
although the reason why is not clear from the legislative record
(Lieder 1983, 1032–33).

When Congress terminated treaty-making with tribes in 1871—although agreements continued to be made until 1914—most Indian property was located (or soon would be) in the territories and remained under the federal government's jurisdiction. As territories prepared for statehood, their leaders pushed for exclusive jurisdiction over all territory, including Indian lands. Emerging states' desires for jurisdiction coincided with the burgeoning assimilation campaign of the federal government to force Indians to integrate into white society. The *Cherokee Tobacco* decision, 70 U.S. (11 Wall.) 116 (1871), confirmed that Indian treaties could implicitly be abrogated by later federal laws. In this context, an enabling act that granted to a new state jurisdiction over all territory within the boundaries might be construed as an express grant to the state of jurisdiction over Indian land, invalidating any treaty provision to the contrary (Davies 1966). Such a scenario arose in 1876 when Colorado was the first state admitted subsequent to the treaty termination measure of 1871. Although Colorado's territorial act contained a disclaimer, the Colorado constitution did not. In 1881 the Supreme Court ruled in *United States v. McBratney*, 104 U.S. 621, that since Colorado had not expressly disclaimed jurisdiction over the Ute Indian Reservation, state law prevailed.

Every state admitted since *McBratney* (except Hawaii) was required to acknowledge that the federal government had "absolute jurisdiction and control" over Indian reservations (Lieder 1983, 1033). Clearly the *McBratney* decision impacted the inclusion of Indian disclaimer clauses. Glen E. Davies, a legal scholar, stresses that the insistence on disclaimers after *McBratney* was a direct response by the federal government to its loss of jurisdiction to the states after the decision (Davies 1966, 137). Lawyer Michael Lieder is more cautious, suggesting that the "conjunction of *McBratney* and the clauses strongly suggests they [the clauses] were a response to that decision" (Lieder 1983, 1033). The 1889 enabling act of North Dakota, South Dakota, Montana, and Washington (25 Stat. 676) was the first such post-*McBratney* law. The disclaimer for these fledgling states says:

That the people inhabiting said proposed States do agree and declare that they forever disclaim all right and title to the unappropriated public lands lying within the boundaries thereof, and to all lands lying within said limits owned or held by any Indian or Indian tribes; and that until the title thereto shall have been extinguished by the United States, the same shall be and remain subject to the disposition of the United States, and said Indian lands shall remain under the *absolute jurisdiction and control of the Congress of the United States* . . . But nothing herein, or in the ordinances herein provided for, shall preclude the said States from taxing as other lands are taxed any lands owned or held *by any Indian who has severed his tribal relations, and has obtained from the United States or from any person a title thereto by patent or other grant, save and except such lands as have been or may be granted to any Indian or Indians under any act of Congress containing a provision exempting the lands thus granted from taxation.* (677; emphasis added)

This provision guarantees that the federal government retained complete and undivided jurisdiction over Indian lands until such time as the Indians were granted their land free and clear of all restrictions. The only times a state could tax an Indian's property under the disclaimers were (1) when an individual Indian had opted to terminate his or her membership with their tribe; or (2) in the case of allotted tribes, once an individual Indian received a patent to an allotment. Unlike most territorial disclaimers, this act never mentions the treaties that established the basis of Indian rights. Nor does it mention any requirement for Indian consent before either the state or federal government could act adversely to Indian rights. These two omissions reflect the general policy tenor of the times, as the federal government was intent on civilizing, privatizing, and Christianizing Indian peoples. Indian consent was rarely sought during this period. Treaty rights, while still theoretically intact during this time, were frequently ignored, often diminished, and sometimes terminated.

However, Oklahoma's act of June 16, 1906, which spliced together
Oklahoma Territory and Indian Territory, did mention treaties and
reads more like the earlier territorial disclaimers. New Mexico and
Arizona's disclaimers, contained in the enabling act of June 20,
1910 (36 Stat. 557), emphasized the states' permanent agreement
never to claim Indian lands or to tax Indian territory so long as
Congress holds it in trust status.[10] Alaska was the last state (1958)
whose enabling act contained an express disclaimer provision.
Although similar to that of New Mexico and Arizona, it had two
distinctive aspects. First, it included not only Indians but Eskimos
and Aleuts as well. Second, a specific property right—the right to
fish—was recognized as being held in trust by the federal government and thus exempt from state jurisdiction.

Constitutional Disclaimers

State constitutions not only protect rights; more importantly, they
"create a framework for state and local government, allocate powers, announce broad policy commitments and, not infrequently,
prescribe the means by which those commitments will be met. At
the most fundamental level, they may embody the political identity
and aspirations of the state's citizenry" (Tarr 1996, xiv). Congress
insisted that disclaimer clauses be inserted in eleven of the eighteen
western states' constitutions (see table 3). Generally, the disclaimer
provisions of the state's enabling acts were simply appended to the
newly drafted constitutions. So, for example, Article 1 of Montana's constitution, called the Compact with the United States,
declares that "all provisions of the enabling act of Congress . . .
including the agreement and declaration that all lands owned or
held by any Indian or Indian tribes shall remain under the absolute
jurisdiction and control of the congress of the United States, continue in full force and effect until revoked by the consent of the
United States and the people of Montana" (Columbia University
1995, 1). In other words, the state was bound to adhere to this clause
until both the federal government and the citizenry of Montana

agreed to modifications. With some stylistic alterations, the constitutional disclaimers of the other western states all closely resembled the disclaimers found in their enabling acts.[11]

STATE DISCLAIMER CLAUSES:
AN OVERLOOKED FACTOR IN TRIBAL/STATE RELATIONS

Notwithstanding their explicit language and legal standing, state disclaimer clauses have been ignored by many commentators (Reed and Zelio 1995), have been narrowly construed and assumed to have little contemporary significance (Pommersheim 1995), have been discussed solely in the context of specific litigation or specific legislation (Carr-Howard 1996; Davies 1966; Goldberg-Ambrose 1975; Lieder 1983; Peterson 1983; Schwartz 1983), or have been discussed only briefly in Indian law texts in sections relating to tribal-state relations (Clinton, Newton, and Price 1991, 500–501; Cohen 1972, 116–17). For example, James Reed and Judy Zelio broadly examine the current condition of state-tribal relations in their 1995 book *States and Tribes: Building New Traditions*, but they fail even to mention disclaimer clauses. The oversight, however troubling to us, is understandable given that the study was published by the National Conference of State Legislatures, which "serves the legislators and staffs of the nation's 50 states, its commonwealths, and territories" (Reed and Zelio 1995, frontispiece). Clearly this publication serves states; it comes as no surprise that the legal interpretations contained within it should also serve states' interests. While correctly acknowledging that "cooperative state-tribal government relationships are difficult to establish," Reed and Zulio questionably assert that states and tribes are "forging their way in a legal wilderness" (ibid., v). The terrain is more a par course than a wilderness, with well-defined trails and clear markers—some of which happen to be expressly worded disclaimer clauses that graphically instruct states not to interfere with tribes or their lands.

On the other hand, Frank Pommersheim (1995), a law professor, discusses tribal-state relations more fully and at least broaches disclaimer clauses. Unfortunately, he takes a shortsighted view of their political and legal significance and fails to explicate their actual or potential value. He notes:

> The second and arguably the most propitious historical moment in which to examine the contours of tribal-state relations is probably the latter part of the nineteenth century, when many states—particularly in the West—joined the Union.[12] The enabling acts admitting most States to the Union . . . provided Congress with ample opportunity to consider the relationship of these new States to Indian people and reservations within their borders. Yet the results proved inadequate and short-lived. Most enabling acts contained only vague "disclaimer clauses" in which the new states generally agreed that "said Indian land shall remain under the absolute jurisdiction and control of the United States." At the time, such a statement undoubtedly seemed sufficient to address the issue since most reservations were comprised almost entirely of Indian land and Indians. States basically had no jurisdiction in Indian country. However, *historical forces and subsequent judicial interpretations have rendered this injunction almost useless.* Courts have not found these disclaimer clauses particularly significant in dealing with the ravages of the allotment policy. (ibid., 142; emphasis added)

We fail to see the force of Pommersheim's assertion that disclaimer clauses were "vague." To the contrary, they were concisely and powerfully explicit. As he acknowledges: "States basically had no jurisdiction in Indian country" (ibid.). The fact that states, courts, and even the federal government have not found it convenient to remember or enforce disclaimer clauses does not diminish their original force of intent or the potential of reviving their meaning. Pommersheim cites only one case to support his view that the clauses are "almost useless," *Arizona v. San Carlos Apache Tribe*, 463 U.S. 545 (1983), a water rights case that examined the effect of the McCarran

Amendment, 66 Stat. 560 (1952), in those states that had disclaimer clauses.[13] The Court held that "the presence or absence of specific jurisdictional disclaimers has rarely been dispositive in our consideration of state jurisdiction over Indian affairs or activities on Indian lands" (463 U.S. 545, 562). By "dispositive" the Court meant "founded in law or subject to legal sanction"; in other words, the Court was not inclined to give much weight one way or another to disclaimer clauses. Despite this swipe at disclaimer clauses' legal weight, the Court did acknowledge and reaffirm the principle that "because of their sovereign status, tribes and their reservation lands are insulated in some respects by a 'historic immunity from state and local control'" (ibid., 570–71). Justice William Brennan stated that the Court "need not resolve" the debate about the original meaning and significance of disclaimer clauses in enabling acts. Indian water rights, said the Court, were subject to state-court authority because of the express language of the McCarran Amendment, regardless of what disclaimer clauses said. One can find other judicial rulings on specific issues—for example, crimes committed by non-Indians and hunting rights cases—where federal and state courts have minimized the legal effect of disclaimer clauses, although they have never completely disavowed them, as Pommersheim seems to do.[14]

We argue that a long line of federal and state case law and statutory law supports the ongoing vitality of state, enabling, and constitutional disclaimer clauses as the most "persuasive considerations as to the lack of state power" in areas such as hunting and fishing rights, taxation, and civil jurisdiction in Indian Country (Cohen 1972, 116; emphasis added).[15] We suggest that at least three things must occur before a state may lawfully attempt to exercise jurisdiction over a tribe: (1) the resident tribe(s) must provide their informed consent before the state may extend its authority; (2) the state must alter its organic laws; and (3) the federal government must consent to the state's alteration of its organic laws and must ensure that the tribes have concurred.

HISTORICAL BACKGROUND OF DISCLAIMERS

The doctrine of federalism has a fluid history, and tribal political fortunes have often hinged on how the balancing contest has worked
out between states and the federal government. From the Articles of
Confederation through the American Revolution to the current
Indian gaming controversies, the colonies—later states—have vied
with the national government for jurisdictional control of Indian
people, their lands, and resources.[16] The contest shows no signs of
immediate resolution.

Tribes, for their part, resent repeated federal and state assertions
of political dominance over their peoples and resources, but insist
upon maintaining a nation-to-nation political relationship with the
federal government in order to maintain tribal sovereign integrity
and to keep at bay states and private or corporate parties who may
have designs on tribal lands, rights, or resources. The federal government, for its part, generally insists that it is a superior sovereign
vis-à-vis the tribes and the states. The federal government has
acknowledged the sovereignty of the tribes through treaties and
the trust relationship and is constitutionally bound to acknowledge
state sovereignty, but vacillates on which of the two entities to support. The states, for their part, are generally unappreciative and frequently resentful of the persistence of tribal nations as separate
geographical, political, and racial enclaves within their borders—
enclaves over whom they have little jurisdiction. States take exception to the federal government's vacillating policy regarding tribes:
Are they to be legally terminated and their members assimilated?
Or are they to be respected as extraconstitutional sovereigns free
of state jurisdiction? Finally, how are the states to cope with the
reality that Indians have citizenship rights in all three polities?

When the U.S. Constitution was drafted, the framers made a clear
and unequivocal declaration. They assumed federal supremacy over
all matters relating to commerce with Indian nations in the commerce clause, thereby relegating states to mere observer status. Some
of the thirteen original states, however, especially Georgia and New

York, acted as if they exercised sovereignty in the area of Indian affairs, and they continued to conduct relations with tribes as if the commerce clause did not exist.[17] Nevertheless, when the Congress of the Confederation enacted the Northwest Ordinance of 1787, which would become one of the most important legal documents of the United States, Congress took pains to note in Article 3 that the federal government would always observe the "utmost good faith" toward Indians and that Indian lands and property would never be taken without tribal consent.[18] Thus, while a few of the thirteen original states contested federal supremacy in the nation's commercial and political affairs with tribes, the Northwest Ordinance (along with the commerce clause and treaty relationship) made it clear that the national government was in charge of the nation's Indian policy.

All new states were admitted "on an equal footing" with the thirteen original states. Equal footing means that new states were guaranteed a republican form of government, adequate lands for schools, a percentage of the net proceeds from the sale of public lands for the construction of roads, and so on. The new states learned quickly, however, that a precondition of territoriality, and then statehood, was the federal government's reservation of power and authority over the field of Indian affairs. The equal footing doctrine, in other words, does not interfere with the federal government's authority under the commerce clause, the property clause, the supremacy clause, or the treaty-making authority.

Although many states have chafed at the Constitution's exclusive placement of Indian policy in the hands of Congress, there have been very few instances where a state has actually expunged or modified its disclaimer clauses. Congress, on a few specific occasions, has delegated a measure of its constitutional authority over Indian affairs to states. Aside from these few exceptions, states have no legitimate constitutional authority inside Indian Country, unless they obtain direct tribal and congressional invitation, an amendment of the state's statutory and constitutional laws, and, arguably, a modification of existing Indian treaties.

WHY THE NEED FOR DISCLAIMERS?

Why did the federal government insist on territorial and state disclaimers? We group the answers to this question into three interrelated categories: expediency, treaties/trust, and exclusion/supremacy.

Expediency

The logic of expediency argues that the federal government only intended to protect Indians in their lands until such time as Indians were ready to be assimilated or the government was ready to remove them. According to Robert Clinton, Nell Jessup Newton, and Monroe Price:

> As the removal policy was winding down, the pace at which states were being settled, formed, and admitted to the union began to outstrip the speed with which the federal government could remove tribes from the states prior to statehood. Thus, beginning with the admission of Wisconsin and Kansas, Congress began to insist that *some* states disclaim authority and jurisdiction over lingering vestiges of Indian country by including such disclaimers in the enabling or statehood legislation in their state constitutions. (1991, 500–501; emphasis in the original)

The authors do not tell us why Congress insisted that only *some* states agree to such a disclaimer. Presumably, as Associate Justice Brennan put it, it had "more to do with historical timing than with deliberate congressional selection" (*Arizona v. San Carlos Apache Tribe of Arizona*, 463 U.S. 545, 562).[19] The expediency argument does not hold up well under temporal scrutiny. If congressional intent to protect Indian lands and peoples is assumed to be fleeting and tied to the removal era (1830s–50s), why was Alaska required to insert a disclaimer clause in its constitution as late as 1956? The expediency argument is not, we would argue, a position that holds much weight morally; nor does it bode well for the continuing health of our Constitution. If constitutional statements as explicit as the commerce clause are to be cavalierly disregarded, what protections does any citizen have?

Treaties/Trust

According to Carole Goldberg-Ambrose, "at the time Congress required the disclaimers they were necessary to protect Indian populations from homesteaders and settlers. By demanding the disclaimers, the federal government acknowledged its obligation to stand between these two hostile groups and prevent continuing exploitation of the Indians" (Goldberg-Ambrose 1975, 570). Congress, she says, "began insisting on disclaimers of state jurisdiction over Indian reservations immediately after United States Supreme Court decisions first indicated the possibility that such jurisdiction could be exercised. Viewed in this light, the disclaimers are more than protection against Indian loss of real property interests; they are congressional insulation against state jurisdiction over reservation Indians" (ibid.).

For example, in *United States v. Stahl*, 27 Fed. Cas. No. 16,373 (1868), a U.S. Circuit Court held that when Kansas was admitted to the Union it came in on an equal footing with the original states. Although the federal government retained title to the land it owned within the state, it relinquished jurisdiction over those lands insofar as the general purposes of government were concerned—with certain exceptions. "The first exception reserved the lands of Indian tribes which had treaties exempting them from state jurisdiction; the second, the power to tax the lands of the United States and of the Indians" (1289).

The treaty dimension receives the shortest shrift in contemporary judicial, state, or congressional discussions about tribal-state relations, yet it is, from a tribal perspective, the most important dimension. The Cherokee Treaty of 1828 contained explicit language in this regard. The Cherokees were guaranteed a "permanent" home in their newly acquired western lands, and they were assured by the federal negotiators that "under the most solemn guarantee

of the United States" their home would remain theirs forever. The
Cherokees were promised that their home "shall never, in all future
time, be embarrassed by having extended around it the lines, or
placed over it the jurisdiction of a Territory or State" (7 Stat. 311).
Three years later the Shawnee Nation negotiated a treaty with the
United States; the Shawnees were guaranteed under Article 10 that
their lands "shall never be within the bounds of any State or territory, nor subject to the laws thereof" (7 Stat. 355). Many other treaties
assured the tribes that their relationship was solely with the federal
government, such as the 1852 treaty with the Apaches, Article 1 of
which states: "Said nation or tribe of Indians through their authorized Chiefs aforesaid do hereby acknowledge and declare that they
are lawfully and exclusively under the laws, jurisdiction, and government of the United States of America" (10 Stat. 979).

The establishment and sanctity of the nation-to-nation relationship between tribes and the federal government is also supported by
the language of congressional reports, such as those accompanying
debates on statehood. In 1888 Representative William Springer of the
Committee on the Territories wrote a report arguing against the
"Admission of Dakota, Montana, Washington, and New Mexico"
(U.S. House 1888). Springer recognized the extraterritorial and non-
taxable nature of Indian Country, which had been confirmed in
Dakota's territorial disclaimer clause of 1861, and he objected to form-
ing states around so many and such large chunks of Indian land.
Dakota's disclaimer clause provided that:

> Nothing in this act contained shall be construed to impair the
> rights or person or property now pertaining to the Indians in
> said Territory, so long as such rights shall remain unextin-
> guished by treaty between the United States and such Indi-
> ans, or to include any territory which, by treaty with any
> Indian tribe, is not, without the consent of said tribe, to be
> included within the territorial limits or jurisdiction of any
> State or Territory; but all such territory shall be excepted out
> of the boundaries and constitute no part of the Territory of

Dakota, until said tribe shall signify their assent to the President of the United States to be included within the said Territory or to affect the authority of the government of the United States to make any regulations respecting such Indians, their lands, property, or other rights by treaty law, or otherwise, which it would have been competent for the government to make if this act had never been passed. (Thorpe 1909, 2846)

Springer was reminding his fellow committee members of both the sovereign and separate proprietary interests of the Indians, who had not consented to any alteration of their land base. He objected to statehood for the Dakotas because nine Indian reservations were included in the territory, the jurisdiction over which was reserved exclusively in the federal government so long as Indian title exists. Springer said that "the State can not tax the lands in these reservations, or derive any advantages from them. These reservations comprise over 26,847,105 acres, or 41,984 square miles . . . White population is prohibited upon all these Indian reservations, and so far as the government and the State of South Dakota is concerned, the Indian reservations might be excluded entirely" (U.S. House 1888, 24).

Exclusion/Supremacy

A few legal scholars have commented on the strength and intent of state disclaimer clauses. Maxwell Carr-Howard asserts that Congress's protection of its absolute control over the nation's relations with tribes was evidenced in the fact that "many western states were given a clear message to avoid any involvement in tribal lands and governments when Congress required, as a condition of their admittance into the Union, that each state 'forever disclaim all right and title to Indian lands within their borders'" (Carr-Howard 1996, 294–95). Michael Lieder corroborates this view by maintaining that the "scanty evidence available indicates that Congress [in making disclaimers] intended only to ensure that the United States retained jurisdiction over Indians and Indian affairs that it already enjoyed in other states" (Lieder 1983, 1031). Finally, Glen Davies (1966) has argued that Congress, as a result of the *McBratney* decision of 1881, required each state admitted to the Union between 1881 and 1912 to guarantee in its constitution that absolute jurisdiction over Indian lands would remain lodged in the federal government until such time as the Indians gained a measure of proprietary independence from federal trust restrictions on their lands.

More evidence supports the exclusion/supremacy rationale for requiring state disclaimers than exists for either the expediency or the treaties/trust rationale. For example, in *The Kansas Indians*, 72 U.S. (5 Wall.) 737 (1866), the Supreme Court combines elements of the exclusion/supremacy and treaties/trust rationales. The Court held that the various treaties made between the Shawnees and other tribes and the United States required that the federal government protect the persons and property of the Indians upon their reservations and that this duty was not terminated by the admission of Kansas into statehood. In the Court's words:

> If the tribal organization of the Shawnees is preserved intact, and recognized by the political department of the government as existing, then they are "a people distinct from others," capable of making treaties, separated from the jurisdiction of Kansas, and to be governed exclusively by the government of the Union. If under the control of Congress, from necessity there can be no divided authority ... *There can be no question of State sovereignty in the case, as Kansas accepted her admission into the family of States on condition that the Indian rights should remain unimpaired and the general government at liberty to make any regulation respecting them, their lands, property, or other rights* ... While the general government has a superintending care over their interests, and continues to treat with them as a nation, the State of Kansas is stopped from denying their title to it. She accepted this status when she accepted the act admitting her into the Union. Conferring

rights and privileges on these Indians cannot affect their situation, which can only be changed by treaty stipulation, or a voluntary abandonment of their tribal organization. As long as the United States recognizes their national character they are under the protection of treaties and the laws of Congress, and their property is withdrawn from the operation of state laws. (755–57; emphasis added)

In a case involving larceny on the Yankton Sioux Reservation, the federal district court ruled in favor of federal jurisdiction over such matters (*United States v. Ewing*, 47 Fed. 809 [1891]). In discussing the impact of the disclaimer clause found in South Dakota's territorial and state organic acts, the Court ruled that the disclaimers were "unquestionably included therein for the purpose of preventing any question arising as to the construed power and control of the United States over the Indian Country" (813). Such absolute power was necessary, said the Court, in order for the United States to fulfill its treaty obligations and other duties to the Indians.

The Supreme Court, in the noted case *United States v. Sandoval*, 231 U.S. 28 (1913), affirmed that the United States has a trust obligation to protect the lands of the Pueblo nations from non-Indian intruders. The Court also held that the disclaimer clause in New Mexico's enabling act unquestionably confirmed that the state assented to the federal government's exercise of exclusive authority to regulate commerce with the Indians. Finally, in *McClanahan v. Arizona State Tax Commission*, 411 U.S. 164 (1973), the Supreme Court again confirmed the exclusive nature of the tribal-federal relationship by holding that "since the signing of the Navajo treaty, Congress has consistently acted upon the assumption that the States lacked jurisdiction over Navajos living on the reservation" (175). This stance was also clearly evidenced in Arizona's disclaimer clause upon the state's entry to the Union that the state would "forever disclaim all right and title to . . . all lands lying within said boundaries owned or held by any Indian or Indian tribes" (ibid.).

The common denominator among all three rationales is congressional intent to retain an exclusive relationship with tribal nations based on treaties, trust, and preemption and the accompanying intent completely to remove states from the government-to-government relation between tribes and the federal government. However, there have been moments when some states have been granted a measure of jurisdiction inside Indian Country, despite extant disclaimers, the ongoing vitality of treaty rights, and absent express tribal consent. These moments have arisen in the ongoing fluid negotiation of federalism—as the balance tips this way to support a strong central government or that way to stress states' rights. The situation has also been influenced by demographic changes (such as non-Indian movement into Indian Country), the independence of federal courts, and the persistence of states that have agitated for greater jurisdiction over Indian lands and their inhabitants. We discuss the moments when the federal government has allowed or authorized state jurisdiction in Indian Country in order of historical occurrence.

FEDERAL DELEGATIONS OF PARTS OF ITS EXCLUSIVE AUTHORITY TO STATES

The first time that federal policymakers acted regarding disclaimer clauses and the territorial sovereignty of Indian tribes was in the Supreme Court ruling *United States v. McBratney*, 104 U.S. 621 (1881). *McBratney* was a criminal case: a non-Indian had murdered another non-Indian on the Ute Indian Reservation, and the question was: who had jurisdiction, the State of Colorado or the United States? The United States argued that existing statutory and treaty law supported federal jurisdiction. The government also cited the disclaimer clause in Colorado's 1861 territorial act. However, neither Colorado's 1875 Organic Act (which admitted Colorado to the Union) nor the 1876 state constitution included disclaimer clauses. The Supreme Court ruled that state law, not federal law, governed the reservation regarding such crimes. It based the ruling on three arguments: (1) because Colorado had been admitted on an equal footing with the original states, (2) because Colorado had not expressly disclaimed jurisdiction over the Ute Reservation, and (3) because no Indians were directly involved in the case.

The Court's reliance on the equal footing doctrine and the absence of disclaimers was unwarranted; these are not sufficient authority to override the federal government's clear authority under the several pertinent clauses of the Constitution. The *McBratney* decision violated the territorial sovereignty of the Ute Nation, ignored the provisions of the Ute treaty, and ignored the congressionally sanctioned exclusive relationship between the Utes and their lands, which had been set aside solely for Indian people.

Four years later, in 1885, the Supreme Court handed down another ruling that recognized some limited state measures of jurisdiction in Indian Country. In *Utah and Northern Railroad v. Fisher*, 116 U.S. 28 (1885), the Court stated that the Idaho Territory had a legitimate interest in regulating the affairs of whites, even if those activities took place within a reservation. In this case, the Court upheld Utah's authority to tax a non-Indian railroad company that ran its line on the Fort Hall Indian Reservation. Idaho's 1863 territorial disclaimer (12 Stat. 808), like Colorado's, protected the treaty rights, resources, and tax exempt status of the Indians, but the Court interpreted the disclaimer to allow the tax on the railroad to stand, because Indians were not directly involved in the case.

The General Allotment Act of 1887 (24 Stat. 388) does not directly deal with state disclaimer clauses, but this powerful policy directive and its amendments did extend state jurisdiction over Indian people in inappropriate ways, and thus it merits some discussion here. The Allotment Act authorized the president to allot reservations in order to individualize Indian lands. The breakup of communally held tribal lands and the assignment of 60 to 180 acre allotments to individual Indian ownership were essential steps in the government's forced assimilation campaign. The act set the stage for subsequent acts and amendments that broke up many reservations (but not all) into individually held lands and eventually granted allotted Indians U.S. citizenship.[20] The grant of citizenship meant that state civil, criminal, and inheritance laws were imposed on the patented Indian allottee, without the allottee's consent. Allotment was a devastating policy that dramatically reduced tribal landholdings. In the process, the government violated tribal sovereignty, Indian treaty rights, and the trust doctrine; exceeded its authority under the commerce clause; and did not require the states with extant disclaimer clauses in their constitutions or enabling acts to amend said documents.

When the Supreme Court handed down *Ward v. Race Horse*, 163 U.S. 504 (1896), a few years later, the erosion of tribal-federal relations and the privileging of states' powers continued. John Race Horse, a Bannock Indian, claimed the right to hunt on his tribe's ceded lands under the 1868 Fort Bridger Treaty. Wyoming, admitted to statehood in 1890, passed a statute regulating hunting throughout the state. Race Horse was prosecuted for killing elk, allegedly in violation of state law, although the elk had been killed on Bannock-ceded lands. The Supreme Court supported Wyoming's position and held that the "privilege" of hunting reserved under the treaty was a "temporary and precarious" one and that Wyoming had jurisdiction to prosecute Race Horse. The Court based its determination for state jurisdiction on the equal footing doctrine, because there was no express reservation in Wyoming's admission act or the state constitution guaranteeing the Indians' hunting rights. *Race Horse* was thought to have been implicitly overruled by several later Supreme Court opinions,[21] but was dramatically revived in 1995 by the 10th Circuit Court of Appeals in *Crow Tribe of Indians and Thomas L. Ten Bear v. Repsis*, 73 F.3d 982 (1995). Fortunately for tribes, the Supreme Court in *Minnesota v. Mille Lacs Band of Chippewa Indians*, 526 U.S. 1722 199, implicitly overruled *Race Horse* when it upheld the Chippewas' 1837 treaty right to hunt, fish, and gather on lands that had been ceded to the federal government.

The next major era when states gained a measure of power over portions of Indian Country was the 1950s, known as the Termination era after the official federal policy from 1953 to the mid-1960s.

Termination legislatively severed federal benefits and support services to certain tribes, bands, and California rancherias and forced the dissolution of their reservations. The policy was embodied in House Concurrent Resolution (HCR) No. 108, passed on August 1, 1953, known simply as the "termination resolution." In the words of Congress:

> Whereas it is the policy of Congress, as rapidly as possible, to make the Indians within the territorial limits of the United States subject to the same laws and entitled to the same privileges and responsibilities as are applicable to other citizens of the United States, to end their status as wards of the United States, and to grant them all of the rights and prerogatives pertaining to American citizenship; and Whereas the Indians within the territorial limits of the United States should assume their full responsibilities as American citizens; Now, therefore, be it Resolved by the House of Representatives (the Senate concurring), That it is declared to be the sense of Congress that, at the earliest possible time, all of the Indian tribes and the individual members thereof located within the States of California, Florida, New York, and Texas, and all of the following named Indian tribes and individual members thereof, should be freed from Federal supervision and control and from all disabilities and limitations specially applicable to Indians. (67 Stat. B132)

Exactly two weeks later Congress enacted a specific measure, Public Law 280 (67 Stat. 588), that conferred upon several states—Arizona, Minnesota, Nebraska, Oregon, and Wisconsin—full criminal and some civil jurisdiction over most reservations within their borders. Congress also consented to the assumption of such jurisdiction by any other state that chose to accept it. Unlike the broadly worded termination policy, P.L. 280 recognized and addressed the disclaimer clause issue. Section 6 explicitly declared:

> Notwithstanding the provisions of any Enabling Act for the admission of a State, the consent of the United States is hereby

given to the people of any State to amend, where necessary, their State constitution or existing statutes, as the case may be, to remove any legal impediment to the assumption of civil and criminal jurisdiction in accordance with the provisions of this Act: Provided, That the provisions of this Act shall not become effective with respect to such assumption of jurisdiction by any such State until the people thereof have appropriately amended their State constitution or statutes as the case may be. (67 Stat. 588)

In authorizing these five states' assumption of jurisdiction, Congress specifically identified states with constitutional or statutory disclaimers and required those states to repeal their disclaimers by a constitutional amendment before the act became operational (Schwartz 1983). Other states not directly named in the measure also had the right, delegated to them by Congress, to assume jurisdiction over reservations and Indian citizens in their borders, but the assumption of such jurisdiction required "the people of the State . . . by affirmative legislative action" to act accordingly. Presumably this meant that states, if they had disclaimer clauses, would have to amend their constitutions or enabling acts.

Goldberg-Ambrose, who has written extensively about P.L. 280, states that tribes were upset with the law because their consent was not required before states assumed jurisdiction.[22] States, for their part, were dissatisfied because they were not given complete jurisdiction, since reservation lands retained their trust status, and tribal lands held in trust may not be taxed by the state. States also learned that treaty rights, such as rights to hunt and fish, survived P.L. 280 and could not be regulated by the state. From another perspective, tribes questioned whether Congress had the authority to delegate its exclusive Indian authority unilaterally to states without tribal consent or a treaty modification. Several cases upheld the state's inherent police power under P.L. 280 even absent legislative acceptance.[23] In other words, state police power was automatically operative "in the absence of congressional action" (Goldberg-Ambrose 1975, 564).

Public Law 280 was immediately controversial because it impaired tribal sovereignty by allowing states to supplant tribal governing authority without tribal consent. Tribal opposition to P.L. 280, with growing awareness among federal policymakers that the act was flawed, led to two important provisions in the 1968 Indian Civil Rights Act (82 Stat.77, 78).[24] The Civil Rights Act required tribal consent before a state could assume jurisdiction. It also stipulated that a state could retrocede all, or any part, of the criminal or civil jurisdiction it had assumed back to the federal government. These actions and judicial interpretations have narrowed the scope of P.L. 280, although states still maintain a dominant presence in criminal law on reservations (Goldberg-Ambrose 1997).

We argue that a stronger case can be built for federal retention of plenary exclusive authority using the commerce, treaty, and supremacy clauses of the Constitution. In our view, exclusive authority may only be delegated to states under several conditions: (1) said action in no way abridges or diminishes tribal sovereignty, and (2) said action is openly consented to by tribes via an amendment to the trust relationship or to extant treaty provisions; or (3) said action may occur but, as the Supreme Court noted in *Parker v. Richard*, 250 U.S. 235 (1919), federal trust protections must accompany the delegation since the state is acting as "the agency selected by Congress and the authority confided to it is to be exercised in giving effect to the will of Congress in respect of a matter within its control. Thus in a practical sense the [state] court in exercising that authority [overseeing oil and gas conveyances of an Indian allottee] acts as a federal agency" (239).

Although tribes continued to question the federal government's authority to vest states with some civil and criminal jurisdiction, Congress was clearly of the view that states could assert jurisdiction if Congress delegated jurisdiction to them, and states amended their constitutions. Orme Lewis, assistant secretary of the interior, said in 1953 that state jurisdiction over Indian Country required congressional consent:

In each instance [states with disclaimer clauses] the State constitution contains an appropriate disclaimer. It would appear
in each case, therefore, that the Congress would be required to
give its consent and the people of each State would be required
to amend the State constitution before the State legally could
assume jurisdiction. (U.S. Senate 1953, 7)

Despite the clarity of the language of P.L. 280 and the congressional record regarding the conditions under which both mandatory (original five states) and optional (all remaining states) states
could assume jurisdiction in Indian Country, six of the eight optional
states with disclaimer clauses (Arizona, Montana, North Dakota,
South Dakota, Utah, and Washington) have passed legislation claiming full or partial jurisdiction over Indian residents on reservation
lands (Goldberg-Ambrose 1975, 569). Of these six states only South
Dakota has amended its constitution as required by the 1953 law.
The noncompliant states claim, despite the law's explicit language,
that a constitutional amendment is not required to assume jurisdiction under P.L. 280. They claim, in fact, that their disclaimers
only require that reservation lands remain under the "absolute jurisdiction and control of the United States." While agreeing that their
disclaimers preclude the alienation or taxation of Indian trust land,
the states also believe that they retain governmental interest over
all lands within their borders and therefore they need not amend
their constitutions or enabling acts, since Congress may repeal P.L.
280 at any time and reclaim jurisdiction (Goldberg-Ambrose 1975,
569–70).

Despite moments when Congress has delegated power over
Indians to states, the preponderance of constitutional, treaty, statutory, and judicial evidence, plus the extraconstitutional status of
tribes as preexisting sovereigns, supports the exclusively federal
character of the relationship between tribes and the United States.
Disclaimer clauses confirm the tribal nation–to–federal nation relationship. They remain the law of the land, and states and state lawmakers are bound by their meaning. We argue that state intrusions

into tribal affairs require tribal consent and federal authorization. States should proceed carefully, respectfully, and legally in their interactions with tribes. There may very well be issues or historic moments that warrant shared jurisdiction, but shared jurisdiction must be founded on agreements that do not violate treaties, the trust doctrine, state disclaimers, or tribal sovereignty. To achieve shared jurisdiction, all parties must agree and treaties, laws, and state constitutions must be appropriately amended.

CONCLUSION

A significant body of historical, legal, and political evidence illuminates the tribal-state relationship and the federal responsibility to oversee that relationship. In 1836 Congress began to insert disclaimer clauses in territorial acts, followed by disclaimer clauses in enabling acts beginning in 1861 and in state constitutions beginning in 1889. As a result, eleven western state constitutions contain a disclaimer clause. Congress apparently was motivated by the Supreme Court's 1881 *McBratney* decision. The Court had found that state law could prevail on an Indian reservation, in cases involving non-Indians, if the state constitution had no disclaimer clause. Disclaimer clauses reiterate exclusive federal authority over Indian affairs, reaffirm tribal sovereignty vis-à-vis the states, and remind states that state sovereignty in the federal system does not extend into Indian Country. Although states have chafed under these directives, disclaimer clauses have helped to protect tribal sovereignty.

Over the last two centuries, however, disclaimer clauses have suffered assaults. Certain congressional policies—such as allotment, termination, and the jurisdictional sharing allowed by P.L. 280—as well as some Supreme Court decisions have eroded the protection that disclaimer clauses afford to tribes. Although allotment was officially abandoned as federal policy in 1934 when Commissioner of Indian Affairs John Collier engineered the passage of the Indian Reorganization Act, assaults on tribes have come from other quarters. Tribes are concerned about the legal health of disclaimer clauses, especially given current controversies over Indian gaming and Indian assertions of sovereign and treaty rights.

Tribes are taking legal, political, and educational steps to protect their sovereignty. Some tribes have worked out accords with states, each party agreeing to respect the sovereignty of the other. The Navajo Nation, for example, in 1994 worked out an accord with the governors of Arizona, New Mexico, and Utah. According to then Navajo president Peterson Zah, "since we must coexist as neighbors we must recognize the sovereignty of one another in order to effectively meet the needs of our common constituents and resolve our common problems."[25] Tribal-state accords augment tribal sovereignty and can be important steps in improving tribal-state relations. State accords that recognize tribes as equal partners are often the result of hard-fought political battles, and compromises on all sides, but they can produce effective results.

Northwest tribes and the states of Washington, Oregon, and Idaho have emerged from difficult years fighting over fishing and shell-fishing rights with intergovernmental resource management plans that have vastly increased the quality of data gathering, biological information, and locally responsive management of fish stocks. The Mashantucket Tribe's lucrative gaming enterprise, Foxwoods Casino, has positively impacted the economy and employment in the state of Connecticut and pumped millions of dollars into local and national charities and nonprofits who depend on private contributions. Gaming tribes in many states have poured money into their own infrastructural needs, but have also given generously to local schools, nonprofits, and arts, health, and social service agencies that serve all citizens of the state.

Despite these positive interactions, tribes are right to be concerned about the health of tribal sovereignty. Treaty-recognized sovereignty, although it is not subject to federal and state constitutions, is being threatened by federal actions as well as state actions. Unfortunately, the Rehnquist Court has presumed since 1989 that states share authority in Indian Country, unless the state has been expressly precluded.[26] Clearly tribes can not rely on the rule of law alone to protect their sovereignty; they must also rely on the "good faith" of federal and state governments to protect tribes' remaining sovereign rights. State disclaimer clauses are an important piece of the protective barrier originally erected around tribes by the federal government, in its role as trustee to tribal beneficiaries. Along with treaties, and constitutional treatment of tribes in the commerce clause, a combination of political, legal, and moral forces must work together to secure to tribes their remaining political, legal, and resource rights.

The constitutionally affixed tribal-federal relationship should remain largely federalized, despite the sporadic case and statutory exceptions discussed in this chapter. Congress will sometimes pass measures that allow state entry into the federalized area of Indian affairs. One example is the Indian Gaming Regulatory Act (IGRA), which requires tribes and states to negotiate compacts for certain types of gaming operations. IGRA's very existence is a reminder to states that the federal government has ultimate responsibility for Indian policies, since states would have no say in Indian gaming without IGRA. Although the Supreme Court's recent decisions tend to place states in a politically superior position to tribes on a growing number of issues, such decisions run contrary to the Constitution's declaration that Indian affairs are a federal prerogative; they also clash directly with a number of western state admission acts and constitutional clauses.

Such decisions also violate the inherent sovereignty of tribes, confirmed in their treaty and trust relations with the federal government. The Supreme Court has confirmed on a number of occasions that tribes are not subject to the United States Constitution, because their sovereignty predates that of the United States and is not derived from the federal Constitution.[27] If tribes are not subject to the federal Constitution, they clearly are not subject to state constitutions that expressly disclaim any jurisdiction over tribes.

CHAPTER SEVEN

"As It Was Intended": The Doctrine of Sovereign Immunity

. . . the Choctaws believe that sovereign immunity for tribes should remain and that legislation seeking a sweeping waiver of tribal immunity is unnecessary and will undermine tribal self-government and self-sufficiency. Furthermore, assertions that the federal, state, and local governments have either abolished or severely restricted the doctrine of sovereign immunity are grossly exaggerated. The tribes are utilizing the doctrine as it was intended and in the same manner as federal, state, and local governments.

PHILLIP MARTIN,
chief of the Mississippi Band of Choctaws, testimony before
Congress, Committee on Indian Affairs, March 11, 1998

The last doctrine to be considered in this book, the doctrine of sovereign immunity, brings into sharp relief many of the issues permeating the contest among sovereigns we have examined in the previous chapters. As prior chapters have demonstrated, the contest in general is about how to define and how to implement tribal sovereignty vis-à-vis federal and state sovereignties. In the case of sovereign immunity, certain powerful politicians—such as former Republican senator Slade Gorton (Washington), who was a member of the Senate Indian Affairs Committee—were concerned that tribes, as sovereign governments, were immune to certain kinds of legal prosecution. Issues highlighted in the struggle over tribal sovereign immunity include tribal-state relations and the status of non-natives who reside or do business on reservations. In other words, the ways in which native and non-native citizens and neighbors perceive one another and interact with one another are at the heart of this story. As we will see, these relations over the past few decades have sometimes been cooperative, but sometimes have been marred by racism and violence.

What is sovereign immunity, exactly? Sovereign immunity means, for example, that a citizen cannot sue the federal government, unless Congress specifies otherwise.[1] To give one concrete illustration, Congress has considered waiving the sovereign immunity of the federal government for military personnel who were injured or made ill as a consequence of military service. Exposure to Agent Orange in the Vietnam War, or to unspecified hazardous biological or chemical agents during the Gulf War, has led to demands that service people be allowed to file suit against the government. This kind of suit requires that Congress expressly waive federal sovereign immunity. State and local governments also possess sovereign immunity. Tribal governments as inherent sovereigns possess sovereign immunity as well, and tribes' inherent sovereignty and sovereign immunity are apparently deep affronts to some Americans' vision of their country.

On March 21, 1998, the *New York Times* boldly declared on its editorial pages that "Senator Slade Gorton has once again declared war on the Indian" ("A Threat to Indian Sovereignty," A14). This declaration of war raises a number of troubling questions. What was the "war" about? Why was Gorton (then a member of the Senate Committee on Indian Affairs) identified as the lead protagonist? Since the phrase "once again" indicates that this was not Gorton's first foray into the battlefield with Indians, what had prompted him on other occasions to wage "war" against native people? Had Gorton acted alone in these encounters? Finally, how did the tribes react to Gorton's battle cry, and what do the states and the federal government have to say?[2]

Senator Gorton had outlined the "war's" major objectives in a bill he introduced in early 1998, misleadingly labeled the "American Indian Equal Justice Act" (S. 1691). Gorton wanted Congress to waive the sovereign immunity of tribal governments in civil lawsuits brought in federal and state courts, and he sought to extend state court jurisdiction over tort and contract claims against tribes.[3] Gorton believed tribal sovereign immunity was inappropriate in five areas of law: torts, contracts, taxation, environmental law, and alleged civil rights violations (Slagle 1998). Senator Ben Nighthorse Campbell (R, Colorado), the lone American Indian in the U.S. Senate and chair of the Committee on Indian Affairs,[4] said at the first of three hearings on sovereign immunity held in Washington, D.C., in 1998 that "S. 1691 . . . is arguably the most meaningful legislation since the Termination Era of the 1940s and 1950s, in my opinion. In fact, some have suggested that it is really a bill of the 1990s for termination" (U.S. Senate 1998a, part 1:1). At a hearing held in Seattle the following month, a raucous crowd of over 500 Indians and non-Indians came to voice their concerns over Gorton's bill.

Senator Campbell's characterization of Gorton's bill as "a bill of the 1990s for termination" clearly illustrates tribal reaction to threats against sovereign immunity. Tribes saw Gorton's action as a direct attack on the sovereignty of their governments, equal in seriousness to the federal termination policies of the 1950s that intended to "terminate" tribes as independent polities with government-to-government relations with the United States. Termination proposed to destroy the tribes as self-governing, land-based sovereigns. Gorton's attempts to waive tribes' sovereign immunity were seen as an equally devastating assault with intent to destroy. The Seattle hearing on S. 1691 "underscored the divide between Indians and non-Indians in the part of the country where most of the nation's tribes reside. White property owners complained that they have no legal recourse in civil disputes with Indian nations, while the tribes lamented that a basic principle of self-government was under attack" (Egan 1998, A12). Many non-Indian neighbors of tribes in western states clearly welcomed Gorton's initiative. The scale and the emotional power of this conflict seemed to provoke martial metaphors from all involved.

Gorton directed a full frontal assault on the doctrine of tribal sovereign immunity in recent years, and in this chapter we focus on this important doctrine to explain why. We agree that the attack on sovereign immunity is the forerunner of an assault on tribal sovereignty. Gorton and others who deny the legal, political, and historical status of tribes as sovereigns are committed to reducing tribal nations to polities with no sovereignty, limited or otherwise—or perhaps even to oblivion. Some proponents of contemporary termination argue that tribes should have no standing at all, as governments, and that Indian individuals should be distinguished by nothing more than a particular "ethnicity," rather than a treaty-based political relationship with the United States.

Gorton's fellow Republicans from the state of Washington went so far as to pass a resolution at the Republican state convention in Spokane on June 17, 2000, calling for the abolition of tribal governments. Like Gorton, other Washington State Republicans were concerned about possible injuries by tribal governments to non-native citizens who reside on or near reservations. According to John Fleming, the Skagit County representative who authored the resolution, the resolution called "on the federal government to 'immediately take whatever steps necessary to terminate all such non-republican forms of government [as tribal councils] on Indian Reservations.'"[5] In an article in the Coeur d'Alene, Idaho, newspaper, Fleming said, "We think it can be done peacefully," but if tribes resist "then the U.S. Army and the Air Force and the Marines and the National Guard are going to have to battle back" (Titone 2000).

Before sending in the Marines, we believe that all Americans should carefully consider what sovereign immunity entails. Why do tribes as sovereigns appear so deeply threatening to Americans such as Fleming and Gorton? Why does the doctrine of sovereign immunity, when exercised by tribes, provoke such extremist posturing? We address these questions here as well as considering former senator Gorton's political career. Gorton has not been alone in the cavalry charge against tribal sovereignty, but his political record reveals several of the fissures in American political life that appear—to some, at least—potentially to threaten the integrity of the nation that native and non-native citizens share. In contrast, we also examine a different view of tribes—as nonthreatening, active participants and partners in America's political landscape—held by such political leaders as Senator Daniel K. Inouye (D, Hawaii, vice-chairman of the Senate Committee on Indian Affairs) and Senator Nighthorse Campbell.

WHAT IS SOVEREIGN IMMUNITY?

The principle of sovereign immunity originated in early English common law, which declared that the king was immune from suit by his subjects. The gist of sovereign immunity was expressed by the popular maxim that "the king can do no wrong." Because law derived from the sovereign—who was supposedly chosen by God and divinely ordained to rule a nation—the sovereign could not be held accountable in courts of his or her own creation (Merkel 1992, 806). Political power in monarchies was lodged in the person of the sovereign, who, in theory, was limited only by his or her relationship to God (Deloria 1979b). In this system, the king or queen, as royal sovereign, was literally "above the law." European nations, and later the United States, transferred their notion of sovereignty and sovereign immunity to tribes during the discovery and early settlement periods. The documentary record is replete with examples of Indian leaders being called "king."[6]

Other rationales besides the English maxim of "the king can do no wrong" have justified the doctrine of sovereign immunity. Some link it to the constitutional doctrine of separation of powers, concluding that sovereign immunity is meant to protect the official actions of the government from undue judicial interference. That is to say, the courts, as one branch of government, cannot enforce judgments against another branch without the latter's consent. In another interpretation, the Supreme Court declared that the doctrine rested "on the logical and practical ground that there can be no legal right as against the authority that makes the law on which the right depends" (*Kawananakoa v. Polyblank*, 205 U.S. 349 [1907]). If the federal authority is the source of all laws and all rights, a citizen cannot assume the right to bring a legal case against the authority that makes the laws. Finally, there is the view that smaller, less economically vibrant governments—such as small towns or poor counties—could be financially ruined without the doctrine of sovereign immunity to protect them from lawsuits (Johnson and Madden 1984).

Sovereign immunity was important to the American founding fathers, as evidenced by Alexander Hamilton's discussion of the nature of sovereignty in the *Federalist* No. 81, where he argued that each state of the Union enjoyed sovereign immunity:

> It is inherent in the nature of sovereignty not to be amenable to the suit of an individual *without its consent.* This is the general sense and the general practice of mankind; and the exemption, as one of the attributes of sovereignty, is now enjoyed by the government of every State in the Union. Unless, therefore, there is a surrender of this immunity in the plan of the convention, it will remain with the States and the danger intimated must be merely ideal. (Hamilton 1961, 487–88; emphasis added)

Hamilton took some pains to articulate clearly that each state enjoyed sovereign immunity as part of its inherent sovereignty and would retain that immunity from suit unless the state expressly surrendered it. The constituent states of the Union recognized the importance of sovereign immunity and incorporated it into the constitutional framework in 1795 with the ratification of the Eleventh

Amendment.[7] The amendment declared that "the judicial power of the United States shall not be construed to extend to any suit in law or equity, commenced or prosecuted against one of the United States by citizens of another State, or by Citizens or Subjects of any foreign state."

The Eleventh Amendment was intended to prevent suits against states by citizens of other states or foreign jurisdictions. What circumstances led to its enactment? *Chisholm v. Georgia*, 2 Dall. (2 U.S.) 419, 478 (1793), is often cited as the first significant case resulting from a conflict between federal jurisdiction and state sovereignty. The plaintiff, a South Carolina citizen named Alexander Chisholm, sued the State of Georgia for the value of some clothing he had supplied to Georgia during the Revolutionary War. Georgia refused to appear in court, claiming sovereign immunity. The Constitution, under Article 3, section 2, extends federal judicial jurisdiction over conflicts between "a State and Citizens of another State." The Supreme Court supported Chisholm and by implication vested sovereignty in the people, over a state. Chief Justice Jay, in dicta,[8] wrote that a suit would not lie against the United States because "there is no power which the courts can call to their aid." The decision sparked fears among states' rights advocates and resulted in Congress passing the Eleventh Amendment. This was the first time that Congress enacted a constitutional amendment to overturn a Supreme Court decision (Hobson 1992). The Eleventh Amendment's guarantee of state sovereign immunity was forcefully reaffirmed by the U.S. Supreme Court in an important constitutional and Indian law case in 1996, *Seminole Tribe of Florida v. Florida*, 517 U.S. 44 (1996). The Court held that states, and state officials, were immune under the Eleventh Amendment from suits brought by Indian tribes—in this case, the Seminole Tribe was trying to enforce the tribal-state compact negotiation requirements of the 1988 Indian Gaming Regulatory Act.

A state may waive immunity from suit if it wishes, by passing a law specifically consenting to suit in state or federal courts. The waiver must be specific and explicit, because the Supreme Court takes sovereign immunity quite seriously and will not lightly infer consent or a waiver. The Court is inclined toward strict construction of statutes that consent to suit. Thus, a state may waive its immunity in its own courts without consenting to suit in federal court—the latter can not be implied from the former (*Great Northern Life Insurance Co. v. Read*, 322 U.S. 47 [1944]).

Like the states, the federal government, as a sovereign, is also generally immune from suit without its consent. Throughout the nineteenth century, sovereign immunity was used to limit suits by individuals against both state and federal governments. In *Cohens v. Virginia*, 6 Wheat. (19 U.S.) 264, 412 (1821), Chief Justice John Marshall, again in dicta, said that "the universally received opinion is that no suit can be commenced or prosecuted against the United States." Chief Justice Marshall addressed the issue even more clearly in *United States v. Clarke*, 8 Pet. (33 U.S.) 436, 444 (1834), when he stated that since the federal government is "not suable of common right, the party who institutes such suit must bring his case within the authority of some act of Congress, or the court cannot exercise jurisdiction over it." Here Marshall articulated that cases could not be brought against the federal government unless congressional legislation allowed the suit. In 1855 Congress allowed such suits when it created a Court of Claims, allowing citizens to file suits against the federal government for injuries caused by government agencies (10 Stat. 612).[9]

Both the states and the federal government gradually came to the conclusion that sometimes "the king *could* do wrong" and that governments did, on occasion, cause injuries. To address injuries and inequities, in 1946 Congress enacted the Federal Tort Claims Act (Title 6 of the Legislative Reorganization Act). The act attempted to reduce the blanket protections of sovereign immunity and to eliminate the practice of congressional representatives introducing private relief bills for constituents who had been injured due to government negligence (Ball 1992, 288). The act expressly authorized individuals to sue the federal government for specified tort claims in federal courts, but placed the burden of proof on the person bringing the suit and contained thirteen exceptions to government liability. In fact, in *Dalehite v. United States*, 346 U.S. 15 (1953), the Supreme Court interpreted one of the exceptions—the discretionary function—in a way that practically ruled out most substantive tort actions against the government. However, while the principle of sovereign immunity frequently bars suits against the government, injured parties may seek damages from individual officials of the United States (or states) who may be personally liable for the judgment (*United States v. New York Rayon Co.*, 329 U.S. 654 [1947]).

To sum up, the doctrine of sovereign immunity has been somewhat eroded by state and federal acknowledgments that they should be accountable for losses they cause. Despite these acknowledgments in particular cases, state and federal governments retain the general power of sovereign immunity itself. Suits may be maintained only by express governmental permission; may be brought only in the manner prescribed by the governments; and are subject to the restrictions imposed by the sovereign (Killian 1987, 759). These are the outlines of sovereign immunity as it has been defined and interpreted for federal and state governments—but what has it meant for tribes?

TRIBAL SOVEREIGN IMMUNITY

Senator Daniel Inouye presided over the first Senate hearing on tribal sovereign immunity in September 1996. Senator Inouye began the day's proceedings by quoting the very disparate views on the subject expressed by Chief Justice William Rehnquist and Associate Justice John Paul Stevens in the 1991 ruling *Oklahoma Tax Commission v. Citizen Band Potawatomi Indian Tribe*, 498 U.S. 505 (1991). Rehnquist, writing for the majority, said that tribes were domestic-dependent nations "which exercise inherent sovereign authority over their members and territories. Suits against Indian tribes are thus barred by sovereign immunity absent a clear waiver by the tribe or congressional abrogation" (509). Stevens, in a concurring opinion, proposed a contrary view of the doctrine, although one that did not single tribes out for special interpretation. He said: "The doctrine of sovereign immunity is founded upon an anachronistic fiction. In my opinion, all governments—Federal, State, and tribal— should generally be accountable for their illegal conduct. The rule that an Indian tribe is immune from an action for damages absent its consent is, however, an established part of our law" (U.S. Senate 1996, 1). Opening with these contrary views on sovereign immunity, Senator Inouye concluded that "whether one views it as anachronistic or relevant in contemporary times, the assertion of sovereign immunity is a right that is jealously guarded by most sovereign governments" (ibid.). Our earlier discussion of state and federal sovereign immunity certainly confirms Inouye's view.

If all sovereign governments jealously guard the doctrine of sovereign immunity, then why is tribal sovereign immunity so controversial? Perhaps it is because tribal sovereign immunity retains more of its vigor in an era when the states and the federal government are limiting their general immunity by enacting specific waivers of their general immunity from tort liability (Canby 1998, 88). The historical and contemporary records show, however, that tribes have also waived their immunity from suit on a number of occasions, and, importantly, the Congress has *forced* waivers of tribal immunity on a number of critical occasions. So the argument that tribal sovereign immunity operates differently from, or retains more vigor than, federal or state sovereign immunity does not seem to hold true. The different sovereigns appear to be on an "even playing field" when it comes to sovereign immunity.[10] We argue that, in reality, the opposition to tribal sovereign immunity is a manifestation of a profound opposition to tribal sovereignty. Before we pursue this argument, however, tribal reliance on sovereign immunity deserves further clarification.

It is important to understand why tribes are reluctant to issue general waivers of their immunity from suit. Tribal governments differ in fundamental ways from state and federal governments— tribal governments directly control or engage in commercial activities far more frequently than other governments. "When," for example, "Billings, Montana . . . might use eminent domain and tax incentives to attract private enterprise, a tribal government might create a tribal agency or entity to operate similar enterprises" (Veeter 1994, 174). On many reservations, direct tribal governmental action is the only way economic development can, or will, happen on Indian lands. Tribal governments are unique in the American political landscape in this and other regards: "They are the only governmental or corporate entities in this society which have two entirely conflicting sets of responsibilities: providing social services for people . . . and running profitable and competitive businesses" (Deloria 1978, S24). Because many tribes are small and impoverished, a forced waiver by the federal government of tribal sovereign immunity would undermine tribal sovereignty and the federal policy of self-determination and could devastate the tribes' limited financial resources. Even tribes that are financially better off, because of gaming dollars or other economic development, are gravely concerned about efforts to force them to waive their general immunity from suit. Gorton's proposed resolution singled tribes out; it did not threaten the power of other sovereigns in the United States—such as states—who must expressly consent to suit or voluntarily waive immunity at their convenience.

The vitality of tribal sovereign immunity has for many years been acknowledged by the Supreme Court, but it is not absolute. On several occasions, the Congress, the Bureau of Indian Affairs, and tribes have enacted laws, policies, or treaties that waive tribal sovereign immunity in limited ways. Senator Gorton was wrong when he claimed in S. 1691 that "the only remaining governments in the United States that maintain and assert the full scope of immunity from lawsuits are Indian tribal governments." As we shall see, there have been many breaches of tribal sovereign immunity—brought about by federal as well as tribal actions—but these breaches have never implied, nor been interpreted to mean, wholesale destruction of the doctrine of sovereign immunity for tribes.

For the most part, the federal government has recognized and supported tribal sovereign immunity as a doctrine of law.

FEDERAL RECOGNITION OF
TRIBAL SOVEREIGN IMMUNITY

As sovereign nations, tribes exercise civil and regulatory jurisdiction over water rights, fish and wildlife, zoning, environmental issues, and nearly every other subject that is also regulated by state, county, or municipal laws. Since almost all tribes have some system of civil dispute resolution, and most have criminal court systems, tribes wield jurisdiction over many areas of law, including torts, contracts, administrative law, and taxation (McCarthy 1998, 486). A host of federal (and tribal) court cases have confirmed that tribes— as de facto, treaty-recognized and constitutionally recognized sovereigns—enjoy the sovereign's common law immunity from suit.[11] Five major U.S. Supreme Court cases acknowledge tribal sovereign immunity.

In *Turner v. United States and Creek Nation of Indians*, 248 U.S. 354, 357–58 (1919), the Court noted that "the Creek Nation [whose political structure had been terminated by Congress in 1906] was recognized by the United States as a distinct political community, with which it made treaties and which within its own territory administered its internal affairs. Like other governments, municipal as well as state, the Creek Nation was free from liability for injuries to persons or property due to mob violence or failure to keep the peace. . . . Such liability is frequently imposed by statute upon cities and counties . . . but neither Congress nor the Creek nation had dealt with the subject by any legislation prior to 1908." Since neither Congress nor the Creek government had passed any law allowing a suit for liability, the tribe's sovereign immunity was judged to be intact.

In *United States v. United States Fidelity & Guaranty Co.*, 309 U.S. 506, 512–14 (1940), the Court was even more emphatic and, as in *Turner*, invoked the federal trust relationship as a reason to protect tribal immunity. "These Indian Nations are exempt from suit without Congressional authorization. It is as though the immunity which was theirs as sovereigns passed to the United States for their benefit, as their tribal properties did. This seems necessarily to follow if the public policy which protects a quasi-sovereignty from judicial attack is to be made effective." Associate Justice Stanley F. Reed went on to elaborate on the issue of consent: "It has heretofore been shown that the suability of the United States and the Indian Nations, whether directly or by cross-action, depends upon affirmative statutory authority. *Consent alone gives jurisdiction to adjudge against a sovereign. Absent that consent, the attempted exercise of judicial power is void*" (514; emphasis added).

The next relevant case, *Santa Clara Pueblo v. Martinez*, 436 U.S. 49 (1978), arose during the halcyon days of Indian activism and social unrest in the 1970s. During this liberal era, Congress attempted to counteract the devastating Termination era and sought, by contrast, to develop Indian tribes' self-governance. One important component of Indian self-determination is the tribe's ability to define its own citizenry. Tribal definitions of tribal membership were at issue in *Santa Clara Pueblo v. Martinez*. Julia Martinez, a full-blooded Pueblo, challenged a tribal ordinance that denied tribal membership to children of female members married to nonmembers. She argued that her tribe's policy violated the equal protection clause of the Indian Civil Rights Act (ICRA). The Supreme Court, through Associate Justice Thurgood Marshall, held that the ICRA did not authorize suits against either the tribe or tribal officials in federal courts. "Indian tribes," said Marshall, "have long been recognized as possessing the common-law immunity from suit traditionally enjoyed by sovereign powers. This aspect of tribal sovereignty, like all others, is subject to the superior and plenary control of Congress. But 'without congressional authorization,' the 'Indian Nations are exempt from suit'" (ibid., 58).[12] Even the dissenting justice, Byron R. White, agreed with the majority that since the ICRA was silent on the question of sovereign immunity, the act did not waive the Pueblos' sovereign immunity (though he did feel that Julia Martinez should be able to sue the governor of the Pueblos). The Court decision meant that Ms. Martinez could not sue her own tribal government.

In the 1991 case *Oklahoma Tax Commission v. Citizen Band of Potawatomi Indian Tribe of Oklahoma*, 498 U.S. 505 (1991), the question before the court was whether a non-Public Law 280 state had the power to tax sales of goods to Indians and nonmembers on federally recognized Indian trust lands.[13] Oklahoma did not dispute that the Potawatomi Tribe generally enjoyed sovereign immunity, but argued that the tribe waived its immunity when it sought an injunction against the state's tax assessment. Chief Justice William Rehnquist, writing for a unanimous court, held that "under the doctrine of tribal sovereign immunity, the State may not tax such sales to Indians, but remains free to collect taxes on sales to nonmembers of the tribe" (ibid., 507). While reaffirming the well-established rule that a tribe, as a sovereign, may not be sued without its consent, the Court did hold that tribal officers could be held liable for damages in actions brought by the state (ibid., 514).[14] In other words, the tribe remained immune from suit, although individual officers of the tribe were not necessarily immune from state action.

Finally, *Kiowa Tribe of Oklahoma v. Manufacturing Technologies, Inc.*, 118 S.Ct. 1700 (1998), upheld the doctrine of sovereign immunity but raised serious questions about the Court's role in making policy, conservative policy in this case, through its decisions. The Kiowa Industrial Development Commission had entered into an agreement with Manufacturing Technologies, an aviation company, to buy stock. The tribe's chairman executed a promissory note in the tribe's name, agreeing to pay $285,000 plus interest. The note was apparently signed outside Kiowa territory in Oklahoma County, although the Kiowas claimed that it was signed on tribal trust land. The tribe defaulted on its commitment to pay the note. When the company brought suit in state court, the Kiowas moved for dismissal for lack of jurisdiction, relying in part on sovereign immunity. The trial court denied the Kiowas' motion for dismissal and ruled in favor of the company. The tribe lost its appeal in the

Oklahoma Court of Civil Appeals, with the court holding that tribes were subject to suit for breaches of conduct involving off-reservation commercial conduct. The Kiowas appealed to the Supreme Court, which found for the Kiowas, ruling that immunity from suit shields the tribe, whether the activity is governmental or commercial, and no matter where the tribal activities occur—inside or outside Indian Country. The Court held that "as a matter of federal law, an Indian tribe is subject to suit only where Congress has authorized the suit or the tribe has waived its immunity" (1702).

The 6-3 decision in *Kiowa* upheld and actually expanded the doctrine of sovereign immunity (to extend to off-reservation lands), but it also contained strong language, written by conservative Associate Justice Anthony Kennedy, which echoes Gorton's disregard for tribal sovereignty. After ruling in favor of the Kiowas, Kennedy gratuitously raised several troubling questions about the doctrine of sovereign immunity's usefulness. He began by stating that the doctrine was "settled law and controls this case," but proceeded to exercise his conservative activism by noting that it "developed almost by accident." An extended quote is necessary to illustrate the degree of the Court's activism as Justice Kennedy sought to influence public policy and public opinion:

> There are reasons to doubt the wisdom of perpetuating the doctrine. At one time, the doctrine of tribal immunity from suit might have been thought necessary to protect nascent tribal governments from encroachments by States. In our interdependent and mobile society, however, tribal immunity extends beyond what is needed to safeguard tribal self-governance. This is evident when tribes take part in the Nation's commerce. Tribal enterprises now include ski resorts, gambling, and sales of cigarettes to non-Indians. . . . In this economic context, immunity can harm those who are unaware that they are dealing with a tribe, who do not know of tribal immunity, or who have no choice in the matter, as in the case of tort victims. These considerations might suggest a need to

> abrogate tribal immunity, at least as an overarching rule.
> Respondent does not ask us to repudiate the principle out-
> right, but suggests instead that we confine it to reservations
> or to non-commercial activities. We decline to draw this dis-
> tinction in this case, as we defer to the role Congress may wish
> to exercise in this important judgment. (ibid.)

The last sentence shows that Kennedy and associates were well
aware that at that very moment Congress was holding hearings on
Gorton's sovereign immunity bill—the Court seemed almost to
anticipate that the legislature would opt to abrogate or severely
diminish tribal sovereign immunity.

While *Kiowa* upheld the doctrine of tribal immunity, it did so
with little enthusiasm and remarkable arrogance about the role
and "place" of tribes in America today. Apparently active participation in modern economic life and, worse yet, economic success
are felt to be grounds to abrogate tribal sovereignty. It is beyond
irony that the tenets of two centuries of federal Indian policy—pur-
portedly, to "civilize," assimilate, and integrate Indians particularly into the nation's economic life—are here perversely twisted
by the Court in its justification for stripping tribes of inherent rights.
Widespread ignorance, perhaps intentional ignorance, of the status
of tribes as sovereigns on the part of the general public is offered as
the rationale for attacking tribal sovereignty.

We cannot help but marvel that this type of attack on tribal sovereignty coincides with tribes' economic successes—in "ski resorts,
gambling, and sales of cigarettes"—after centuries of oppression
and poverty. Could it be that competition in the marketplace, from
Indians, is really that hard to swallow? We are also left to ponder
how the Court will rule in a future case, now that Congress has
decided for the moment *not* to force a waiver of the doctrine. The
justices on a number of occasions have stated that sovereign immunity is "judge-made law." Does that mean that judges may "unmake"
a doctrine if they believe it no longer serves compelling need, or if
they believe it threatens mainstream economic domination of tribes?

Unfortunately, the historical evidence indicates that this kind of judicial policy-making is a real possibility.

WAIVERS OF TRIBAL SOVEREIGN IMMUNITY

Tribal nations, the historical evidence conclusively shows, are sovereign entities wielding legislative, executive, and judicial powers both comparable to and different from powers exercised by states and the federal government. As a result of conflicting doctrines, and conflicting interpretations of doctrines, the federal government has acknowledged the separate pre- and extraconstitutional nature of tribal sovereignty—including sovereign immunity—yet has simultaneously empowered itself (through doctrines such as discovery, trust, and plenary power) to impose its will on tribes, even over strenuous tribal objections. As a result, on the one hand, some federal cases have held that Congress *can* waive a tribe's immunity from suit, though the waiver must be clearly expressed.[15] On the other hand, at the 1996 sovereign immunity hearing, a lead attorney for the BIA admitted that there was *no* conclusive legal evidence supporting the federal government's right forcibly to waive a tribe's immunity.

Senator Inouye had asked Robert T. Anderson, associate solicitor for the Division of Indian Affairs in the Department of Interior, whether Congress had the power to waive tribal sovereign immunity and, if so, whether Anderson knew of any court cases that upheld the legality of such a federal waiver. Anderson replied: "I'm not aware of such a case, but I believe that it is certainly within Congress' power and really is a matter of horn book Federal Indian law that Congress, having the ultimate authority to terminate the Federal-tribal relationship, likely has the authority to eliminate tribal sovereign immunity under various circumstances" (U.S. Senate 1996, 10). Unable to cite any supporting cases to bolster his "belief," Anderson could only recite the federal government's self-assumed plenary power vis-à-vis tribes.

In an even more telling exchange, Senator Inouye raised a critical issue (one Gorton has seemed unwilling to acknowledge), the established trust relationship between the United States and Indian tribes. Inouye asked: "Mr. Anderson, would you agree that an integral part of the Federal Government's trust responsibility to tribes is to protect their sovereignty, which also includes the protection of their sovereign immunity?"

Anderson replied: "Yes; I would, Mr. Chairman. I'd add that the Federal Government has an obligation to protect tribal trust resources: land, water, hunting and fishing rights, and that sovereign immunity is integral to the protection of those resources on the part of the tribes. Therefore, it's critical that tribal immunity be preserved and that the United States support that immunity" (ibid.). Despite the status of the federal government as trustee of tribal lands, resources, and rights, the United States has on several occasions violated the trustee/beneficiary relationship by declaring that tribes are not immune from suits by the United States; by forcing tribes to cede lands or accept diminishments of their resources; and by insisting that tribes waive aspects of their sovereign immunity. There is interesting, and federally self-serving, lack of reciprocity in this relationship. Tribes are allegedly not immune from suit by the federal government in federal courts, but the federal government insists on its own immunity from suit in tribal court.

Many examples of forced federal waivers of tribal sovereign immunity can be found if we review American legal history. One example can be culled from a little-known aspect of federal Indian policy known as the depredation claims system, which lasted from 1790 to 1920 (Skogen 1996). Theoretically designed to prevent retaliation and to maintain peace on the frontier, the claims system was established to compensate Indians and whites who suffered depredations. "Depredation" meant the destruction or plundering of property. The first law to include a depredations provision was the Indian Trade and Intercourse Act (1 Stat. 137, enacted 1790), in a provision designed to protect Indians against the crimes of white settlers: "any person who shall go into any town, settlement, or territory belonging to any nation or tribe of Indians, and shall commit any crime upon or trespass against the person or property of

any peaceful and friendly Indian . . . shall be proceeded against."
In 1796 Congress passed the first Indian Depredations Act to protect against acts committed by members of Indian tribes.

The act was designed to protect Indians and whites, although it
very soon became a system that white settlers attempted to exploit
for economic purposes. Section 14 dealt with Indian depredations:
"if any Indian or Indians belonging to any tribe in amity with the
United States, shall come over or across the boundary line of any
State . . . and take, steal, or destroy any horse, horses, or other property belonging to any inhabitant . . . or shall commit any murder,
violence, or outrage upon any inhabitant, it shall be the duty of
such inhabitant . . . to make application to [the government] . . . to
redress this grievance." The government, when furnished the necessary proof of a depredation, would seek satisfaction of the claim
from the Indians. If that was unsuccessful, then the government
guaranteed payment to the injured party. Importantly, this statute
did not apply to all tribes, only those "in amity," in peace and
friendship with the United States.[16]

In 1855 Congress created the Court of Claims so that a citizen
could seek legal redress against the government for injuries caused
by government agents, and in 1891 Congress designated the Court
of Claims as the proper venue for depredations suits (Skogen
1996, 126). The U.S. attorney general was required to defend the
interests of the United States and the accused Indians. According
to section 6 of the act, awards against Indians and their trust agent,
the United States, were to be charged against Indian treaty and
trust funds. Within three years, more than 10,841 preexisting
claims were transferred to the Court of Claims. When the process
finally ended in 1920, nearly 11,000 Indian depredation cases had
been filed, and thousands more had been dealt with administra-
tively by the executive branch. Altogether, the United States
awarded approximately $5.5 million to claimants. In depredations
cases, the tribes' sovereign immunity was waived by the acts of
Congress that authorized the system and that assigned depredations to the Court of Claims. Tribal consent was necessary neither

to pursue suits nor to drain treaty and trust funds in the payment of reparations.[17]

The federal government has waived tribal sovereign immunity in other contexts as well, even in the case of trust resources such as water rights, although the grounds on which it has done so are problematic. For instance, in 1952, Senator Patrick McCarran (D, Nevada) introduced an amendment to address water-rights apportionment. Through the so-called McCarran Amendment (66 Stat. 549, 560), Congress waived its sovereign immunity on a limited basis and gave state courts the authority to determine water rights comprehensively. This important law authorized state courts to adjudicate *all* federally secured water rights, including Indian water rights, in a river or other water source that traverses the state. The act reads: "Consent is given to join the United States as a defendant in any suit (1) for the adjudication of rights to the use of water of a river system or other source, or (2) for the administration of such rights, where it appears that the United States owns or is in the process of acquiring water rights by appropriation under State law" (ibid.).

Although the McCarran act said nothing explicitly about Indian water rights, the Supreme Court held in 1971 that the McCarran Amendment applied to "all water rights the United States then had or might in the future acquire" (Deloria and Wilkins 1999, 131).[18] According to this argument, Indian water rights were subject to state court adjudication "because the United States holds Indian water rights in its own name under the Winters Doctrine and Indian rights are an equitable-use, not a legal title" (ibid.). No evidence from 1952, when the McCarran act was introduced, indicates that Congress intended for Indian water rights—a major trust resource—to be subject to state court adjudication. But the Court, nearly twenty years later, chose to interpret the McCarran act to mean that the United States, as trustee, had waived its immunity and allowed its "reserved water rights" to be adjudicated in state court. By extension, since Indian water rights are "reserved water rights," the tribes waived their immunity as well. This "accidental" congressional waiver of tribal sovereign immunity has taken a mighty toll on Indian reserved water rights in the West, since state courts have historically been much less hospitable toward Indian reserved rights than federal courts (Burton 1991).

Other federal waivers of tribal immunity have occurred over the years. Under the Indian Civil Rights Act of 1968 (82 Stat. 77), Congress waived tribal sovereign immunity by granting to any person incarcerated by a tribe the privilege of the writ of habeas corpus in a federal court; the federal habeas corpus writ is an order to test the legality of one's detention by a tribe. This was the only appeal remedy provided by Congress under the act. Tribal sovereign immunity from suit is also abrogated under the Resource Conservation and Recovery Act, which Congress enacted to remedy national problems caused by hazardous waste and solid waste disposal. Under the act, citizens are permitted to file lawsuits against persons, municipalities, states, or other governmental entities if they are alleged to be in violation of the act's provisions. Tribes, said the Court, are considered "municipalities" for purposes of this act and can therefore be sued (*Blue Legs v. B.I.A.*, 867 F.2d 1097 [8th Cir. 1989]). A number of lower federal courts have held that by conducting gaming under the Indian Gaming Regulatory Act a tribe waives its sovereign immunity for the limited purposes of maintaining compliance with that law.[19] And some cases have determined that the term "sue and be sued" found in many Indian Reorganization Act tribal corporate charters constitutes a waiver of tribal sovereign immunity.[20]

As noted earlier, tribes have the inherent power to waive their sovereign immunity voluntarily, though such a waiver must be explicitly stated. "Increased economic development involving nontribal entities has resulted in tribal governments voluntarily waiving tribal immunity and providing protections to non-Indians and non-members interest as necessary. For example, in its gaming compact with the State of Arizona, the Yavapai-Apache Nation agreed to establish procedures for the disposition of tort claims arising from alleged injuries to patrons of its gaming establishment" (U.S.

Senate 1996, Testimony of Susan Williams, 136). The evidence presented here puts the lie to Gorton's contention that tribes "assert the full scope of immunity from lawsuits." In fact, "it is clear that tribes are not cloaked with an impermeable shield of sovereign immunity from suit" (ibid.). While tribes retain immunity generally, the Congress on a number of occasions has ignored the doctrine or has acted unilaterally to waive it to benefit white settlers or state governments. Tribes themselves have also acted to grant limited waivers when it has seemed appropriate.

As Chairman Joseph A. Pokootas of the Confederated Tribes of the Colville Reservation put it in his testimony before the Committee on Indian Affairs in Seattle on April 7, 1998:

> The Colville Tribes has to deal with non-Indians every day. To insure that everyone who comes into contact with or could be affected by Colville Tribal governmental actions is fairly treated, the Colville Tribes has adopted a Civil Rights Ordinance . . . To be sure that its Civil Rights Act could be enforced easily and readily by any person (member or not), the Tribes waived its sovereign immunity with respect to any action brought under the Civil Rights Act against a Tribal officer or employee for the purpose of securing declaratory or injunctive relief. The Tribes went further and allowed recovery for damages where the Tribes carries an enforceable policy of liability insurance that covers the alleged wrongful action. (U.S. Senate 1998b, pt. 2: 1249)

Chairman Pokootas's testimony, and similar testimony by other tribal leaders, apparently had little influence on Gorton's antagonistic stance toward tribal sovereignty. What were the roots of his position?

SENATOR GORTON AND THE ROLE OF THE SENATE COMMITTEE ON INDIAN AFFAIRS

Thomas Slade Gorton—whose ancestors include Slade Gorton, cofounder of Gorton's of Gloucester, a fish-processing company in

Massachusetts—was born in Chicago and resides in Bellevue, Washington.[21] He received a law degree from Columbia University in 1953 and served in the army, the air force, and the air force reserve. Gorton practiced law until he ran for public office; he was first elected to the Washington State House in 1956, where he served until 1968. During those years, he helped draft legislation that— had it been passed—would have declared state jurisdiction over Indian reservations. Then and now, Gorton believes that *any* tribal jurisdictional authority over non-Indians who live or work on reservations is too much authority. In 1968 Gorton was elected state attorney general, a position he held for three four-year terms, until 1980. In his capacity as attorney general, his "Indian fighter" mentality evolved, largely over the issue of Indian treaty fishing rights. During these years, Gorton developed his view of Indian people as "supercitizens," undeserving recipients of special rights and privileges.

Gorton brought a number of suits against tribes in Washington, challenging their treaty-specified fishing rights. The tribes won a major legal and political victory in 1974, when a federal district court held in *United States v. Washington* that the Indians, under the treaties negotiated by territorial governor and authorized federal agent Isaac Stevens in the 1850s, were entitled to half of the allowable catch of fish in the state each year. Gorton was frustrated by the decision in *U.S. v. Washington*, also known as the *Boldt* decision after the presiding federal court judge, George Boldt, whose ruling the Supreme Court upheld. Gorton was not alone in his frustrations. Non-native commercial fishers who harvested salmon, sport fishers who angled for steelhead trout, and others vociferously protested the case as it wound through the courts. Confrontations between native and non-native fishers were violent and ugly, and state agencies balked at enforcing the federal court's ruling.

> The state enforced its regulations sporadically and generally with little effect: when the state issued citations to non-Indians, the lower state courts dismissed them. Frequently, the

state's agencies set forth regulations which did not permit Indians an equal share. As a result, the Federal District Court had to intervene again and again to force state compliance with the Boldt decision. In response, the state attorney general repeatedly appealed Judge Boldt's rulings. (Cohen 1986, 89–90)

The state attorney general was Slade Gorton. When the Ninth Circuit Court of Appeals affirmed the Boldt decision in June 1975 (the Supreme Court declined to review *U.S. v. Washington* in January 1976), the court stated:

The record in this case, and . . . others, makes it crystal clear that it had been the recalcitrance of Washington State officials (and their vocal non-Indian commercial and sports fishing allies) which produced the denial of Indian rights requiring intervention by the District Court. This responsibility should neither escape notice nor be forgotten. (Cohen 1986, 90–91)[22]

The extreme, and sometimes violent, anti-Indian sentiments expressed by some during those years left a bitter legacy that tribal leaders, state officials, and intertribal, interagency, and international fisheries managers have worked diligently for decades to overcome. They have not forgotten how Slade Gorton played on inflamed public emotions during the difficult *U.S. v. Washington* years. Those were vitriolic and polarizing times; perhaps Gorton was scarred by that legacy as well.

When Gorton was elected to the U.S. Senate in 1980 (defeating the powerful Democrat Warren G. Magnuson), he gained a national platform from which to articulate his antitreaty and anti-tribal sovereignty positions. He was appointed to two important committees, Appropriations and Commerce, during his first term. Although Gorton was defeated in 1986, he was reelected in 1988 when GOP senator Daniel J. Evans, a former governor who had won a special election in 1983 to succeed the late senator Henry M. "Scoop" Jackson, surprisingly announced his retirement. The party leadership could not persuade Representative Sid Morrison and Representative Rod Chandler to run and so turned to Gorton, who easily won the party's nomination. Gorton then defeated the Democratic challenger, Representative Mike Lowry, in 1988, after spending more than $1 million on advertisements, successfully reversing voter perceptions of him as "arrogant," which had led to his 1986 defeat.[23]

During his tenure as U.S. senator, Gorton introduced legislation that—had it been successful—would have terminated Indian treaty rights to fish for steelhead trout. Additionally, in 1992, he introduced a measure that would have required greater federal court review of tribal court rulings (McCarthy 1998). Gorton's political career had developed from early perceptions of him as a fairly liberal Republican to a more conservative stance in recent years: antitribal sovereignty, pro-states' rights, anti-federal powers. In 1994 Gorton benefited from the Republican Revolution led by Newt Gingrich and was reelected. He joined other conservative lawmakers in attempting to relax environmental regulations and rewrite the Endangered Species Act, he supported strong military defense, and he participated in budget cuts to reduce the role of the federal government in state and private citizens' affairs.

When Gorton was elected to a third term, he was appointed to the Budget, Energy and Natural Resources, and Indian Affairs committees (in addition to his memberships on the Appropriation, Commerce, Science, and Transportation committees). Gorton was named chair of the important Interior Appropriations Subcommittee during the 104th Congress. From his position as chair, Gorton began his repetitive and powerful attacks on tribal rights. In 1995 he attempted, through an amendment attached as a rider to the Department of Interior's Appropriation bill, H.R. 1977,[24] to take away self-governance funds of the tribes and to punish tribes for filing a lawsuit, if a tribal government's actions adversely impacted the rights of non-Indian reservation residents (for example, those who own rights to water, electricity, or other utilities within the borders of a reservation where the tribal government provides utility services to non-Indian users). The act would have denied tribes the right to raise garbage or sewer fees for non-Indian residents. A year later, Gorton focused his attack on tribal sovereign immunity, and once again he used a legislative rider attached to Interior's fiscal year 1997 appropriations bill as his mechanism. His proposal, section 329, reads as follows:

> In cases in which the actions or proposed actions of an Indian tribe or its agents impact, or threaten to impact, the ownership or use of the private property of another person or entity, including access to such property that might arise from such impacts or which impact the receipt of water, electricity, or other utility to such property, an Indian tribe receiving funds under this Act or tribal official of such tribe, acting in an official capacity, shall—No. 1, be subject to the jurisdiction, orders, and decrees of the appropriate State court of general jurisdiction or Federal district courts for requests of injunctive relief, damages or other appropriate remedies; and No. 2, *shall be deemed to have waived any sovereign immunity as a defense* to such court's jurisdiction, orders and decrees. (U.S. Senate 1996, 1; emphasis added)

A second provision inserted by Gorton into the rider was equally troublesome to tribes. He proposed that a process known as "means-testing" be applied to tribes: it would have denied federal money to tribes if their incomes were above a certain level and would have forced tribes to report their income in order to receive government benefits. Gorton's proposals seriously alarmed those tribes with gaming revenues.

Since the development of tribal gaming operations in the 1970s, and the increase of some gaming tribes' income, state and federal governments have demanded that tribal income levels be disclosed. Tribes have taken the position that, as sovereign governments, their income is their own business. They fear that disclosure could lead to loss of federal income and to envious states—afraid of loss of income to state lotteries, for example—seeking ways to punish tribes. Gorton and others sought to cut federal program funds that are still critical to tribal agencies and populations, because of a perceived "abundance" of gaming revenue. In reality, gaming revenues are still quite recent and are unevenly distributed across tribes, and the economic challenges facing tribes remain immense. Tribes face the legacy of generations of underfunding, deferred maintenance, and serious infrastructural needs, which on many reservations have never been met by federal agencies or monies. Federal monies are still necessary to run many programs, while gaming revenues are being used to build infrastructure. Many reservations, for example, lack any fire-protection agencies—before tribal gaming revenues allowed tribes to establish fire departments, homes simply burned to the ground. Other infrastructure that the federal government has never adequately funded includes roads, water systems, education, senior housing, senior care, and day care, among others. Gorton's proposals ignited tribal and non-Indian protest; when the bill was brought before the full Senate Appropriation Committee, Gorton agreed to delete his provisions so that the Committee on Indian Affairs (CIA) could conduct a hearing on the issue of waiving tribal sovereign immunity.

The CIA held a hearing in September 1996 on tribal sovereign immunity in Washington, D.C. Indian people and their allies and tribal governments testified in favor of retaining sovereign immunity, while opponents, including states, argued against. No clear "winner" emerged, leaving Gorton dissatisfied. In July 1997 he renewed his efforts via appropriations riders to strip away tribes' legal immunity from suit or face the loss of up to $767 million in federal dollars, about half the budget for daily tribal operations. The rider once again required tribal nations to report their income (Gray 1997, A20). After intense lobbying from tribes and important lawmakers, Gorton agreed to drop his rider in exchange for the Senate's promise to hold additional hearings on the immunity question and to schedule a vote by the early summer of 1998.

Hearings were held in March, April, and May of 1998 in Washington, D.C., Minneapolis, and Seattle. While the hearings were ongoing, Gorton broke his promise and introduced S. 1691 to waive the sovereign immunity of tribes. The committee's markup of S. 1691 was set for May 20, 1998, but on that day Gorton terminated action on his own bill, choosing instead to advance his agenda through separate bills. Accordingly, on July 14, 1998, Gorton introduced, with no cosponsors, five bills, each designed dramatically to diminish some part of tribes' inherent authority to govern their lands and residents of those lands. The five measures addressed civil rights (S. 2298), contracts (S. 2299), state tax collections within Indian country (S. 2300), environmental issues (S. 2301), and tort liability insurance (S. 2302). For example, S. 2298, a bill to amend the American Indian Civil Rights Act, would have granted the U.S. district courts jurisdiction over any civil rights action brought against a tribe. In order to be enforceable, the act would have waived tribal sovereign immunity.

These bills were all referred to the Committee on Indian Affairs, where they expired for lack of action at the end of the 105th Congress. Other members of the committee, who have a different vision of tribes than Gorton, prevailed in this instance. It is worth taking a closer look at some of the other players on the committee, and at the history and nature of the committee itself, to understand the political processes at work here. The Senate Select Committee on Indian Affairs was established in 1977, succeeding a complex variety of prior committees established over the years, beginning in 1820. The select committee established in 1977 had a temporary two-year lifespan; extensions were granted periodically until the committee achieved permanent status in 1984. In 1993, pursuant to a resolution introduced by Senator Inouye and Senator John McCain (R, Arizona), the word "select" was dropped from the committee's title, to reflect the committee's permanent status (Wilkins 1995).

The committee (like its predecessor select committee) exercises broad authority over all aspects of federal Indian policy: its job is diverse and complicated, and the committee is one of the busiest in the Senate. Like other congressional committees, the Indian Affairs Committee is "at the heart of governance in the federal government. Committees, the subdivisions of legislatures, prepare legislation for action by the respective houses and they also may conduct investigations" (Wilkins 1995, 29). Since the 1940s membership on the committee has been dominated by senators from western states, where the majority of Indian people reside, and votes have more often reflected regional, rather than partisan, patterns (ibid.).

Senator Daniel K. Inouye has served in the U.S. Senate since 1962 and has served on the Committee for Indian Affairs for years. He chaired Indian Affairs from 1987 until 1994, when Republicans gained control of the Senate, and he remains the vice-chair. Although he was allied with Gorton on some issues, such as federal support for the military, Inouye's record reveals a strikingly different view of indigenous rights and nations, and he is known as "an activist and defender of Indian rights" (*Congressional Quarterly Weekly Report* 1994). Born in Honolulu in 1924, Inouye received his law degree from George Washington University Law School in 1952. He served in the legendary "Nisei regiment," the 442d Infantry Regimental Combat Team in Europe, and was awarded the Congressional Medal of Honor. Inouye served in the Hawaii Territorial House of Representatives, the Territorial Senate, and the U.S. Congress before his election to the U.S. Senate (Congressional Information Service 2000; Elving 1988).

As a senator, Inouye is perhaps best known to most Americans for his role on the Watergate Committee in 1973–74, but to native people he is renowned for his dogged, long-term support for indigenous languages, education, religious rights, economic development, land claims—all the myriad, real-life details that make up self-determination and sovereignty for tribal people and governments. He successfully supported establishment of the National Museum of the American Indian, the last Smithsonian Institution museum to be erected on the Mall in Washington, D.C., and he unsuccessfully has labored to strengthen the American Indian Religious Freedom Act (National Journal 1995). Inouye's "private, personal style" has been characterized as "quietly relentless." "He is one Democrat who does not casually take the Senate floor or adopt a forward position on an issue. When he does, he usually prevails" (Elving 1988, 1). Fortunately for Indian people, Inouye's careful rationalism and unassuming tenacity have stood them in good stead in his tenure on the Committee for Indian Affairs.

Despite the countervailing weight of senators such as Inouye, Gorton continued his war against Indian sovereignty. In the first session of the 106th Congress, on March 4, 1999, he introduced another bill, again without cosponsors, called the "State Excise, Sales, and Transaction Tax Enforcement Act of 1999" (S. 550). S. 550 proposed to waive the sovereign immunity of tribes so that states could collect taxes on goods or services purchased from Indian tribes by non-tribal members. Gorton frequently uses the rhetoric of "equality" to mask his real agenda of curtailing the sovereign powers of tribes. As he put it in a misleadingly titled editorial in the *Washington Post* on September 16, 1997, "Equal Justice for Indians, Too": "though tribal sovereign immunity has lofty antecedents, its present day application is both anachronistic and unjust" (A17).

We hold that sovereign immunity is neither "anachronistic" nor "unjust." The history of tribal sovereign immunity reveals that this doctrine is an inherent tribal right, retained as part of the panoply of rights and powers of tribes as sovereign nations.

WHAT IS THE FATE OF TRIBAL SOVEREIGN IMMUNITY?

Gorton's attacks on sovereign immunity relied on the principal criticism that nonmembers who live or work on Indian land may be treated unfairly by tribal governments or their judicial systems. In his opening remarks on S. 1691 at the 1998 Seattle hearing, Gorton said that "the question raised by this bill is whether or not on the eve of the 21st century there should remain governments operating under the American flag and under the jurisdiction of the United States that will remain entirely irresponsible for their actions, unable to be taken to court by people who feel aggrieved by those actions" (3). But as Robert Anderson, former associate solicitor for the BIA, said in his testimony on S. 1691:[25]

> The proposed legislation would provide for a sweeping waiver of tribal immunity ... The administration opposes such

a unilateral waiver of tribal immunity. The administration supports and recognizes, as the law has for a couple of hundred years, Indian tribes as one of the three sovereigns . . . Indian tribes have made great strides with respect to development of law enforcement, institutions, tribal courts, and other institutions . . . to address the needs of tribal members and non-members alike . . . tribal immunity is necessary not only to protect the tribal revenues, as States and the Federal Government rely on immunity to protect their revenue, but also to prohibit undue interference with the orderly administration of governmental processes. (ibid., 7)

An alternative to Gorton's radical approach to tribal sovereign immunity was introduced by Senator Ben Nighthorse Campbell, the chair of the Committee on Indian Affairs, in the spring of 1999, titled the Indian Tribal Economic Development and Contract Encouragement Act. This measure became law on March 14, 2000 (114 St. 46). The broad purpose of this act was to "encourage Indian economic development, to provide for the disclosure of Indian tribal sovereign immunity in contracts involving Indian tribes, and for other purposes" (U.S. Senate 1999).[26] The Senate Report accompanying the bill in September 1999 noted that "over the last several years, the Committee has held extensive hearings on tribal sovereign immunity" and that the committee's members have divergent views on the "value, effect, and even the purpose and justification for the doctrine" (ibid., 12). Rather than try to reconcile these divergent views, the Committee on Indian Affairs stressed that the bill "builds upon an apparent agreement that Indian tribes and their contracting partners are generally best served if questions of immunity are addressed, resolved, or at least disclosed when a contract is executed" (ibid., 13).

A key provision of the act declares that a tribe entering into a covered contract must include a specific statement of its sovereign immunity policy. In his statement introducing S. 613, Senator Nighthorse Campbell referred to his concern over "those who may enter into agreements with Indian tribes knowing that the tribe retains immunity but at a latter time insists [*sic*] that they have been treated unfairly by the tribe raising the immunity defense" (ibid., 13). Under the terms of S. 613, any party entering into a contract with a tribe that requires federal approval is guaranteed to be informed about tribal immunity. While the act imposes a requirement on tribes, it does not affect the rights of either the tribe or the contracting party—it only requires that rights be explicitly stated or "disclosed." Whether an explicit statement of a tribe's sovereign immunity policy would satisfy Gorton or not is uncertain, but businesses will not be able to make the argument that "they didn't know" that tribes had sovereign immunity.

One encouraging sign of Senate recognition of tribal sovereignty is the passage of S. Res. 277 on June 27, 2000. Also sponsored by Senator Nighthorse Campbell, the resolution—titled "Commemorating the 30th Anniversary of the Policy of Indian Self-Determination"—begins:

> Whereas the United States of America and the sovereign Indian Tribes contained within its boundaries have had a long and mutually beneficial relationship since the beginning of the Republic;
> Whereas the United States has recognized this special legal and political relationship and its trust responsibility to the Indian Tribes as reflected in the Federal Constitution, treaties, numerous court decisions, federal statutes, executive orders, and course of dealing;

and goes on to refer to the Special Message to Congress on Indian Affairs delivered by President Richard M. Nixon on July 8, 1970. Nixon's Special Message articulated "a new, more enlightened Federal Indian policy grounded in economic self-reliance and political self-determination" (S. Res. 277). The resolution concludes: "That the Senate of the United States recognizes the unique role of the Indian Tribes and their members in the United States, and commemorates the vision and leadership of President Nixon, and every succeeding President, in fostering the policy of Indian Self-Determination" (ibid.).

Clearly the vision of tribes embodied in this resolution is quite a different vision than Gorton's. Here tribes are not to be feared; tribal governments are not bent on injuring non-native residents or neighbors; Indian people are not "supercitizens" who greedily demand it all; nor are tribes conspiring to strip "real" Americans of rights or prerogatives. Tribes are also not superhuman, perfect, unimpeachable, omniscient, or even living cosmically in balance with nature. In these regards, tribal governments and tribal citizens are remarkably, and even disturbingly, like other governments and other citizens: human, imperfect, struggling to survive, and hoping to prosper. In these human endeavors, tribes and tribal citizens would each proudly say, as Gorton has said, "I believe very strongly in the rule of law" (Pianin 2000). One consequence of that belief, coupled with growing economic and political clout, is that tribes worked together and with the support of others helped defeat Gorton in his bid for reelection in the fall of 2000.

> The Quinault, Jamestown S'Klallam and other tribes came together . . . to form the First American Education Project, a Washington state nonprofit group that is aggressively raising funds for a media campaign against Gorton, who spent $4.8 million to win his last election and hopes to raise $7 million this time. The Indians' campaign will include TV, radio and newspaper issue ads highlighting Gorton's environmental record and his assault on Indians' rights. (Pianin 2000)

It remains to be seen what might happen in the wake of Gorton's defeat and with the Senate now evenly divided between Democrats and Republicans. Since Republicans still control the House of Representatives, and with a Bush presidency facilitated by the conservative Supreme Court, tribes certainly cannot afford to relax. One thing is clear, however. Tribes can and will actively proceed to defend their sovereignty and exercise their belief in the rule of law: in the rule of tribal law and the rule of American law.

CONCLUSION

We began by defining a sovereign by the powers of self-government, self-definition, self-determination, and self-education. The connections and interdependencies of the modern world deny the possibility of a self-contained, unfettered sovereign, but limited sovereignties exist all around us: the United States of America, the individual states that constitute the nation, and the senior sovereigns, American Indian tribes who have called this country home for millennia. Tribes, states, and the United States are bound together by a complex web of overlapping jurisdictions, contested boundaries, reciprocal obligations, unilateral power plays, greed, generosity, self-interest, common goals, competition, cooperation, occasionally hideous violence, and occasionally glorious celebration. The political history of sovereignty in this shared nation tells the story of a mighty contest among sovereigns. Unfortunately, both federal Indian policy and many state histories have historically been built on a foundation of racism, ethnocentrism, and misperceptions—or lies—about Indian people. As a result, judicial bodies inappropriately make policy; bureaucratic bodies inappropriately oppress tribal governments and attempt to destroy tribal histories, identities, and languages; and political bodies inappropriately attempt to legislate tribes out of existence. We believe it is possible to rise above the errors of our shared history and resolve some of the conflicts among these competing sovereigns. Our belief in this possibility is rooted in the historical record and in the inherent rights of each tribal nation, as an original sovereign, to exercise political, economic, and cultural self-determination.

Rising above our errors requires generous cooperation, tough-minded resolve, and mutual respect for the inherent sovereignty of our partners. Mutual respect demands that indigenous perspectives achieve their rightful place in federal Indian policy and law. Tribal sovereignty is inherent. It existed prior to the constitutional beginnings of the United States of America, so it is by definition extra-constitutional in nature, since tribes were recognized as nations distinct from the United States, and Indians as individuals were not generally incorporated as citizens. Tribal sovereignty has been recognized constitutionally as well, most importantly through the treaty, commerce, and property clauses. When President Nixon outlined, in 1970, the United States' intention to recognize and foster tribal self-determination, he may not have realized it, but he was speaking to generations of Indian people who struggled, fought, and died to preserve and protect tribal sovereignty over the centuries. He vindicated their vision and their perseverance, but tribal sovereignty is still threatened, despite gains in tribal self-determination and social, political, and economic progress. Republican control of the House, a split Senate, a Republican president, a rising tide for the states in the federal-state balance of powers, and Supreme Court conservatism from the 1980s onward are all causes for concern.

It is time to call for a just, accurate, and humane understanding of the status of Indian tribes and Indian people in America. American Indian people are not merely another "minority," defined as an ethnic group or an economic class, because tribes possess a nation-to-nation political relationship with the federal government. That unique political relationship is founded on the principle of tribal sovereignty, on the facts of treaty negotiation and ratification, and on the contractual and voluntary federal assumption of a trust responsibility and relationship to tribes. The reality that underlies the political relationship is the transfer of land from tribes to the

United States. The United States did not "give" tribes rights or lands. Tribes possessed both. Tribes were defined as "domestic, dependent nations" by Chief Justice John Marshall in 1831 and 1832, but they were in reality "distinct, independent" nations, which Marshall noted more accurately in 1832. All congressional and judicial delusions over the meaning of "plenary" aside, the federal government does not possess complete and unhindered powers over tribes. Like all sovereigns, tribes' sovereignty operates within constraints: tribes retain some measures of external powers (i.e., powers to deal with other governments) as well as some measures of internal sovereignty (i.e., powers over their own lands and the people who live on or traverse those lands).

Treaties are constitutionally privileged as the supreme law of the land and are legally binding statements of federal and tribal intent and responsibilities. Treaty modification or abrogation requires mutual consent; or if unilaterally undertaken, it requires explicit expression of intention. Since treaties are constitutionally acknowledged federal pledges, it is a federal mandate to defend treaties, the nations who signed them, and the provisions of treaties from attack or threat from others, such as states, corporate interests, or others. The United States' handling of Indian affairs and relations is firmly situated in the hands of the federal government, specifically Congress. When legal disputes over treaties arise, three canons of construction direct the courts to: (1) resolve ambiguities expressed in treaties in favor of Indians; (2) interpret treaties as the Indians themselves would have understood them; and (3) liberally construe treaties in favor of the tribes. Each of these "canons" stands for a system of fundamental rules that the Court agrees to recognize and use in its interpretation of written instruments. The courts should not make public policy through a judicial decision-making process, but leave that to the appropriate—and constitutionally specified—arena of congressional action. Our examination of several key doctrines of law and policy makes it clear that federal policymakers have vacillated in their stance on indigenous nationhood, despite the prior existence of tribes and their recognition as national powers by Europeans, as well as the United States, in a multitude of diplomatic arrangements from the 1660s onward.

Each of the doctrines of law we have examined has a complex history and is pivotal in either destabilizing or stabilizing Indian rights and resources. Doctrines that have been interpreted in ways that damage indigenous rights include discovery, plenary power, and implied repeals. Doctrines that have been more accurately implemented to support the U.S. commitment to tribal sovereignty include trust, reserved rights, and state constitutional disclaimers. We offer our analyses in order to clarify the lessons of history, and we apply indigenous perspectives and principles to shape our recommendations for the future of each doctrine.

THE DOCTRINE OF DISCOVERY

A European notion of the doctrine of discovery proposes that European nations whose representatives "discovered" American lands gained absolute legal title to, and ownership of, American soil. We call this definition of the doctrine of discovery the *expansive* definition. The expansive definition of discovery allows indigenous nations an occupancy or possessory right to lands, but judges them too incompetent to manage those lands and in need of a benevolent guardian who holds full legal title. The more extreme *absolute* definition of discovery assumes complete conquest and denies any possibility that indigenous nations possessed aboriginal title, or even use and occupancy rights, to their lands. The expansive and absolute senses of discovery strip tribes and individuals of their complete property rights. Defined as such, the doctrine grants full legal title and ownership to the "discovering" European nations, while a less complete but still superior title was "inherited" by the United States of America, reducing tribes to mere "tenants." We consider these notions to be legal fictions.

An accurate definition of the doctrine of discovery grants "discovering" European nations (and their American successor) an exclusive, preemptive right to be the first purchaser of Indian land, should a tribe agree to sell any of its territory. The preemptive doctrine granting an exclusive right of first purchase is legally and historically the most authentic understanding of the term, based on the following factors: (1) the pragmatic realities of colonial interaction between native nations and Spain, France, Great Britain, and the United States overwhelmingly indicate that all these political "sovereigns" recognized indigenous title to land; (2) the federal government of the United States continued European practices of treaty-making with Indian tribes, and treaty negotiations and language convincingly illustrate further confirmation of indigenous land rights; and (3) relevant Supreme Court decisions (with the exception of *Johnson v. McIntosh* in 1823) persuasively argue that the United States does not hold a legal title superior to that of the tribes.

The doctrine of discovery was a mechanism that helped to regulate colonial claims, as it gave the quickest and most powerful European nation the upper hand over other European claimants to land and as it disregarded any aboriginal land rights. The doctrine of discovery, when defined as an exclusive principle of benevolent paternalism or, as it was in the *McIntosh* decision, as an assertion of federal ownership of fee-simple title to all the Indian lands in the United States, is a clear legal fiction that needs to be explicitly stricken from the federal government's political and legal vocabulary. A doctrine of discovery that purports to assign instantaneous ownership of Indian lands to European/American nations, and which hopes to reduce Indians to a status as simple tenants in their aboriginal homelands, runs contrary to common sense and to the force and continued vitality of tribal sovereignty. It is also inimical to congressional and executive policy pronouncements and Supreme Court precedent and is directly at odds with the bulk of extant European and U.S. treaty provisions, which abundantly demonstrate that tribes possessed full and complete legal title to their lands.

The political branches of the federal government—the Congress and the executive—are constitutionally charged with establishing and maintaining the treaty relationship with tribes and with overseeing federal Indian policy. It is time for Congress and the executive to act. The federal government should turn away from legacies of conquest and benevolent paternalism by explicitly disavowing the absolute and expansive definitions of the discovery doctrine. Tribal nations, as they begin the twenty-first century, must be acknowledged as the true owners of the lands they have inhabited since time immemorial. Land is the foundation for tribal societies and tribal identity—it is the essential resource necessary for cultural, political, and economic development and self-determination. Congressional, presidential, and judicial endorsements of a preemptive discovery doctrine are a necessary first step in reformulating Indian policy so that it is based on justice, humanity, and "the actual state of things."

THE TRUST DOCTRINE

A web of closely related terms has been used to describe the relationship between tribal governments and the United States government: trust, trust doctrine, trust duty, trust relationship, trust responsibility, trust obligation, trust analogy, ward-guardian, and beneficiary-trustee. We argue that several of these terms are coeval—the trust *relationship*, for example, is equal to the trust *responsibility*—based on the foundational notion of federal *responsibility* to *protect or enhance* tribal assets (including fiscal, natural, human, and cultural resources) through policy decisions and management actions. Several of these terms are definitely not equivalent: the "guardian-ward" relationship is a seriously reduced and dangerously paternalistic "version" of the "trustee-beneficiary" relationship. "Trust" entails two important constraints on the trustee. One, the federal government, as "trustee" of Indian tribes' assets, is responsible to manage *in the best interests* of tribes, that is, for tribal benefit. Two, the trust responsibility is legally mandated—it cannot be sloughed off as a "mere" moral directive.

An appropriate and necessary definition of trust is an indigenous definition, shaped by native understandings and political realities. An indigenous vision of trust, such as the Cherokee understanding explicated in chapter 2, is rooted in a commitment to protect tribal interests. Even the nonindigenous trust doctrine, however slippery the notion has been over time, has a long history as a legal doctrine. Historically, as Vine Deloria, Jr., has demonstrated, the doctrines of discovery and trust have been linked. As long as any government lays claim to Indian lands based on the doctrine of discovery, then that government willingly assumes a role as protectorate of Indian nations.

As protector, the federal government may—in fact, does—wield extraordinarily broad power over tribal lands, resources, and rights. That power is constrained, however, by the political and moral promises made by the 1787 Northwest Ordinance, where the federal government pledged utmost good faith toward the Indians, the passage of laws founded in justice and humanity, and the preservation of peace and friendship. Many other congressional, executive, and judicial decisions have molded the power of the protector as well, but to articulate a meaningful notion of trust we must turn to native sources and native ideas. As a model case, we turn to the vision of trust developed by the Cherokee Nation and people.

The Cherokees are not "emblematic" of Indian nations—theirs is only one example of an indigenous version of trust—but it is an example of how one native nation has consistently expressed what it expects from the United States. What did—and do—the Cherokees expect?: a recognition of Cherokee self-government, sovereignty, rights, and territorial integrity, and federal status as *advisor* to the Cherokees in matters that would serve the best interest of the Indians. Moreover, a tribal sense of trust holds that the rights or lands guaranteed by treaty or agreement last in perpetuity (unless otherwise specified), or until such time as the two parties mutually agree to change the agreement's conditions. Treaty-based rights endure through time because U.S. law has endured through time. They do not exist in law today by virtue of a "time warp" any more than the Constitution does. Ironic as it may seem, Indian peoples and nations believe in the U.S. rule of law, however imperfectly it may have been implemented over time.

The indigenous vision of trust authorizes and allows both parties—the United States and the tribe—to do only what is diplomatically agreed or consented to. Any unilateral action that adversely affects either party violates the trust. One nation may voluntarily assume certain responsibilities, but these are acceptable only so long as the receiving party finds them in its best interest.

THE DOCTRINE OF PLENARY POWER

A central paradox or "irreconcilability" in Indian law and policy stems from the federal government's conflicting claims: one claim to exercise plenary power (unlimited power) over tribes, tribal resources, and Indian affairs; and another claim to support the inherent sovereignty of Indian nations. In history, and in contemporary life, one claim tends to gain ground at the expense of the other. One way to solve the irreconcilability is to understand that plenary power is an *exclusive*, but not absolute, power of Congress—exclusivity is constitutionally based and appropriate and does not impute any power to the executive or judicial branches of the federal government, nor to the states. *Preemptive* plenary power, where Congress preempts the action of states toward tribes, is also constitutionally based and appropriate. However, plenary power defined as *unlimited and absolute* power over tribes is insupportable, for several reasons.

The unlimited-absolute definition of plenary power creates a constitutional problem—nowhere does the Constitution empower the United States with unlimited authority over tribal governments, their resources, and their peoples. Additionally, absolute plenary power is undermined by the facts of history: the numerous and myriad moments when agencies, branches, or divisions of the federal government have recognized and supported the sovereign rights of tribes. Finally, plenary power understood as unlimited federal power cannot be a viable political doctrine in a democracy founded on the principles of limited government. The Constitution limits the powers of both the federal and state governments to those powers that the Constitution very explicitly names.

Plenary power as an exclusive power of Congress is constitutionally supported, explicitly by the commerce clause and implicitly by the treaty clause. Exclusive plenary power is the definition Congress uses most frequently in enacting Indian-specific legislation or when enacting Indian preference laws. Plenary power is also appropriately a *preemptive* power, where federal powers "preempt" or supersede state powers or jurisdictions. Unfortunately, over time the Supreme Court has redefined "plenary" from its constitutionally moored meanings of exclusive and preemptive to its highly problematic—unconstitutional, in our view—definition as unlimited and absolute. Through judicial decisions in cases such as *Lone Wolf v. Hitchcock*, it seems that the Supreme Court has intentionally acted politically, to ensure that federal power would outweigh tribal power. Even when plenary power was defined as unlimited/absolute, however, the federal government did not always wield the power as an absolute bludgeon, a testament to the government's adherence to the rule of law, and at least sporadic support for treaty rights.

The Supreme Court's assertion of congressional "full, entire, complete, absolute, perfect, and unqualified" authority over tribes and Indians is incorrect. "Absolute" political power is irreconcilable with democracy, is irreconcilable with the treaty and trust relationship, and is irreconcilable with tribal sovereignty. In order to improve government-to-government relations the United States must resolve to use plenary power only in its *exclusive* and *preemptive* senses. It is time explicitly to renounce absolute plenary power because it violates the democratic principles of enumerated powers, limited government, consent of the governed, and the rule of law.

THE DOCTRINE OF RESERVED RIGHTS

Tribes today possess a range of rights and prerogatives that derive from their inherent sovereignty; some of these rights were explicitly recorded in treaties. These are aptly known as "reserved rights," since they can be understood as rights that tribes had and never surrendered—they are rights or prerogatives that tribes reserved to themselves and never transferred to another sovereign, such as the United States. Tribes do not exercise rights because Congress granted them rights. Tribes exercise rights based on their original and indigenous sovereignty. Reserved rights include property rights, such as the right to hunt, or gather, or fish; and political rights, such as the power to regulate domestic relations, tax, administer justice, or exercise civil and criminal jurisdiction. A judicially supported and historically accurate vision of the reserved rights doctrine, based on the Tenth Amendment to the Constitution, sees *all rights* as reserved rights, except those specifically given up in a treaty or similar agreement. Tribal reserved rights are currently under sustained attack and will continue to be vulnerable to governmental and judicial assaults until tribally reserved rights attain a status comparable to the Tenth Amendment, which reserves rights to the states. This may require a constitutional amendment that would enshrine reserved treaty rights.

The federal government as *trustee* of tribal interests must seriously pursue its moral, legal, and fiscal responsibilities as designated legal agent acting in the interests of tribes, the legal owners of reserved rights.

THE DOCTRINE OF IMPLIED REPEALS

The central question of implied repeals is: who has the power to change or terminate treaties? In tribal-federal treaty relations, both parties must consent to treaty changes or abrogation. On the federal side of the equation, only the political branches may modify or abrogate treaty rights, since the political branches—specifically the president and the Senate—negotiate and ratify treaties. We deny the political or judicial authority of the Supreme Court to end or modify Indian treaty rights through resort to the doctrine of implied repeal. When cases arise where treaty language disagrees with, or contradicts, the language of later congressional or state statutes, the Court must uphold the federal government's treaty obligations, based on the trust doctrine and the good faith doctrine as articulated in the 1787 Northwest Ordinance. If the Court severs specific Indian treaty rights based on implied repeals, and does so without a specific legislative mandate, the Court violates the Constitution and acts contrary to the acknowledged trust relationship with tribes. In sorting out irreconcilable differences between treaty provisions and statutory provisions, the Supreme Court should uphold the treaty and interpret the statute in conformity with the context in which the treaty was negotiated.

Tribal consent should be a necessary component of any negotiated amendment to a treaty or agreement. Treaties are solemn and binding pacts, and breaking them should not be taken lightly or, if at all avoidable, unilaterally. Mutual, consensual, and voluntary action through the same political/diplomatic channels that characterize treaty negotiation is the desired and rational approach. We can turn to the Supreme Court's decision in *The Kansas Indians* for a reasonable idea of how Indian treaties/agreements may be changed: Indian treaties and the rights affirmed or created by treaty provisions may be modified, amended, or terminated only through bilateral treaty stipulations, by purchase, or by voluntary abandonment by the tribal organization. Changes in treaties/agreements require that Congress enact statutes with exact language specifying modification or elimination of treaty provisions.

DISCLAIMERS IN TRIBAL-STATE RELATIONS

The federally mandated disclaimer clauses found in a number of state organic acts and constitutions, eschewing any state jurisdiction over Indian affairs, lands, and peoples, do not constitute the same kind of legal doctrine examined in other chapters. They are, however, important legal and political defenses available to tribes when states threaten tribal sovereignty. Disclaimer clauses explicitly and unambiguously proclaim the supremacy of the tribal government–to–federal government relationship over any inappropriate intrusion by the states. Disclaimer clauses offer a potentially potent defense for tribes against the states as the American national federalist model of government shifts toward privileging state powers. Despite historic fluctuation between sometimes protecting tribes from states and sometimes fostering state intrusions into tribal life, the federal government must act as the lone constitutional authority to deal with indigenous nations.

Tribes and states have rarely had collegial and cooperative political or social relations, but states cannot assert jurisdiction over tribal affairs simply because they want to. State assertions of superiority over tribes violate the doctrine of inherent tribal sovereignty, are contrary to judicial precedent, run afoul of the treaty relationship, damage the federally recognized trust doctrine, and breach the doctrine of federal supremacy in the field of Indian affairs outlined expressly in the commerce clause, and implicitly in the treaty clause, of the Constitution. Collegial and cooperative tribal-state relations are entirely possible while retaining federal supremacy (over the subject of Indian affairs) and tribal sovereignty, as numerous tribal leaders and state officials can attest. Collegiality and cooperation require mutual respect and a political will to work toward common goals, but those are humane challenges, not insurmountable obstacles.

Congress is ultimately responsible for leading the states, since the Constitution vests the political branches of the *federal* government with the authority to exercise and administer this nation's Indian policy. Congress must make it clear that states cannot disregard their fundamental laws. Disclaimer clauses are the rule of law, and states cannot assume inappropriate jurisdiction unless the treaty and trust relationships are seriously modified, or without tribal and federal consent. If Congress does act on occasion to delegate its constitutionally vested authority over Indian affairs to states, it must attach the existing treaty and trust obligations that bind the tribes and the United States. Congress cannot unilaterally terminate its treaty and trust commitments by delegating those commitments to the states—such action requires a mutually agreed upon treaty modification with the tribes' informed consent.

THE DOCTRINE OF SOVEREIGN IMMUNITY

Sovereign immunity means that a government cannot be sued without its own consent—this type of immunity from suit is accepted in Western law as a necessary attribute, or prerogative, of inherent sovereigns. Tribes are protected by sovereign immunity just as are other governmental entities, such as the federal government or the governments of states, counties, cities, and townships. Some non-native Americans feel deeply threatened and affronted by tribal exercise of sovereign immunity and demand that tribes surrender—or be forcefully stripped of—their immunity from suit. Tribes and their supporters feel that attacks on sovereign immunity are merely the skirmishes in a war to destroy tribal sovereignty entirely.

While all governments guard their sovereign immunity, tribes are particularly vulnerable governments for a number of reasons. Unlike the federal and state governments, tribal governments strive to be "all things to all people." They govern, to be sure. They administer a plethora of programs that derive from their own national goals as well as from federal and state agencies: job training, education, health services, housing, and so on. They administer their own programs, if they have the funds and infrastructure: fire and police protection, education, mental health services, senior care and housing, day care, disabled care, community development, and so on. They also run businesses: timber, fishing, mining, and agricultural industries; light industry; cottage industries and arts cooperatives; and so on. A few tribes have large populations, large land bases, and resources for economic development, but many, many tribes are small, poor, and isolated. They cope with the multitude of tribal government responsibilities when their total population might be 500 to 5,000 people. How many similarly sized American communities could do as well or better? Despite these facts, tribes demand no special interpretation or implementation of sovereign immunity. Charges that tribal sovereign immunity is somehow "different" are simply false.

Just as all governments guard sovereign immunity, all governments occasionally waive immunity in specific circumstances, and tribes are no exception to that rule. Waivers have sometimes been forcibly imposed by the federal government and sometimes been voluntarily issued by tribes for specific economic or other reasons. The prerogative to guard or to waive tribal sovereign immunity is an inherent right and a necessary component of successful self-determination, self-government, and economic development.

HAVING REVISITED THE PAST, WE LOOK TOWARD THE FUTURE

Like many American Indians, we believe strongly in the rule of law: law that is exercised by tribal governments; law as it is exercised by the states and federal government; and the law that is constituted by shared rules or contracts—treaties, agreements, memoranda of understanding—negotiated by these sovereigns. We believe that the uneven ground can be smoothed, but not by suppressing history or oppressing people. We believe that uneven, and inequitable, power relations can be brought into balance. We believe strongly in the possibility of justice in America.

We know, deeply, the lessons of history and the realities of the present, and both those sources tell us we probably ought to be less optimistic. Why do we resist the impulse? Like many in America, we will not let go of the possibility—of justice, of respect for someone different than ourselves, of equal opportunity. Perhaps some Americans are uncomfortable that Indians, as the original inhabitants and possessors of all American lands, still exist. Perhaps some Americans feel threatened by the ongoing vitality of tribes, as governments, and Indians, as people, because they have not yet come to terms with their own history. We must acknowledge the past, in order to do better. All Americans need to realize that tribes, as governments, and Indians, as human beings, are modern, pragmatic, deeply committed to their traditions, forever tied to their ancestral lands, hopeful, hard-working, and generous—some might say—to a fault. Like all human beings, as individuals we are flawed, but to a remarkable degree, given the shared history of America, we remain optimistic.

NOTES

INTRODUCTION

1. For more information about Plymouth and the history of the Mayflower, as well as local native populations, see the website of Plimoth Plantation, the living history museum that recreates and interprets "Pilgrim" and Wampanoag history, at http://www.plimoth.org/.

2. American Indian tribes are not the only ones to bear the brunt of judicial conservatism, which affects other minority and powerless groups as well (Kairys 1993).

3. For tribes as political entities, see *Morton v. Mancari*, 417 U.S. 535 (1974); for tribes as defined by race relations, see *United States v. Rogers*, 45 U.S. (4 How.) 567 (1846), *United States v. Celestine*, 215 U.S. 278 (1909), and *United States v. Nice*, 241 U.S. 591 (1916).

4. We use the terms "American Indian," "Indian," "Native American," and "native" interchangeably to indicate the indigenous populations of the mainland United States (we do not discuss the political or social standing of native Hawaiians). Since our discussion is restricted to the United States, for example, we do not include the term "First Nations" used in Canada. These terms are all inadequate to describe the linguistic, cultural, and ethnic diversity of the populations they encompass.

5. An *absolute* sovereign cannot exist, since all nations are accountable to their citizens, to other units of government, and to the international community.

1. "THE LAW OF NATIONS": THE DOCTRINE OF DISCOVERY

1. *Oneida Indian Nation of Wisconsin v. State of New York*, 649 F.Supp. 420, 424 (1986).

2. Full legal ownership is also known as fee-simple ownership, in which the inheritor has unqualified ownership and sole power of disposition of a parcel of land.

3. *Worcester v. Georgia*, 31 U.S. (6 Pet.) 515, 543 (1832).

4. For works by indigenous scholars, see, for example, Deloria and Lytle 1983, 2–6; Robert T. Coulter, as cited in Wilmer 1993, 1; Williams 1990, 99–201; and Wilkins 1994b, 159–81. For works by nonindigenous scholars, see, for example, Newton 1980, 1222; and Ball 1987, 24–26.

5. See chapter 3 for discussion of plenary power and chapter 2 for discussion of trust.

6. See *County of Oneida v. Oneida Indian Nation of New York State*, 470 U.S. 226 (1985); *New Mexico ex rel. Reynolds v. AaModt*, 618 F.Supp. 993 (1985); *Bear v. United States*, 611 F.Supp. 589 (1985); *Oneida Indian Nation of Wisconsin v. New York*, 649 F.Supp. 420 (1986); *Oneida Indian Nation of New York v. New York and Various State Agencies*, 860 F.2d 1145 (1988); and *Alabama-Coushatta Tribe v. United States*, 1996 U.S. Claims Lexis 128 (1996). State courts have also grappled with the doctrine: see *In re Wilson*, 30 Cal. 3d 21 (1981); *In re Rights to Use Water in Big Horn River System*, 753 P.2d 76 (1988); and *State v. Elliott*, 159 Vt. 102 (1992).

7. See Wilkins 1994c, 349–68; and 1997b, 24–31.

8. *Tee-Hit-Ton v. United States*, 348 U.S. 272, 289–90.

9. Two exceptions here would be the various Pueblo peoples who hold fee-simple title to their lands under grants from the Spanish and Mexican governments (these lands were later placed under trust by the federal government) and the Eastern Cherokees. For Pueblo land title, see Dozier 1970 and Sando 1976, 1992. The Eastern Band of Cherokees of North Carolina purchased land with individual funds that were at first held under single title, next by a private trustee, then by the band itself when it incorporated, and finally by the federal government when it was asked by the Cherokees to place the land under federal trust status. For Eastern Cherokee land issues, see Finger 1991; McLoughlin 1986; and Royce 1887.

10. For Spanish policy, see Forbes 1960; Hanke 1949; Spicer 1962; and Williams 1990. For French policy, see Delage 1993; Kennedy 1950; and Wade 1988. For Great Britain's Indian policy, see Jacobs 1972; and Jennings 1975. Vaughan 1979– is an excellent compilation of British and early American treaties, as well as a number of Dutch treaties with northeastern tribes.

11. Jennings 1984, cited in Williams 1997, 20.

12. See also Jones 1988, 185–94.

13. Wade oversimplifies; the French did not entirely lack racial prejudice, but it took different forms than the British strict segregationism and the Spanish obsession with "sangre puro," miscegenation, and degrees of blood. A close reading of the Jesuit Relations (Jesuits 1959) sheds some light on this. See also Van Kirk 1980 and R. White 1991.

14. There is evidence that the French negotiated written treaties with tribes in 1622, 1653, 1665, and 1701. See the index of Thwaites 1896–1901 for reference to several of these. See also O'Callaghan 1853–87, vol. 3, for a verbatim transcript of a treaty between the French and the Iroquois (121–25), and vol. 9, for the records of several of other treaties with the Iroquois (44–47).

15. O'Callaghan 1853-87, vol. 3, 125.

16. For views of British segregation of native communities, see Axtell 1981; Ronda 1977; and Simmons 1979.

17. See Prucha 1994, 42–54, for his discussion of the Treaty of Fort Stanwix and treaties with the western Indians.

18. Examples include the Treaty with the Six Nations (October 22, 1784: 7 Stat., 15); Treaty with the Wyandots (January 21, 1785: 7 Stat., 16); Treaty with the Cherokees (November 28, 1785: 7 Stat., 18); Treaty with the Choctaws (January 3, 1786: 7 Stat., 21); Treaty with the Chickasaws (January 10, 1786: 7 Stat., 24); and Treaty with the Shawnees (January 31, 1786: 7 Stat., 26).

19. The other participatory tribes were the Delawares, Ottawas, Chippewas, Potawatomies, and the Sac Nation.

20. The other tribes were the Delawares, Shawnees, Ottawas, Chippewas, Potawatomies, Miamis, Eel River, Weas, Kickapoos, Piankeshaws, and Kaskaskias.

21. Congress, via an appropriation rider (16 Stat., 566), arguably terminated the president's capacity to negotiate further treaties with tribes in 1871, although existing treaties were to remain legally binding.

22. For autobiographical information on Marshall, and commentary on his importance to American law outside Indian law, see G. White 1991.

23. In treaties, tribes sometimes agreed to preemption. In this case, Marshall simply imposed his judgment without tribal consent.

24. See, e.g., Burke 1969 and Norgren 1996.

2. "WITH THE GREATEST RESPECT AND FIDELITY": THE TRUST DOCTRINE

1. Judicial schizophrenia is evident in the debate over trust. There is also case law that states that in the absence of explicit treaty, agreement,

or statutory language no enforceable relationship of trust pertains between tribes and the federal government. As a federal court held in *Gila River Pima-Maricopa Indian Community v. United States*, 140 F.Supp. 776 (1956), "whether or not the legal relationship of guardian and ward exists between a particular Indian tribe and the United States depends, we think, upon the express provisions of the particular treaty, agreement, executive order, or statute under which the claim presented arises . . . [and] in the absence of some language in a treaty, agreement or statute spelling out such a relationship, the court seems to have meant merely that the relationship between the Indians and the Government is 'similar to' or 'resembles' such a legal relationship and that doubtful language in the treaty or statute under consideration should be interpreted in favor of the weak and dependent Indians" (780–81). This decision was reaffirmed fourteen years later in a Federal Court of Appeals case involving the same parties (427 F.2d 1194 [1970]).

2. See, for example, the innumerable memorials, letters, and testimony by tribal people to Congress documented in U.S. Congress, *American State Papers: Indian Affairs* (2 vols., 1832, 1834). See also *Documents Relating to the Negotiation of Ratified and Unratified Treaties with Various Indian Tribes, 1801–1869*, Record Group 75 in the National Archives, Washington, D.C., and the many documents indexed in Johnson 1977. This invaluable compilation chronologically sequences a wide array of congressional documents, reports, hearings, memorials, and numerous executive reports, documents, and other governmental items. An enormous corpus of twentieth-century public documents expresses a sense of tribal attitudes toward the trust doctrine. See the multivolume, multiyear set of the U.S. Senate's *Survey of Conditions of the Indians in the United States* (1928–40); transcripts and expert testimony relating to the Indian Claims Commission; the numerous records and briefs submitted by Indians and their attorneys during the long history of litigation; and letters and memorials submitted to the Bureau of Indian Affairs, the Congress, and the president over various issues. Compilations of speeches and oral history also contain clear testimony relating to the indigenous visions of trust: see, for example, the Doris Duke Oral History Collection, Western History Collection, University of Oklahoma.

3. See King 1979. Schisms among the Cherokee people have included conflict among the Old Settler Cherokees, the Treaty Party, and Ross Party Cherokees in the early 1800s; the division within the Western Cherokees during the U.S. Civil War, when some Cherokees supported the Union and others negotiated treaties with the Confederacy; the opposition posed by the Keetowah Society (led by Redbird Smith in the late 1800s) to allotment

and to dissolution of the tribal government of the Western Cherokees; the separation between the Eastern Band of Cherokees in western North Carolina and the Western Cherokees in eastern Oklahoma; and the late 1990s constitutional crisis pitting then–principal chief Joe Byrd against other segments of the Cherokee Nation government.

4. Georgia was essentially agreeing to a western boundary. The state's claims to land derived from its history as a British colony, when northern and southern boundaries had been established, but claims to land stretched off into an unmapped and unknown western horizon.

5. Eli Whitney's invention of the cotton gin in 1793 made the production of cotton commercially profitable on a scale never before possible. Agricultural land values rose as demand increased, and rich agricultural lands within the Cherokee nation were the envy of Georgia's white citizens.

6. A reading of the oral arguments indicates that Wirt was referring to the Indian Removal Act of May 28, 1830, which has a proviso in section 7 that says: "Provided, That nothing in this act contained shall be construed as authorizing or directing the violation of any existing treaty between the United States and any of the Indian tribes."

7. There have been some modifications in precedents in recent years, however. See *Williams v. Lee*, 358 U.S. 217 (1959), and *Brendale v. Confederated Tribes and Bands of the Yakima Indian Nation*, 492 U.S. 408 (1989).

8. See Glancy 1996 for a fictionalized account of the Trail of Tears from a Cherokee perspective; see also Foreman 1972 for an overview of the removal of the Choctaw, Creek, Chickasaw, Cherokee, and Seminole peoples; and Debo 1972 for the history of U.S. betrayal of these tribes after their reestablishment in Indian Territory.

9. David Wilkins has a copy of this unpublished letter.

10. The Cherokee language is a member of the large Iroquoian language family.

11. See Steele 1992; White 1991.

12. See *Lyng v. Northwest Indian Cemetery Protective Association*, 484 U.S. 439 (1988); *Cotton Petroleum Corporation v. New Mexico*, 490 U.S. 163 (1989); *Employment Division v. Smith*, 494 U.S. 872 (1990); *Duro v. Reina*, 110 S.Ct. 2053 (1990); *County of Yakima v. Yakima Nation*, 112 S.Ct. 683 (1992); *South Dakota v. Bourland*, 113 S.Ct. 2309 (1993); *Hagen v. Utah*, 114 S.Ct. 958 (1994); *Seminole Tribe v. Florida*, 517 U.S. 44 (1996); *Strate v. A-1 Contractors*, 520 U.S. 438 (1997); *Cass County, Minnesota v. Leech Lake Band of Chippewa Indians*, 118 S.Ct. 1904 (1998); *Alaska v. Native Village of Venetie Tribal Government*, 118 S.Ct. 948 (1998).

3. "SUCH AN OUTRAGE": THE DOCTRINE OF PLENARY POWER

1. For the purposes of this chapter we focus on tribes rather than individual Indians since the commerce clause empowers Congress to oversee the federal government's commercial relations with Indian *tribes*, and countless treaties were negotiated with tribal nations, not with individual Indians. Also, historically the federal government's most destructive acts have been aimed at the breakup of tribal nations as sovereign collectivities. For instance, Indian removal, the allotment of Indian lands, and the termination of tribal recognition in the 1950s are all examples of the United States acting to destroy, or at the very least destabilize, tribal nations. There is, however, compelling evidence that the courts and Congress have asserted plenary power over Indian individuals as well, even after they became citizens of the United States. As the attorney general for the United States said in his brief to the Supreme Court in *Perrin v. United States* (1914), "the fact that some or all of these Indians may have become citizens under the provisions of the allotment act of 1887 does not in any way affect the power of Congress to protect them against their appetites (which are not altered by the investiture of citizenship) or to protect the neighboring white inhabitants, whose safety would be affected by excessive indulgence of the Indian appetite." The attorney general was speaking about the Indians' alleged "appetite" for alcohol.

2. The Constitution does not explicitly grant the federal government the power to regulate Indian affairs. It only states that Congress shall be the branch with the power to "regulate commerce with foreign nations . . . and with the Indian tribes" (Article 1, sec. 8, cl. 3). The commerce and treaty clauses of the Constitution serve as the primary bases for the exercise of federal power over Indian affairs. The treaty clause (Article 2, sec. 2, cl. 2) grants the president the authority to make treaties, with the "advice and consent" of the Senate. No explicit reference is made to Indians, but the United States followed European examples in treating with Indian tribes.

3. In Deloria 1985a, see especially chapter 7, "The Plenary Power Doctrine"; in Shattuck and Norgren 1991, see especially chapter 3, "The Transformation of Indian Law: Trusteeship, Plenary Power, and the Political Question Doctrine."

4. Special thanks to Professor Vine Deloria, Jr., for bringing this list of infrequently cited laws to our attention. See the following documents and their provisions for explicit examples of Congress admitting its limitations regarding tribal lands, rights, and resources, absent unequivocal tribal consent. These examples clearly show that tribes were far from passive actors

in their bilateral relationship with the United States, even though they were in a weakened military and economic state vis-à-vis the United States:

(1) Treaty with Mixed Bands of Bannacks [sic] and Shoshones. October 14, 1863—this treaty was not ratified by the U.S. Senate due to tribal resistance (Kappler 1941, 693).

(2) Agreement with the Crows, May 14, 1880 (Kappler 1904, vol. 2, 1063). This agreement was not ratified and was replaced by an agreement of June 12, 1880, which was ratified April 11, 1882 (22 Stat. 42).

(3) U.S. Statute. "An Act to graduate the price and dispose of the residue of the Osage Indian trust and diminished-reserve lands . . . ," March 3, 1881 (21 St. 509). See the attached proviso, which reads: "Provided, however, That no proceeding shall be taken under this act until two-thirds of the adult males of said Osage Indian tribes shall assent to the foregoing provisions."

(4) U.S. Statute. "An Act to divide a portion of the reservation of the Sioux Nation of Indians in Dakota into separate reservations and to secure the relinquishment of the Indian title to the remainder," April 30, 1888 (25 St. 94). See section 24, which states: "That this act shall take effect only upon the acceptance thereof and consent thereto by the different bands of the Sioux Nation of Indians . . . and upon failure of such proof [vote by adult Indians] and proclamation [issued by the president] this act becomes of no effect, and null and void."

(5) U.S. Statute. "An Act to ratify and confirm an agreement with the Muscogee or Creek band of Indians, and for other purposes," March 1, 1901 (31 St. 861). See the preamble, which states in relevant parts: "That the agreement negotiated between the Commission to the Five Civilized tribes and the Muscogee or Creek tribe . . . as herein amended, is hereby accepted, ratified, and confirmed, and the same shall be of full force and effect when ratified by the Creek National Council."

5. Of course, history is replete with examples where federal officials ignored the doctrine of tribal consent and acted unilaterally.

6. At the present, there is no indication that the Supreme Court is willing to weaken Congress's plenary authority over tribes in the ways it has weakened plenary authority over states.

7. Tribal reservations are lands held in trust by the federal government, just as military reservations are. The Navajo reservation was established

by the treaty of 1868 and, as such, is an area where federal jurisdiction supersedes state jurisdiction (exceptions to this rule occur in specifically circumscribed exceptions, such as the grant of criminal jurisdiction to certain states over certain reservations that was legislated through Public Law 280).

8. See chapter 6 for a fuller discussion of these important, if little known, disclaimer clauses.

9. Even if the Constitution granted such a power to Congress, we would argue that tribes are not subject to the Constitution, since they were not parties to its establishment.

10. By "extraconstitutional" and "extralegal" we mean factors that are not derived from the Constitution. These may include nonconstitutional doctrines or legal constructs such as the alleged "wardship" and/or "dependent" status of Indians; the use of the "doctrine of discovery" to justify extensions of federal power over Indians and their resources; the presumption of plenary power not related to Indian commerce; the alleged "incorporation" of Indians into the American polity; or the racial constitution of a reservation or Indian community, to name but a few. See Carter 1976; Fetzer 1981; and Wilkins 1997a for examples of "extra" factors and their implications for tribal sovereignty.

11. Dred Scott was a slave who lived for nine years with his owners in states where slavery was illegal. After returning to Missouri, Scott sued for freedom for himself and his family. The case reached the Supreme Court, which ruled against the Scotts. "On March 6th, 1857, Chief Justice Roger B. Taney delivered the majority opinion of the U.S. Supreme Court in the Dred Scott case. Seven of the nine justices agreed that Dred Scott should remain a slave, but Taney did not stop there. He also ruled that as a slave, Dred Scott was not a citizen of the United States, and therefore had no right to bring suit in the federal courts on any matter. In addition, he declared that Scott had never been free, due to the fact that slaves were personal property; thus the Missouri Compromise of 1820 was unconstitutional, and the Federal Government had no right to prohibit slavery in the new territories. The court appeared to be sanctioning slavery under the terms of the Constitution itself, and saying that slavery could not be outlawed or restricted within the United States" (Moore 1999).

12. See also the important "reserved rights" cases, *U.S. v. Winans* (1905) and *Winters v. U.S* (1908), which are discussed in more detail in chapter 4.

13. The two "minor exceptions" are Supreme Court decisions that supported individualized Indian property rights. First, *Choate v. Trapp*, 224 U.S. 665 (1912), held that a 1908 federal statute that purported to remove

restrictions on alienation and taxation of some land allotments to citizens of the Five Civilized Tribes without payment of just compensation violated the Fifth Amendment. Second, *Hodel v. Irving*, 481 U.S. 704 (1987), held that a federal statute that provided for escheatment (the reversion of property to the tribe in the absence of legal heirs) of individual Indian fractional land interest without the payment of just compensation to individual Indians also violated the Fifth Amendment (Pommersheim 1995).

14. More importantly, while these two decisions were victories for individual Indian property rights, it is clear that the Court still concedes that Congress retains plenary power over tribal governments as sovereign bodies. As a leading liberal lawyer, Charles Wilkinson, recently admitted: "No Supreme Court case has yet overturned any statute as being beyond Congress's authority, and that record may well remain safe under the new regime, both for statutes that burden and statutes that benefit Indians" (Wilkinson 1987, 82).

4. "TREATIES AS COVENANTS": THE DOCTRINE OF RESERVED RIGHTS

1. Numerous news articles and web sites address this recent issue (the Makahs successfully killed a young gray whale on May 17, 1999). The official Makah site, "Makah Whaling: Questions and Answers," is available at http://www.makah.com/whales.htm (although in December 2000 it had not been updated since the summer of 1998). The Northwest Indian Fisheries Commission (NWIFC) web site posts the "Makah Management Plan for Makah Treaty Gray Whale Hunting for the Years 1998–2002," available at http://www.nwifc.wa.gov/whaling/whaleplan.html. The NWIFC was established in the wake of the Boldt Decision, as *U.S. v. Washington* is commonly known in the Pacific Northwest; it is the intertribal agency that regulates Northwest native fisheries—in addition to tribal, state, federal, and international levels of regulation. The "Makah Whaling News and Information Page," available at http://www.geocities.com/Yosemite/7431/whaling.htm, is a compilation of different views of the controversy; it is managed by "one small 'nuclear' family of the Makah nation." Anti-whaling positions can be found at sites maintained by the West Coast Anti-Whaling Society at http://www.anti-whaling.com/backgroundArticles.htm and by the Sea Shepherd Conservation Society at http://www.seashepherd.org/home.html. Regional news coverage is posted on the web by the newspaper Oregonian, at http://oregonlive.com/speical/issues/makah.html.

2. For more on reactions against hunting and fishing, see Williams and Neubrech 1976.

3. See the many legal definitions of what constitutes Indian Country, or Indian reservations, in Murchison [1901] 1973, 5–20. In 1999 there were 278 reservations, in 32 states, formally recognized by the federal government. Broadly, reservations are tracts of land expressly set aside or reserved for Indian nations by some federal action, typically with the concurrence of the tribe(s). Many Indian reservations were created during the treaty era, when tribes were persuaded or coerced to cede a majority of their original homelands, reserving a much smaller portion of their territory as a specific reservation. Other Indian reservations were created by presidential executive orders in the late nineteenth and early twentieth centuries. Still others have been created by congressional acts; and since the 1934 Indian Reorganization Act, the secretary of the interior has been empowered to establish, expand, or restore Indian reservations.

4. The Rehnquist Court emphasizes a concept known as dual federalism, the idea that the states and the national government have separate spheres of authority, and each is considered supreme in its own sphere.

5. There are 27 federally recognized tribes in the state of Washington, and 10 federally recognized tribes in Oregon (as well as additional groups who lack federal recognition). The recognized entities are, in several cases, confederations of what historically were autonomous tribes or bands. State of Washington: Confederated Tribes of the Chehalis Reservation, Confederated Tribes of the Colville Reservation, Confederated Tribes and Bands of the Yakama Indian Nation, Hoh, Jamestown Band of S'Klallam, Kalispel, Lower Elwha, Lummi, Makah, Muckleshoot, Nisqually, Noocksack, Port Gamble Indian Community, Puyallup, Quileute, Quinault, Samish, Sauk-Suiattle, Shoalwater Bay, Skokomish, Spokane, Squaxin Island, Stillaguamish, Suquamish, Swinomish, Tulalip Tribes, Upper Skagit. State of Oregon: Burns Paiute, Confederated Tribes of the Coos, Lower Umpqua, and Siuslaw Indians, Confederated Tribes of the Grand Ronde Community, Confederated Tribes of the Siletz Reservation, Confederated Tribes of the Umatilla Reservation, Confederated Tribes of the Warm Springs Reservation, Cow Creek Band of Umpqua, Coquille, Klamath (United States 1996, 58212–15). For examples of treaties, see the Treaty of Medicine Creek, December 26, 1854 (10 Stat. 1132), the Treaty of Point Elliot, January 26, 1855 (12 Stat. 927), the Treaty of Point-no-Point, January 26, 1855 (12 Stat. 933), the Treaty with the Makah, January 31, 1855 (12 Stat. 939), Treaty with the Walla Walla, Cayuse, etc., June 9, 1855 (12 Stat. 945).

6. Access by native people to these "usual and accustomed grounds and stations" was strictly regulated according to inheritance, intermarriage, and agreements among native communities (typically villages were the meaningful politically autonomous units throughout this region). See Boxberger 1989; Stewart 1977; Suquamish Museum 1985; Suttles 1987; and Wright 1992 for in-depth discussions of native fishing in the Pacific Northwest. In recent years, the case *U.S. v. Washington* has been in the forefront of Northwest Coast debates over reserved rights. We do not discuss the case here in any detail, but that is not a reflection on its importance. Other cases are more pertinent to the development of our arguments concerning how, and why, courts have interpreted the reserved rights doctrine in various ways. *U.S. v. Washington* is critically important in several ways, however, that should at least be mentioned: (1) in the weight given to native testimony and to the ethnographic and historic evidence amassed by native and non-native scholars and expert witnesses; (2) in the co-management model and regulatory agencies and mechanisms developed cooperatively by tribes, intertribal agencies, the states, and the federal government (and Canada as well, in international treaty negotiations); and (3) in the degree of federal court supervision of the development, direction, and implementation of the co-management model.

7. "Yakima" is an alternative spelling that was commonly used prior to the 1990s.

8. White based his reading of the equal footing doctrine on the 1883 case of *Escanaba Co. v. Chicago*, 107 U.S. 678 (1883).

9. See Peroff 1982 for a discussion of Menominee struggles with termination.

10. The Menominee Nation was not as successful, however, in 1998 when it attempted to secure judicial recognition of its *off-reservation* hunting and fishing rights. Off-reservation rights had been explicitly recognized in an 1831 treaty, but the 1831 treaty provisions were held to have been extinguished by removal provisions included in later treaties (*Menominee Indian Tribe of Wisconsin v. Thompson*, 161 F.3d 449 [1998]).

11. See Newton 1980 and Wilkins 1997a, 166–85, for two accounts that question the legal rationale used in the *Tee-Hit-Ton* decision.

12. *Crow Tribe of Indians and Thomas L. Ten Bear v. Repsis*, 73 F.3d 982 (10th Cir. 1995).

13. The Supreme Court also indulged its inclination to privilege the accrual of income from natural resources in the *Lyng* decision. In that case, the survival of native religion was deemed less important than the federal government's right to turn a profit from timber sales.

14. For (1) see, e.g., *McClanahan v. Arizona State Tax Commission*, 411 U.S. 164, 174 (1973). For (2) see, e.g., *Choctaw Nation v. Oklahoma*, 397 U.S. 620, 631 (1970). For (3) see, e.g., *Tulee v. Washington*, 315 U.S. 681, 684–85 (1942).

15. See, e.g., *Confederated Bands of Ute Indians v. United States*, 330 U.S. 169, 179 (1947), *United States v. Dion*, 476 U.S. 734, 739–40 (1986), and *Menominee Indian Tribe v. Thompson*, 161 F.3d 449, 457 (1998).

5. "JUSTICES WHO BENT THE LAW": THE DOCTRINE OF IMPLIED REPEALS

1. In *Minnesota v. Mille Lacs Band of Chippewa Indians* (119 S.Ct. 1187), handed down on March 24, 1999, the Court in a 5-4 ruling upheld the Chippewas' 1837 treaty right to hunt, fish, and gather on 13 million acres of land the eight Chippewa bands had ceded to the federal government in central Minnesota. In upholding these treaty rights, Associate Justice Sandra Day O'Connor reiterated that "Congress may abrogate Indian treaties, but it must clearly express its intent to do so." Quoting from *U.S. v. Dion* (476 U.S. 734 [1986]), O'Connor stated that "there must be clear evidence that Congress actually considered the conflict between its intended action on the one hand and Indian treaty rights on the other, and chose to resolve that conflict by abrogating the treaty." There is, said O'Connor, "no such 'clear evidence' of congressional intent to abrogate the Chippewa treaties here."

2. As discussed in chapter 2, our definition of trust holds that the federal government is under the legal and moral obligation to protect Indian lands, waters, minerals, and all other natural resources. It is also obligated to protect and encourage tribal self-government; to assist the tribes in their movement toward economic independence; and to provide social programs and services to raise the standard of living of Indian people to a level comparable to what the majority enjoys (U.S. Congress 1977, 136). The trust relationship, however, is not and cannot be uniform across tribes. No two tribal entities enjoy exactly the same relationship with the federal government: there are variations in when and why a tribe first established its political relationship with a European power (typically Spain, France, or Great Britain) or with the United States; what the relative strengths or weaknesses of the tribal nation were at the time it negotiated its relationship and whether these shifted over time; and whether or not a treaty/treaties were ever negotiated and/or ratified.

3. The majority criterion refers to the fact that every conflict in society invariably is a dispute between a majority of those eligible to participate and a minority or minorities or else it is a dispute between or among

minorities only. Thus the outcome of the Court's decisions must either (1) accord with the preferences of a minority—counter to those of a majority; (2) accord with the preferences of a majority—counter to those of a minority; or (3) accord with the preferences of one minority, counter to another minority (Dahl 1957, 281–82). Dahl discussed the popular view that the Supreme Court's primary role is to protect the rights of minorities against the tyranny of the majority. His analysis of decisions where the Court declared portions of federal legislation unconstitutional showed, however, that "the policy views dominant on the Court are never for long out of line with the policy views dominant among the lawmaking majorities of the United States" (285). Dahl found that "the evidence is not impressive" that the Court has protected fundamental or natural rights and liberties against the tyranny of some lawmakers. As Jonathan Casper (1976) would later show, Dahl wrote his analysis during the politically repressive era of McCarthyism and before the Warren Court had begun to render decisions favoring fundamental rights of minorities against tyrannical or indifferent majorities. Casper also correctly chided Dahl for his exclusion of data (he did not examine cases involving statutory construction or cases arising out of state and local legislation) and for his reliance on a policy framework that was rooted in influence or power. Dahl's "winners or losers" approach, Casper asserted, "imposes an artificial distinction that obscures a dynamic process in which even 'losers' contribute importantly to outcomes that eventually emerge" (Casper 1976, 62).

4. See, e.g., *Worcester* (1832), *Crow Dog* (1883), and *Choate v. Trapp* (1912).

5. Quoted in O'Brien 1995, 114.

6. See, e.g., *U.S. v. Holliday*, 70 U.S. (3 Wall.) 407 (1866); *U.S. v. Old Settlers*, 148 U.S. 427 (1893); *Stephens v. Cherokee Nation*, 174 U.S. 445 (1899); *Cherokee Nation v. Hitchcock*, 187 U.S. 294 (1902); *Lone Wolf v. Hitchcock*, 187 U.S. 553 (1903); *U.S. v. Rickert*, 188 U.S. 432 (1903); *Blackfeather v. U.S.*, 190 U.S. 368 (1903); *Matter of Heff*, 197 U.S. 488 (1905); *U.S. v. Hitchcock*, 205 U.S. 80 (1907); *Tiger v. Western Investment Co.*, 221 U.S. 286 (1911); *U.S. v. Sandoval*, 231 U.S. 28 (1913); *Johnson v. Gearlds*, 234 U.S. 422 (1914); *U.S. v. Nice*, 241 U.S. 591 (1916); *U.S. v. Waller*, 243 U.S. 452 (1917); *Brader v. James*, 246 U.S. 88 (1918); and *U.S. v. Boylan*, 265 Fed. 165 (1920).

7. Even during this period Congress dealt with tribes in a qualitatively different way than it dealt with foreign affairs. The difference had to do with the unique political relationship with tribes that had already evolved, rooted in the political doctrines of consent, good faith, and trust, as laid out in congressional policy pronouncements, Supreme Court cases

such as the Cherokee cases (*Cherokee Nation v. Georgia*, 1831, and *Worcester v. Georgia*, 1832), and presidential proclamations and annual messages acknowledging the federal government's moral obligations to protect tribes.

8. See, e.g., Newton 1984, for a good analysis of the relationship between the Supreme Court and the Congress. The Rehnquist Court generally is less deferential to the Congress than its predecessors in many areas of law, including Indian affairs, and has challenged Congress's presumption of commerce power especially as it relates to—or is seen as interfering with—the rights of states to control their affairs. Nevertheless, in Indian affairs, there remains a presumption on the part of the Court that the federal government, and particularly the Congress, has superior standing in relation to tribes and may act accordingly.

9. The Supreme Court placed some limitation on the congressional plenary power doctrine in the 1914 decision *Perrin v. United States*, 232 U.S. 478, by establishing the "pure arbitrariness" test. The Court, while affirming that Congress had tremendous authority over Indian affairs, nevertheless stated that "[a]s the power is incident only to the presence of the Indians and their status as wards of the Government, it must be conceded that it does not go beyond what is reasonably essential for their protection, and that, to be effective, its exercise must not be purely arbitrary but founded upon some reasonable basis" (486).

10. For a good discussion of the treaty proceedings, see Jones 1966.

11. A legal term closely related to the implied repeal doctrine, implicit divestiture, proposes that tribes were "implicitly divested" of certain sovereign powers by their geographic incorporation within, and allegedly dependent relationship upon, the federal government. It was first used by Chief Justice Rehnquist in *Oliphant v. Suquamish*, 435 U.S. 191 (1978). For cases involving the implied repeal doctrine, see, e.g., *Decoteau v. District Court*, 420 U.S. 425 (1975), *Rosebud Sioux v. Kneip*, 430 U.S. 584 (1977), *U.S. v. Dion*, 106 S.Ct. 2216 (1986), *Oregon Department of Fish & Wildlife v. Klamath Indian Tribe*, 473 U.S. 753 (1985), *South Dakota v. Bourland*, 113 S.Ct. 2309 (1993), and *Hagen v. Utah*, 1145 S.Ct. 958 (1994).

12. An example was a 1995 federal court of appeals decision, *Crow Tribe of Indians v. Repsis*, 73 F.3d 982, that reinvigorated the 1896 Supreme Court opinion, *Ward v. Race Horse*, 163 U.S. 504, which had constricted Indian treaty rights and laid out a vision of tribal-state relations that elevated states' rights to a preeminent role above treaty rights. In *Race Horse* the Court had declared that treaty rights were nothing more than "temporary and precarious" privileges and that they could be terminated at any time

by Congress. Although *Race Horse* was thought to have been "implicitly" overruled by later opinions, *Crow Tribe* held that all the doctrines enunciated in *Race Horse* were "alive and well." Fortunately for tribes, the Supreme Court in *Minnesota v. Mille Lacs Band of Chippewa Indians*, 119 S.Ct. 1187 (1999), without expressly overruling *Race Horse*, dramatically weakened its holding. The Court said that "*Race Horse* rested on a false premise [and] as this Court's subsequent cases have made clear, an Indian tribe's treaty rights to hunt, fish, and gather on state land are not irreconcilable with a State's sovereignty over the natural resources in the State."

13. See, e.g., *U.S. ex rel. Hualapai Indians v. Santa Fe Pacific Railroad*, 314 U.S. 339 (1941), and *Bryan v. Itasca Co.*, 426 U.S. 373 (1976).

14. The federal government has on many occasions acted to abrogate or diminish the rights of other nations, including tribal nations, by not ratifying previously negotiated treaties (e.g., the eighteen treaties negotiated between the federal government and various California tribes); by failing to enact necessary legislation to implement particular treaty provisions; by failing to carry out treaty mandates (e.g., fishing rights of Washington, Oregon, and Wisconsin tribal members); or by enacting later laws that implicitly overrode earlier treaty rights (Kiowas, Comanches, and Apaches in Oklahoma). See volume 2 of Deloria and DeMallie (1999), especially chapters 13 and 14, which detail treaties and agreements rejected by Congress and Indian nations.

15. Vine Deloria, Jr., in response to a query by Senator Daniel Inouye in 1987, on whether any Indian treaties had not been violated, said that "there are technical attorneys' interpretations which are that various articles are specifically violated. I think the spirit of all the treaties or the pledge of good faith between Indians and the U.S.—that spirit has certainly long since been destroyed" (U.S. Senate 1988, 29). Regarding U.S. violations of foreign treaties, see Christopher Joyner's chapter "International Law" (Joyner 1992). Joyner details U.S. intervention in the affairs of many Third World countries, despite avowed support for the doctrine of nonintervention. Examples include U.S. intervention in Guatemala in 1954, Cuba in 1961, the Dominican Republic in 1965, Chile in 1973, Granada in 1983, and Panama in 1989. According to Joyner, between 1900 and 1930 the United States intervened militarily on some sixty occasions in several Caribbean and Central American states. The Indian treaty-termination rider attached to the 1871 Indian Appropriation Act declared that "hereafter no Indian nation or tribe within the territory of the U.S. shall be acknowledged or recognized as an independent nation, tribe, or power with whom the U.S. may contract by treaty." This measure, however, recognized the ongoing validity of

previously ratified Indian treaties (16 St. 544, 566). Consult Deloria and DeMallie (1999, vol. 1, chapter 6, "The End of Treaty-Making") for detailed examination of this critical period. Also, see Rice 1977 for a persuasive argument that Congress's action to end treaty-making with tribes is of questionable constitutionality. More importantly, the practice of treaty-making, termed agreements, continued from 1872 to 1914. The only difference between the two is that agreements require ratification by both Houses, while treaties need only be ratified by the Senate.

16. See, for example, Article 8 of the 1868 treaty between the Northern Cheyennes, Northern Arapahoes, and the United States (15 Stat., 655); and Article 10 of the 1868 Navajo Treaty with the United States (15 Stat., 667).

6. "NO REASONABLE PLEA":
DISCLAIMERS IN TRIBAL-STATE RELATIONS

1. "Indian Country" is that area within which Indian laws and customs, and federal laws relating to Indians, are generally applicable. It is also defined as all the land under the supervision and protection of the U.S. government that has been set aside primarily for the use of Indians, including all Indian reservations and any other area under federal jurisdiction and designated for Indian use.

2. Tribes, as preexisting polities, exercise a number of political and legal powers that only sovereigns may yield, such as the power to adopt a form of government; to define the conditions of tribal citizenship/membership; to regulate the domestic relations of the tribe's citizens/members; to prescribe rules of inheritance with respect to personal property; to levy duties, taxes, or fees on tribal citizens and noncitizen residents; and to administer justice. See the Solicitor's Opinion 1934, 445–77, for details.

3. The trust doctrine or responsibility, as defined by the Supreme Court in *Seminole v. United States*, holds that there is a "distinctive obligation of trust incumbent upon the Government in its dealing with these dependent and sometimes exploited people. . . . In carrying out its treaty obligations with the Indian tribes, the Government is something more than a mere contracting party. Under a humane and self-imposed policy which has found expression in many acts of Congress, and numerous decisions of this Court, it has charged itself with *moral obligations of the highest responsibility and trust. Its conduct, as disclosed in the acts of those who represent it in dealing with the Indians, should therefore be judged by the most exacting fiduciary standards*" (316 U.S. 286, 296–97, 1942). The commerce clause declares that Congress alone has the power to "regulate commerce with

foreign nations, and among the several states, and *with the Indian tribes*" (emphasis added).

4. Most nonwestern states, of course, do not have disclaimer clauses mentioning Indian tribes. This absence of language should not be interpreted as giving those states jurisdiction over Indian tribes or lands in their borders, unless specific congressional legislation declares as much. The constitutional and historical evidence discussed later in this chapter pointedly shows that the federal government, and Congress in particular, has wielded jurisdiction over the nation's Indian policy since the birth of the country. Even nondisclaiming states are bound, under the Constitution, to the reality that the treaty relationship and the Constitution's various clauses—treaty, property, supremacy, and commerce—clearly allocate jurisdiction in the field of Indian policy to the federal government, not state governments.

5. Tribal authority is preconstitutional because it predates the birth of the United States and continues to this day. It is extraconstitutional because it does not stem from the federal or state constitutions or the nonindigenous population who created those documents, but it flows from the will of each indigenous tribal community.

6. Two years later, in *United States v. Sutton*, 215 U.S. 291 (1909), the Court construed Washington State's enabling act disclaimer clause to mean that the federal government retained exclusive jurisdiction and control over the matter of liquor introduction within a reservation.

7. There are, of course, several historical examples (discussed later) where Congress explicitly delegated to certain states jurisdiction over particular tribal nations and their members.

8. The Supreme Court in *Parker v. Richard*, 250 U.S. 235 (1919), held as much when it determined that state courts act practically as a federal agency when Congress delegates authority to them to act regarding Indian oil and gas royalties. "That the agency which is to approve or not is a state court is not material. It is the agency selected by Congress and the authority confided to it is to be exercised in giving effect to the will of Congress in respect of a matter within its control. Thus in a practical sense the court in exercising that authority acts as a federal agency.... Plainly, the restrictions have the same force and operate in the same way as if Congress had selected another agency, exclusively federal, such as the Superintendent of the Five Civilized Tribes" (239).

9. In addition to disclaiming jurisdiction over Indians, several territorial acts exclude Indians from official population counts for determining congressional representatives. See, for example, Wisconsin's statute (5 Stat. 10), Article 1, sec. 2, clause 3; and the Fourteenth Amendment, sec. 2.

10. The clause, however, did include a brief reference to Indian lands recognized by "any prior sovereignty," a recognition that many Pueblos and Spaniards in New Mexico had received land grants from Spain, the title to which was to be respected under federal law (36 Stat. 559).

11. Idaho and Wyoming, admittedly without enabling acts, each nevertheless included clauses that looked very similar to those of the other disclaiming states.

12. The first moment, he asserts, is the precedent established in *Worcester v. Georgia* of an exclusive tribal-federal relationship.

13. The McCarran act waived the sovereign immunity of the United States as to comprehensive state water rights adjudication.

14. See, for example, *United States v. Ward*, 28 Fed. Cas. No. 16,639 (1863).

15. Examples of federal and state case law include *The Kansas Indians*, 72 U.S. (5 Wall.) 737 (1866); *Harkness v. Hyde*, 98 U.S. 476 (1878); *Wau-Pe-Man-Qua v. Aldrich*, 28 Fed. 489 (1886); *United States v. Partello*, 48 Fed. 670 (1891); *United States v. Ewing*, 47 Fed. 809 (1891); *United States v. Rickert*, 188 U.S. 432 (1903); *United States v. Winans*, 198 U.S. 371 (1905); *Dick v. United States*, 208 U.S. 340 (1908); *Winters v. United States*, 207 U.S. 564 (1908); *United States v. Sutton*, 215 U.S. 291 (1909); *United States v. Sandoval*, 231 U.S. 28 (1913); *United States v. Yakima County*, 274 Fed. 115 (1921); *United States v. Ferry County*, 24 F.Supp. 399 (1938); *United States v. Board of Commissioners*, 26 F.Supp. 270 (1939); *State v. Arthur*, 261 P.2d 135 (1953); *Martinez v. Southern Ute Tribe*, 249 F.2d 915 (1957); *Williams v. Lee*, 358 U.S. 217 (1959); *Kennerly v. District Court*, 400 U.S. 423 (1971); *McClanahan v. Arizona State Tax Commission*, 411 U.S. 164 (1973); and *Chino v. Chino*, 90 N.M. 203 (1977). For an example of statutory law, see the Buck Act, July 30, 1947, 61 Stat. 644, which exempts much of Indian Country and Indian entities from state taxation.

16. For more on gaming controversies, see Mason 2000.

17. See Norgren 1996 for an excellent analysis detailing Georgia's efforts to deal directly with the Cherokee Nation in a way that openly challenged the federal government's authority in the field.

18. See Onuf 1987 and Elazar 1988 for more on the Northwest Ordinance. The Northwest Ordinance provided for three stages of government for the territories and states into which the region was to be divided. First, authority was to be exercised by appointees of the national government. In the second stage, authority was to be shared by these appointees and a representative assembly with the governor still appointed by the president. Finally, the state was to be admitted to the Union on an equal footing with the old states (Gates 1968, 317). The third stage was fulfilled only

after the territory had attained a population of 60,000 free inhabitants, adopted a constitution, and created a republican form of government and after determining the qualifications for voting and holding office.

19. Justice Brennan here is referring to the *McBratney* decision, 104 U.S. 621 (1881), which appears to have played a pivotal role in determining which states were required to have disclaimers.

20. Allotments were usually held in trust for individual Indians by the federal government for some period; the standard was twenty-five years. It was assumed that this "grace" period, when lands would remain free from state or local taxation, would better enable the adjustment of Indian people into local polities and economies. At the end of the trust period (or earlier, if the allottee demonstrated "competence," graduated from an Indian school, or had a sufficient degree of white blood to be considered "competent"), the trust restrictions were lifted and the allottee was issued a deed to his or her property—a fee-simple title. At that point, the allottee was termed "patented" and was granted U.S. citizenship.

21. *United States v. Winans*, 198 U.S. 371 (1905); *Winters v. United States*, 207 U.S. 564 (1908); *Dick v. United States*, 208 U.S. 340 (1909); *Seufert Bro's Co. v. United States*, 249 U.S. 194 (1919); and *Tulee v. Washington*, 315 U.S. 681 (1942). The editors of the 1982 revised edition of Felix Cohen's *Handbook of Federal Indian Law* state that the *Ward* ruling had "temporarily confused" the import of disclaimer clauses, but that the court in *Dick v. United States* had restored clarity to the situation, without expressly overruling the *Ward* precedent (268, note 72).

22. Goldberg-Ambrose (1975, 1997) acknowledges that P.L. 280 was the "most direct evidence of congressional intent with respect to state jurisdiction" but that this did not prevent both tribes and the states from expressing their dissatisfaction with the measure (Goldberg-Ambrose 1975, 538). The issue of tribal consent was addressed by amendments to the act in 1968, the Indian Civil Rights Act (ICRA; 82 Stat. 77). The ICRA provided that future assertions of state jurisdiction under P.L. 280 required the Indians' consent. States were also allowed to return jurisdiction to the federal government if they desired.

23. See, for example, Goldberg-Ambrose (1975, 563); and the cases she cites. See also *Agua Caliente Band of Mission Indians Tribal Council v. City of Palm Springs*, 347 F.Supp. 42 (C.D. Cal. 1972), and *Anderson v. Britton*, 212 Ore. 1 (1957).

24. The equally controversial Indian Civil Rights Act imposed many provisions of the U.S. Bill of Rights on tribal governments, regulating government regulations with reservation residents.

25. David Wilkins has copies of the accord and Zah's memorandum describing the policy.

26. See, for example, *Cotton Petroleum Corporation v. New Mexico*, 490 U.S. 163 (1989); *Brendale v. Confederated Tribes and Bands of the Yakima Indian Nation*, 109 S.Ct. 2994 (1989); and *County of Yakima v. Yakima Indian Nation*, 112 S.Ct. 683 (1992).

27. See, for example, *The Kansas Indians*, 72 U.S. (5 Wall.) 737 (1867); *Ex parte Crow Dog*, 109 U.S. 556 (1883); *Elk v. Wilkins*, 112 U.S. 94 (1884); *Talton v. Mayes*, 163 U.S. 376 (1896); *United States v. Wheeler*, 435 U.S. 313 (1978); and *Santa Clara Pueblo v. Martinez*, 436 U.S. 49 (1978).

7. "AS IT WAS INTENDED":
THE DOCTRINE OF SOVEREIGN IMMUNITY

1. We discuss the conditions of sovereign immunity in more detail later in this chapter. Suffice it to say at this point that there are exceptions to the rule we have stated in very general terms.

2. Gorton was defeated in his reelection bid in December 2000 by a Democrat, Maria Cantwell, by 2,229 votes out of nearly 2.5 million cast. His loss created a 50-50 tie in the new Senate. Although Gorton carried a majority of Washington State's rural counties, Cantwell, who was supported by American Indian tribes, environmentalists, tribal lawyers, and abortion-rights activists, carried the more populated urban counties. Washington State's tribes and national Indian leaders were so anxious to oust Gorton that they organized a nonprofit group in 1999, the First American Education Project, composed of several state tribes, and pledged to raise $2 million in an independent campaign fund to deny Gorton a fourth term. In August 2000 a $100,000 television ad campaign was begun in which tribes accused Gorton of sacrificing the state's environmental health for campaign contributions from the oil and mining industries. As W. Ron Allen, a member of the Jamestown S'Klallam tribe in Washington State and first vice-president of the National Congress of American Indians, declared: "We want to make a strong statement that if you attack the tribes, there will be consequences" ("Recount Seals Senate Race in Washington for Democrat," *New York Times*, December 2, 2000, A8; Eric Pianin, "Indian Tribes Target an Enemy," *Washington Post*, April 10, 2000, 14; and Ross Anderson, "Tribal Ads Criticize Gorton," *Seattle Times*, August 15, 2000, B2).

3. "Tort" refers to a wrongful act, injury, or damage where the defendant may be liable, but where no breach of contract has occurred. A civil suit would be brought in case of breach of contract. Gorton was targeting situations where tribes might be liable (e.g., for personal injuries or prop-

erty damages a nontribal member might suffer while on reservation lands). Contract claims would cover cases where an individual or company has contracted with a tribe.

4. As of August 2000, the members of the Senate Committee on Indian Affairs were Ben Nighthorse Campbell (R, Colorado), chair; Daniel K. Inouye (D, Hawaii), vice-chair; Frank H. Murkowski (R, Arkansas); John McCain (R, Arizona); Slade Gorton (R, Washington); Pete V. Domenici (R, New Mexico); Craig Thomas (R, Wyoming); Orrin G. Hatch (R, Utah); James Inhofe (R, Oklahoma); Kent Conrad (D, North Dakota); Harry Reid (D, Nevada); Daniel K. Akaka (D, Hawaii); Paul Wellstone (D, Minnesota); and Byron L. Dorgan (D, North Dakota).

5. In Fleming's view, tribal councils are "non-Republican" (and therefore, he argues, unconstitutional) because non-native residents on reservations are denied representation in the ruling government since they cannot vote in tribal elections. Fleming lives within the boundaries of the Swinomish Reservation in western Washington.

6. For example, Metacom, a sachem of the Wampanoag Confederacy in Massachusetts in the late 1600s, was called "King Philip" by the English (Grinde and Johansen 1991, 3).

7. Proposed by congressional resolution in March 1794, the Eleventh Amendment was ratified less than a year later, in February 1795.

8. "In dicta" refers to the opinion of the justices that is attached to the actual judgment, or "holding," of the Court in any particular case. The attached arguments express the opinion of the ruling majority or of the minority, which is known as the dissent. Either way, the attached opinions do not carry the weight of law. They are, however, frequently quoted or referred to in subsequent court interpretations or rulings—they can be influential, and legal scholars debate the influence they should exert. "Dicta" is the plural of "dictum" or "obiter dictum," a Latin expression meaning "said in passing."

9. This act established a federal court composed of five judges, with jurisdiction over the nation.

10. In fact, states that have waived their own immunity from tort liability must nevertheless respect the immunity of the tribes, and, conversely, tribes must also honor states' immunity from suit in tribal court. As discussed earlier, as a result of the *Seminole* decision, tribes are barred by the Eleventh Amendment from suing states (for failing to negotiate gaming contracts) in federal court without state consent, even when Congress has authorized such suits through the Indian Gaming Regulatory Act.

11. See, e.g., *Puyallup Tribe, Inc. v. Washington Game Dept.*, 433 U.S. 165 (1977); *Weeks Construction, Inc., v. Oglala Sioux Housing Authority*, 797 F.2d 668 (8th Cir. 1986); *Pan American Co. v. Sycuan Band of Mission Indians*, 884 F.2d 416 (9th Cir. 1989); *Morgan v. Colorado River Indian Tribes*, 103 Ariz. 425 (1968); *In re Greene*, 980 F.2d 590 (9th Cir. 1992); *Three Affiliated Tribes v. Wold Eng'g*, 476 U.S. 887 (1986); *Public Service Co. of Colorado v. Shoshone-Bannock Tribes*, 30 F.3d 1203 (9th Cir. 1994); *U.S. v. Red Lake Band of Chippewa Indians*, 827 F.2d 380 (8th Cir. 1987), cert. denied 485 U.S. 935 (1988); *Fletcher v. U.S.*, 116 F.3d 1315 (10th Cir. 1997); *U.S. v. Yakima Tribal Court*, 806 F.2d 853 (9th Cir. 1986), cert. denied 481 U.S. 1069 (1987); *Montgomery v. Flandreau Santee Sioux Tribe*, 905 F.Supp. 740 (D.S.D. 1995). A number of precedents have emerged from this corpus of myriad cases: for example, a tribe's waiver of its sovereign immunity must be unequivocal; it applies in both state and federal courts; it extends to claims for declaratory and injunctive relief, not just damages, and it is not defeated by a claim that the tribe acted beyond its power; states must honor the immunity of the tribes; tribes are not immune from suits by the federal government; a court may adjudicate the rights of individual tribal members; tribal officials acting within the scope of their authority share the tribal nation's immunity from suit; conducting gaming under the Indian Gaming Regulatory Act constitutes a limited waiver of sovereign immunity for the purpose of keeping in compliance with the act.

12. Marshall went on to note that "nothing on the face of Title I of the ICRA purports to subject tribes to the jurisdiction of the federal courts in civil actions for injunctive or declaratory relief. . . . In the absence here of any unequivocal expression of contrary legislative intent, we conclude that suits against the tribe under the ICRA are barred by its sovereign immunity from suit" (ibid., 59).

13. As discussed in chapter 6, P.L. 280 delegated some powers and jurisdictional rights from the federal government to certain states. Oklahoma, however, was not one of those states.

14. This rule emerged out of *Ex parte Young*, 209 U.S. 123 (1908), which held that the federal courts were not precluded by the Eleventh Amendment from restraining state officers from enforcing state laws deemed to be in violation of the federal Constitution. In other words, the *Young* doctrine holds that actions against individual government officials engaging in illegal activity are not actions against the sovereign and may proceed.

15. See, for example, *Northern States Power Co. v. Prairie Island Mdewakanton Sioux Indian Community*, 991 F.2d 458 (8th Cir. 1993).

16. The 1796 law expired in two years, but was reenacted on March 3, 1799 (4 Stat. 731). The Indian depredations laws changed over the years. Section 14 of the 1796 act was superseded by the act of June 30, 1834, which charged the commissioner of Indian affairs with supervising the process of indemnification whenever a tribe failed to compensate an injured white party. The most important aspect of the 1834 act was the provision that the payment made by the federal government to satisfy white claimants could be deducted from any annuities a tribe was entitled to receive.

17. Besides depredations claims cases, at least one Indian treaty contained a provision permitting a payment of claims against a tribe out of tribal annuities to compensate those who had property taken or destroyed. Article 4 of the Cherokee Treaty of January 26, 1794, provided that "the said Cherokee nation, in order to evince the sincerity of their intentions in future, to prevent the practice of stealing horses, attended with the most pernicious consequences to the lives and peace of both parties, do hereby agree, that for every horse which shall be stolen from the white inhabitants by any Cherokee Indians, and not returned within three months, that the sum of fifty dollars shall be deducted from the said annuity of five thousand dollars" (7 Stat. 43). In some cases the commissioner of Indian affairs acted unilaterally to take money from tribes to pay for depredations. Commissioner Ely S. Parker, a Seneca himself, "had few qualms about paying depredation claims and unhesitatingly used Indian funds for that purpose. When in 1870 the Comanches, Kiowas, and Apaches complained that they received fewer annuity goods in 1869 than 1868, Parker explained that in the year before he took office all their treaty funds had been used to purchase goods for them. However, their 1869 annuity was decreased by a depredation payment of $30,000 which of course greatly reduced the amount applicable for the purchase of goods" (Skogen 1996, 197).

18. This ruling was made in companion cases, *United States v. District Court for the County of Eagle*, 401 U.S. 520, and *United States v. District Court for Water Division*, No. 5, 401 U.S. 527.

19. *Montgomery v. Flandreau Santee Sioux Tribe*, 905 F.Supp. 740 (D.S.D. 1995).

20. See, e.g., *Merrion v. Jicarilla Apache Tribe*, 617 F.2d 537, 540 (10th Cir. 1980), aff'd on other grounds, 455 U.S. 1300 (1982); *Rosebud Sioux Tribe v. A. & P. Steel, Inc.*, 874 F.2d 550 (8th Cir. 1989).

21. Biographical information comes from Duncan and Lawrence 1997, 1516–18.

22. The inaction of the state attorney general's office against non-Indian fishers who flouted the Boldt decision encouraged major illegal

fisheries, or "outlaw" fishing, "for years following the decision" (Cohen 1986, 93).

23. Gorton's 1986 loss "turned out to be a blessing in disguise, he said, because he had become too aloof and detached from the average voter. . . . he told audiences that he had learned his lesson 'well and for good.' His [1988] campaign theme was 'common sense, caring and conviction' " (Associated Press Political Service 1999).

24. Attaching riders is often criticized as a dubious way to make public policy, since the rider often bears little relation to the subject of the bill it rides upon and typically is subject to little or no debate. Despite the objections, it is a time-honored congressional strategy to accomplish legislative action.

25. After the 1996 hearing, Anderson left the BIA, moved west, and became a counselor to the secretary of the interior.

26. One of the most important "other purposes" was to amend the Indian Reorganization Act of 1934 so that tribes no longer have to get the secretary of interior's approval to hire an attorney.

References

American Friends Service Committee. 1975. *Uncommon Controversy: Fishing Rights of the Muckleshoot, Puyallup, and Nisqually Indians*. Seattle: University of Washington Press.

Anderson, Ross. 2000. Tribal Ads Criticize Gorton. *Seattle Times*, August 15, B2.

Associated Press Political Service. 1999. AP Candidate Bios, Thomas Slade Gorton. LEXIS-NEXIS Academic Universe.

Axtell, James. 1981. *The European and the Indian: Essays in the Ethnohistory of Colonial North America*. New York: Oxford University Press.

Ball, Howard. 1992. Federal Tort Claims Act. In *The Oxford Companion to the Supreme Court*, ed. K. L. Hall, 288–89. New York: Oxford University Press.

Ball, Milner S. 1987. Constitution, Court, Indian Tribes. *American Bar Foundation Research Journal* 1: 1–139.

Berman, Howard R. 1978. The Concept of Aboriginal Rights in the Early History of the United States. *Buffalo Law Review* 27: 637–67.

Biolsi, Thomas. 1992. *Organizing the Lakota*. Tucson: University of Arizona Press.

Black's Law Dictionary. 1979. 5th ed. St. Paul, Minn.: West Publishing Co.

Boxberger, Daniel. 1989. *To Fish in Common: The Ethnohistory of Lummi Indian Salmon Fishing*. Lincoln: University of Nebraska Press.

Brodeur, Paul. 1985. *Restitution: The Land Claims of the Mashpee, Passamaquoddy, and Penobscot Indians of New England*. Boston: Northeastern University Press.

Burke, Joseph C. 1969. The Cherokee Cases: A Study in Law, Politics, and Morality. *Stanford Law Review* 21: 500–531.

Burton, Lloyd. 1991. *American Indian Water Rights and the Limits of Law.* Lawrence: University Press of Kansas.

Byler, William. 1977. The Destruction of American Indian Families. In *The Destruction of American Indian Families,* ed. S. Unger, 1–11. New York: Association on American Indian Affairs.

Campisi, Jack. 1985. The Trade and Intercourse Acts: Land Claims on the Eastern Seaboard. In *Irredeemable America: The Indians' Estate and Land Claims,* ed. Imre Sutton, 337–62. Albuquerque: University of New Mexico Press.

Canby, William C., Jr. 1998. *American Indian Law.* 3rd ed. St. Paul, Minn.: West Publishing Co.

Carr-Howard, Maxwell. 1996. Tribal-State Relations: Time for Constitutional Stature? *New Mexico Law Review* 26: 293–321.

Carter, Nancy Carol. 1976. Race and Power Politics as Aspects of Federal Guardianship over American Indians: Land-Related Cases, 1887–1924. *American Indian Law Review* 4: 197–248.

Casper, Jonathan. 1976. The Supreme Court and National Policy Making. *American Political Science Review* 70 (1): 50–63.

Chambers, Reid P. 1975. Judicial Enforcement of the Federal Trust Responsibility to Indians. *Stanford Law Review* 27: 1213–49.

Champagne, Duane. 1992. *Social Order and Political Change: Constitutional Governments among the Cherokee, the Choctaw, the Chickasaw, and the Creek.* Stanford: Stanford University Press.

Clark, Blue. 1994. *Lone Wolf v. Hitchcock: Treaty Rights and Indian Law at the End of the Nineteenth Century.* Lincoln: University of Nebraska Press.

Clinton, Robert N., Nell Jessup Newton, and Monroe E. Price. 1991. *American Indian Law.* 3rd ed. Charlottesville, Va.: Michie Co.

Cohen, Fay. 1986. *Treaties on Trial: The Continuing Controversy over Northwest Indian Fishing Rights.* Seattle: University of Washington Press.

Cohen, Felix S., ed. 1972. *Handbook of Federal Indian Law.* Albuquerque: University of New Mexico Press.

———. 1982. *Handbook of Federal Indian Law.* Revised ed. Edited by Rennard Strickland et al. Albuquerque: University of New Mexico Press.

Collins, Richard B. 1989. Indian Consent to American Government. *Arizona Law Review* 31: 365–87.

Columbia University. 1995. Legislative Drafting Research Fund. *Constitutions of the United States: National and State.* Dobbs Ferry, N.Y.: Oceana Publications.

Congressional Information Service, Inc. 2000. Member Profile Report, 106th Congress, Senator Daniel K. Inouye D-HI.

Congressional Quarterly Weekly Report. March 5, 1994. 1994 Committee Supplement: Senate Indian Affairs 52 (9): 1–2.

Congressional Record. 1903. Washington, D.C.: Government Printing Office.

Coulter, Robert T. 1977. The Denial of Legal Remedies to Indian Nations under U.S. Law. *American Indian Journal* 3 (September): 5–11.

Coulter, Robert T., and Steven M. Tullberg. 1984. Indian Land Rights. In *The Aggressions of Civilization,* ed. Sandra L. Cadwalader and Vine Deloria, Jr., 185–213. Philadelphia: Temple University Press.

Dahl, Robert. 1957. Decision-making in a Democracy: The Supreme Court as a National Policy-maker. *Journal of Public Law* 6: 279–95.

Davies, Glen E. 1966. State Taxation on Indian Reservations. *Utah Law Review* (July): 132–51.

Debo, Angie. 1972. *And Still the Waters Run: The Betrayal of the Five Civilized Tribes.* Princeton: Princeton University Press.

Delage, Denys. 1993. *Bitter Feast: Amerindians and Europeans in Northeastern North America, 1600–64.* Vancouver, B.C.: University of British Columbia Press.

Deloria, Sam. 1978. Introduction. In *La Confluencia,* Special Issue on Indian Tribal Sovereignty and Treaty Rights, S23–S26. Albuquerque, N.M.: La Confluencia.

Deloria, Vine, Jr. 1979a. *A Brief History of the Federal Responsibility to the American Indian.* Department of Health, Education, and Welfare, Office of Education, OE Publication No. 79-02404. Washington, D.C.: Government Printing Office.

———. 1979b. Self-Determination and the Concept of Sovereignty. In *Economic Development in American Indian Reservations,* ed. R. D. Ortiz, 22–28. Albuquerque: University of New Mexico Press.

———. 1980. Anthologies: Main Course or Left-overs? *Journal of Ethnic Studies* 8: 111–15.

———. 1985a. *Behind the Trail of Broken Treaties: An Indian Declaration of Independence.* Austin: University of Texas Press.

———. 1985b. The Distinctive Status of Indian Rights. In *The Plains Indians of the Twentieth Century,* ed. Peter Iverson, 237–48. Norman: University of Oklahoma Press.

———. 1988. Beyond the Pale: American Indians and the Constitution. In *A Less Than Perfect Union,* ed. Jules Lobel, 249–67. New York: Monthly Review Press.

———. 1989. Laws Founded in Justice and Humanity: Reflections on the Content and Character of Federal Indian Law. *Arizona Law Journal* 31: 203–23.

———. 1992. Trouble in High Places: Erosion of American Indian Rights to Religious Freedom in the United States. In *The State of Native America,* ed. M. Annette Jaimes, 267–90. Boston: South End Press.

———. 1994. Treaties. In *Native America in the Twentieth Century: An Encyclopedia,* ed. Mary B. Davis, 646–49. New York: Garland Publishing Co.

———. 1996. Reserving to Themselves: Treaties and the Powers of Indian Tribes. *Arizona Law Review* 38: 963–80.

Deloria, Vine, Jr., and Raymond DeMallie. 1999. *Documents of American Indian Diplomacy: Treaties, Agreements, and Conventions, 1775–1979.* 2 vols. Norman: University of Oklahoma Press.

Deloria, Vine, Jr., and Clifford M. Lytle. 1983. *American Indians, American Justice.* Austin: University of Texas Press.

———. 1984. *The Nations Within: The Past and Future of American Indian Sovereignty.* New York: Pantheon Books.

Deloria, Vine, Jr., and David E. Wilkins. 1999. *Tribes, Treaties and Constitutional Tribulations.* Austin: University of Texas Press.

Dozier, Edward P. 1970. *The Pueblo Indians of North America.* New York: Holt, Rinehart, and Winston.

Duncan, Philip D., and Christine C. Lawrence, eds. 1997. *Congressional Quarterly's Politics in America, 1998: The 105th Congress.* Washington, D.C.: Congressional Quarterly Press.

Editorial. 1995. Gambling Fever: Gambling Should Remain an Indian Monopoly. *Arizona Daily Star,* February 19, 2D.

Edmunds, R. David. 1996. Tecumseh. In *Encyclopedia of North American Indians,* ed. F. Hoxie. New York: Houghton Mifflin Co.

Egan, Timothy. 1998. Debate about Tribal Rights Turns Rancorous. *New York Times,* April 8.

Elazar, Daniel J., ed. 1988. Land and Liberty in American Society: The Land Ordinance of 1785 and the Northwest Ordinance of 1878. *Publius: The Journal of Federalism* 18: entire issue.

Elving, Ronald D. 1988. The Quiet Insider: Hawaii's Daniel Inouye Wields a Private, Personal Power. *Congressional Quarterly Weekly Report* 46(16) (April 16): 1–3.

Engdahl, David E. 1976. State and Federal Power over Federal Property. *Arizona Law Review* 18: 283–384.

Estin, Ann Laquer. 1984. *Lone Wolf v. Hitchcock:* The Long Shadow. In *The Aggressions of Civilization: Federal Indian Policy since the 1880s,* ed.

Sandra L. Cadwalader and Vine Deloria, Jr., 216–45. Philadelphia: Temple University Press.

Feldman, Glenn M. 1993. The Great Casino Controversy: Indian Gaming in Arizona. *Arizona Attorney* 29(11): 19–23.

Fetzer, Philip Lee. 1981. Jurisdictional Decisions in Indian Law: The Importance of Extra-legal Factors in Judicial Decision-making. *American Indian Law Review* 9: 253–72.

Finger, John R. 1991. *Cherokee Americans: The Eastern Band of Cherokee in the Twentieth Century*. Lincoln: University of Nebraska Press.

Fisher, Louis. 1990. *Constitutional Structures: Separated Powers and Federalism*. Vol. 1. New York: McGraw Hill.

Forbes, Jack D. 1960. *Apache, Navajo, and Spaniard*. Norman: University of Oklahoma Press.

Foreman, Grant. 1972. *Indian Removal: The Emigration of the Five Civilized Tribes*. 2d ed. 1982. Norman: University of Oklahoma Press.

Gates, Paul W. 1968. *History of Public Land Law Development*. Washington, D.C.: U.S. Government Printing Office.

Gibson, Charles. 1988. Spanish Indian Policies. In *History of Indian-White Relations*, ed. Wilcomb E. Washburn, 96–102. Vol. 4 of *Handbook of North American Indians*. Washington, D.C.: Smithsonian Institution.

Gitlin, Jay. 1994. Empires of Trade, Hinterlands of Settlement. In *The Oxford History of the American West*, ed. Clyde Milner II et al., 79–113. New York: Oxford University Press.

Glancy, Diane. 1996. *Pushing the Bear: A Novel of the Trail of Tears*. New York: Harcourt Brace and Co.

Goldberg-Ambrose, Carole E. 1975. Public Law 280: The Limits of State Jurisdiction over Reservation Indians. *UCLA Law Review* 22: 535–94.

———. 1997. *Planting Tail Feathers: Tribal Survival and Public Law 280*. Los Angeles: American Indian Studies Center.

Gray, Jerry. 1997. Senate Shelves Proposals to Restrict Indian Legal Protection. *New York Times*, September 17.

Green, L. C. 1975. North America's Indians and the Trusteeship Concept. *Anglo-American Law Review* 4: 137–62.

Grinde, Donald A., Jr., and Bruce E. Johansen. 1991. *Exemplar of Liberty: Native America and the Evolution of Democracy*. Los Angeles: American Indian Studies Center.

Hall, Gilbert L. 1981. *Duty of Protection: The Federal Indian Trust Relationship*. 2d ed. Washington, D.C.: Institute for the Development of Indian Law.

Hamilton, Alexander. 1961. *The Federalist Papers*. New York: New American Library.

Hanke, Lewis. 1949. *The Spanish Struggle for Justice in the Conquest of America*. Philadelphia: University of Pennsylvania Press.

Harring, Sidney L. 1994. *Crow Dog's Case: American Indian Sovereignty, Tribal Law, and United States Law in the Nineteenth Century*. New York: Cambridge University Press.

Hobsbawm, Eric. 1973. Peasants and Politics. *Journal of Peasant Studies* 1: 3–22.

Hobson, Charles F. 1992. Chisholm v. Georgia. In *The Oxford Companion to the Supreme Court of the United States*, ed. K. L. Hall, 144. New York: Oxford University Press.

Horowitz, David. 1978. *The First Frontier: The Indian Wars and America's Origins, 1607–1776*. New York: Simon and Schuster.

Horsman, Reginald. 1988. United States Indian Policies, 1776–1815. In *History of Indian-White Relations*, ed. Wilcomb Washburn, 29–39. Vol. 4 of *Handbook of North American Indians*. Washington, D.C.: Smithsonian Institution Press.

Jacobs, Wilbur R. 1972. *Dispossessing the American Indian: Indians and Whites on the Colonial Frontier*. New York: Scribners.

———. 1988. British Indian Policies. In *History of Indian-White Relations*, ed. Wilcomb E. Washburn, 5–12. Vol. 4 of *Handbook of North American Indians*. Washington, D.C.: Smithsonian Institution Press.

Jennings, Francis. 1975. *The Invasion of America: Indians, Colonization and the Cant of Conquest*. Chapel Hill: University of North Carolina Press.

———. 1984. *The Ambiguous Iroquois Empire: The Covenant Chain Confederation of Indian Tribes with English Colonies from Its Beginning to the Lancaster Treaty of 1744*. New York: W. W. Norton.

Jesuits. Letters from Missions (North America). 1959. *Jesuit Relations and Allied Documents: Travels and Explorations of the Jesuit Missionaries in New France, 1610–1791*. New York: Pageant Book Co.

Johnson, Ralph W., and James M. Madden. 1984. Sovereign Immunity in Indian Tribal Law. *American Indian Law Review* 12: 170–71.

Johnson, Steven L., comp. 1977. *Guide to American Indian Documents in the Congressional Serial Set: 1817–1899*. New York: Clearwater Publishing Co.

Jonaitis, Aldona. 1991. *Chiefly Feasts: The Enduring Kwakiutl Potlatch*. Seattle: University of Washington Press; New York: American Museum of Natural History.

Jones, Dorothy V. 1982. *License for Empire: By Treaty in Early America*. Chicago: University of Chicago Press.

————. 1988. British Colonial Indian Treaties. In *History of Indian-White Relations*, ed. Wilcomb E. Washburn, 185–94. Vol. 4 of *Handbook of North American Indians*. Washington, D.C.: Smithsonian Institution Press.

Jones, Douglas C. 1966. *The Treaty of Medicine Lodge: The Story of the Great Treaty Council as Told by Eyewitnesses*. Norman: University of Oklahoma Press.

Joyner, Christopher. 1992. International Law. In *Intervention into the 1990s: U.S. Foreign Policy in the Third World*, ed. Peter Schraeder, 229–44. Boulder, Colo.: Lynne Reinner Publishers.

Kairys, David. 1993. *With Liberty and Justice for Some: A Critique of the Conservative Supreme Court*. New York: New Press.

Kappler, Charles, comp. 1904. *Indian Affairs: Laws and Treaties*. Vol. 2, *Treaties*. Senate Document #319, 58th Congress, 2d session, serial 4624. Washington, D.C.: Government Printing Office.

————. 1904–41. *Indian Affairs: Laws and Treaties*. 5 vols. (1904, 1904, 1913, 1929, 1941). Washington, D.C.: Government Printing Office.

Kennedy, John H. 1950. *Jesuit and Savage in New France*. New Haven: Yale University Press.

Killian, Johnny H., ed. 1987. *The Constitution of the United States: Analysis and Interpretation*. Washington, D.C.: Government Printing Office.

King, Duane H., ed. 1979. *The Cherokee Indian Nation: A Troubled History*. Knoxville: University of Tennessee Press.

Kramer, Karl J. 1986. The Most Dangerous Branch: An Institutional Approach to Understanding the Role of the Judiciary in American Indian Jurisdictional Determination. *Wisconsin Law Review* 5–6: 989–1038.

Krauss, E. P. 1983. The Irony of Native American "Rights." *Oklahoma University Law Review* 8: 409–49.

Kurland, Philip B., and Gerhard Casper. 1978. *United States Supreme Court: Landmark Briefs and Arguments of the Supreme Court of the United States. Constitutional Law*. Vol. 2. Washington, D.C.: University Publications of America.

Lazarus, Edward. 1991. *Black Hills/White Justice*. New York: Harper Collins Publishers.

Lieder, Michael. 1983. Adjudication of Indian Water Rights under the McCarran Amendment: Two Courts Are Better Than One. *Georgetown Law Journal* 71: 1023–61.

Lomawaima, K. Tsianina. 1994. *They Called It Prairie Light: The Story of Chilocco Indian School*. Lincoln: University of Nebraska Press.

Mankiller, Wilma, and Michael Wallis. 1993. *Mankiller: A Chief and Her People*. New York: St. Martin's Press.

Mason, W. Dale. 2000. *Indian Gaming: Tribal Sovereignty and American Politics*. Norman: University of Oklahoma Press.

McCarthy, Robert J. 1998. Civil Rights in Tribal Courts: The Indian Bill of Rights at Thirty Years. *Idaho Law Review* 34: 465–515.

McDonald, Forrest. 1992. Tenth Amendment. In *The Oxford Companion to the Supreme Court of the United States*, ed. K. L. Hall, 861–64. New York: Oxford University Press.

McDonnell, Janet A. 1991. *The Dispossession of the American Indian, 1887–1934*. Bloomington: Indiana University Press.

McLaughlin, James. 1910. *My Friend the Indian*. Boston: Houghton/Mifflin Co.

McLoughlin, William G. 1986. *Cherokee Renascence in the New Republic*. Princeton, N.J.: Princeton University Press.

McLuhan, T. C. 1971. *Touch the Earth*. New York: Simon and Schuster.

Merkel, Philip C. 1992. Sovereign Immunity. In *The Oxford Companion to the Supreme Court of the United States*, ed. K. L. Hall, 806–7. New York: Oxford University Press.

Metz, Sharon. 1990. A Legacy of Broken Promises. *Sojourners* (June): 16–20.

Milner, Clyde A., II, et al., eds. 1994. *The Oxford History of the American West*. New York: Oxford University Press.

Moore, Bob. 1999. The Dred Scott Decision. In Web Site of the Jefferson National Expansion Memorial, St. Louis, Mo. Available at http://www.nps.gov/jeff/ocv-dscottd.htm.

Murchison, Kenneth S., comp. [1901] 1973. *Digest of Decisions Relating to Indian Affairs*, vol. 1. *Judicial*. Milwood, N.Y.: Kraus Reprint Co.

Nabokov, Peter. 1991. *Native American Testimony*. New York: Viking Penguin.

Nagel, Joanne. 1996. *American Indian Ethnic Renewal: Red Power and the Resurgence of Identity and Culture*. New York: Oxford University Press.

National Journal. 1995. The States and Congressional Districts: Their Governors, Senators and Representatives: Hawaii. *In The Almanac of American Politics 1996*. Available online at http://nationaljournal.com/almanac/.

Nelson, Michael C. 1977. *The Winters Doctrine: Seventy Years of Application of "Reserved" Water Rights to Indian Reservations*. Tucson, Ariz.: Office of Arid Land Studies.

News from Indian Country. March 1995, 2.

Newton, Nell J. 1980. At the Whim of the Sovereign: Aboriginal Title Revisited. *Hastings Law Journal* 31: 1215–85.

———. 1982. Enforcing the Federal-Indian Trust Relationship after *Mitchell*. *Catholic University Law Review* 31: 635–83.

———. 1984. Federal Power over Indians: Its Sources, Scope, and Limitations. *University of Pennsylvania Law Review* 132: 195–288.

———. 1992. Indian Claims in the Courts of the Conqueror. *American University Law Review* 41: 753–854.

———. 1993. Let a Thousand Policy-Flowers Bloom: Making Indian Policy in the Twenty-first Century. *Arkansas Law Review* 46: 25–75.

Norgren, Jill. 1996. *The Cherokee Cases: The Confrontation of Law and Politics*. New York: McGraw-Hill.

Nugent, Walter. 1994. Comparing Wests and Frontiers. In *The Oxford History of the American West*, ed. Clyde A. Milner II et al., 803–33. New York: Oxford University Press.

O'Brien, David M. 1995. *Constitutional Law and Politics: Struggle for Power and Governmental Accountability*, 2d ed. Vol. 1. New York: W. W. Norton & Co.

O'Callaghan, E. B., ed. 1849–51. *Documentary History of the State of New York*. 4 vols. Albany: Weed, Parsons & Co.

———. 1853–87. *Documents Relative to the Colonial History of the State of New York*. 15 vols. Albany, Weed, Parsons & Co.

Onuf, Peter S. 1987. *Statehood and Union: A History of the Northwest Ordinance*. Bloomington: Indiana University Press.

O'Toole, Francis J., and Thomas Tureen. 1971. State Power and the Passamaquoddy Tribe: A Gross National Hypocrisy? *Maine Law Review* 23: 1–39.

Peroff, Nicholas C. 1982. *Menominee Drums: Tribal Termination and Restoration, 1954–1974*. Norman: University of Oklahoma Press.

Peterson, Mark R. 1983. *Northern Cheyenne Tribe v. Adsit*: Are State Jurisdictional Disclaimers Still the Indian's Assurance of Federal Jurisdiction? *Golden Gate University Law Review* 13: 329–43.

Pianin, Eric. 2000. Indian Tribes Target an Enemy. *Washington Post National Weekly Edition*, April 10, 14.

Pomeroy, Earl S. 1947. *The Territories and the United States: 1861–1890*. Philadelphia: University of Pennsylvania Press.

Pommersheim, Frank. 1995. *Braid of Feathers: American Indian Law and Contemporary Tribal Life*. Berkeley: University of California Press.

Prucha, Francis P. 1962. *American Indian Policy in the Formative Years: The Trade and Intercourse Acts, 1790–1834*. Lincoln: University of Nebraska Press.

———. 1984. *The Great Father: The United States Government and the American Indian*. 2 vols. Lincoln: University of Nebraska Press.

———. 1985. *The Indian in American Society*. Berkeley: University of California Press.

———, ed. 1990. *Documents of United States Indian Policy*. 2d ed. Lincoln: University of Nebraska Press.

———. 1994. *American Indian Treaties: The History of a Political Anomaly*. Berkeley: University of California Press.

Recount Seals Senate Race in Washington for Democrat. 2000. *New York Times*, December 2, A8.

Reed, James B., and Judy A. Zelio. 1995. *States and Tribes: Building New Traditions*. Denver: National Conference of State Legislators.

Rethinking the Trust Doctrine in Federal Indian Law. 1984. *Harvard Law Review* 98: 422–40.

Rice, George W. 1977. Indian Rights: 25 U.S.C. Sec. 77: The End of Sovereignty or a Self-Limitation of Contractual Ability? *American Indian Law Review* 5: 239–53.

Ronda, James P. 1977. "We Are Well As We Are": An Indian Critique of Seventeenth-Century Christian Missions. *William and Mary Quarterly* 34(1): 66–82.

Royce, Charles C. 1887. The Cherokee Nation of Indians: A Narrative of Their Official Relations with the Colonial and Federal Governments. In *Annual Report of the Bureau of Ethnology, 1883–1884*, 121–378. Washington, D.C.: Government Printing Office.

Rubio, Raul. 1995. Symington's Threat to Indian Gaming Echoes Past. *Tucson Citizen*, June 2, 15A.

Sando, Joe S. 1976. *The Pueblo Indians*. San Francisco: Indian Historian Press.

———. 1992. *Pueblo Nations: Eight Centuries of Pueblo Indian History*. Santa Fe, N.M.: Clear Light Publishers.

Scheiber, Harry N. 1992. Federalism. In *The Oxford Companion to the Supreme Court of the United States*, ed. Kermit L. Hall, 278–87. New York: Oxford University Press.

Schwartz, William P. 1983. State Disclaimers of Jurisdiction over Indians: A Bar to the McCarran Amendment? *Land and Water Law Review* 18: 175–99.

Scott, James C. 1985. *Weapons of the Weak: Everyday Forms of Peasant Resistance*. New Haven: Yale University Press.

Shattuck, Petra T., and Jill Norgren. 1979. Political Uses of the Legal Process by Black and American Indian Minorities. *Howard Law Journal* 22: 25–35.

———. 1991. *Partial Justice: Federal Indian Law in a Liberal Constitutional System*. Providence, R.I.: Berg Publishers.

Simmons, William S. 1979. Conversion from Indian to Puritan. *New England Quarterly* 52(2): 197–219.

Simpson, J. A., and E. S. C. Weiner, eds. 1989. *Oxford English Dictionary*. 2d ed. Oxford, England: Clarendon Press.

Skogen, Larry C. 1996. *Indian Depredation Claims, 1796–1920*. Norman: University of Oklahoma Press.

Slagle, Allogan. 1998. The Assault on Sovereign Immunity Continues. *News from Native California* 2(4): 45.

Solicitor's Opinion. October 25, 1934. Powers of Indian Tribes. *Opinions of the Solicitor*. Vol. 1. 55 I.D. 14. Washington, D.C.: U.S. Department of the Interior.

Spicer, Edward. 1962. *Cycles of Conquest: The Impact of Spain, Mexico, and the U.S. on the Indians of the Southwest, 1573–1960*. Tucson: University of Arizona Press.

Steele, Ian K. 1992. *Warpaths: Invasions of North America*. New York: Oxford University Press.

Stewart, Hilary. 1977. *Indian Fishing: Early Methods on the Northwest Coast*. Seattle: University of Washington Press.

Strickland, Rennard. 1975. *Fire and the Spirits: Cherokee Law from Clan to Courts*. Norman: University of Oklahoma Press.

Suquamish Museum. 1985. *The Eyes of Chief Seattle*. Port Madison, Wash.: Suquamish Museum.

Suttles, Wayne. 1987. *Coast Salish Essays*. Seattle: University of Washington Press.

Tarr, G. Alan, ed. 1996. *Constitutional Politics in the States: Contemporary Controversies and Historical Patterns*. Westport, Conn.: Greenwood Press.

Thomas, Cyrus. 1899. Introduction. In *Indian Land Cessions in the United States*, comp. Charles C. Royce, 527–61. Eighteenth Annual Report of the Bureau of American Ethnology, 1896–97, part 2. Washington, D.C.: Government Printing Office.

Thorpe, Francis N., ed. 1909. *The Federal and State Constitutions, Colonial Charters, and Other Organic Laws of the States, Territories, and Colonies*. 7 vols. Washington, D.C.: Government Printing Office.

Thwaites, Reuben G., ed. and trans. 1896–1901. *The Jesuit Relations and Allied Documents*. 73 vols. Cleveland: Burrows Brothers.

Titone, Julie. 2000. Resolution Would End Tribal Sovereignty. *Spokesman Review*, Coeur d'Alene Idaho, July 3 (available at http://www.spokane.net).

Tuttle, Stephen. 1992. Hypocrisy in Arizona? You Bet. *Arizona Republic*, May 24, C3.

United States. 1854. *Official Opinions of the Attorneys General of the United States*. Vol. 6. Washington, D.C.: Government Printing Office.

———. 1873. *Official Opinions of the Attorneys General of the United States*. Vol. 13. Washington, D.C.: Government Printing Office.

———. 1980. *The Complete Oral Arguments of the Supreme Court of the United States*. Frederick, Md.: University Publications of America.

———. 1994. *Weekly Compilation of Presidential Documents*. Washington, D.C.: Government Printing Office.

———. 1996. *Federal Register*. Vol. 61, no. 220 (November 13). Washington, D.C.: Government Printing Office.

United States Commission on Civil Rights. 1981. *Indian Tribes: A Continuing Quest for Survival*. Washington, D.C.: Government Printing Office.

U.S. Congress. 1832. *American State Papers: Foreign Relations*. Vol. 6. Washington, D.C.: Gales & Seaton.

———. 1834. *American State Papers: Indian Affairs*. Vol. 2. Washington, D.C.: Gales & Seaton.

———. 1977. Special Report. *American Indian Policy Review Commission: Final Report*. 2 vols. Washington, D.C.: Government Printing Office.

U.S. Congress. House. 1888. Committee on Territories. *Admission of Dakota, Montana, Washington, and New Mexico into the Union*. 50th Congress, 1st sess. Washington, D.C.: Government Printing Office.

———. 1903. *Agreement and Memorial of the Kansas (or Kaw) Indians of Oklahoma*. Document No. 452, 57th Congress, 1st sess., March 11, 1902. Washington, D.C.: Government Printing Office.

———. 1978. Committee on Interior and Insular Affairs. *House Report No. 1386*. 95th Congress, 2d sess. Washington, D.C.: Government Printing Office.

U.S. Congress. Senate. 1928–40. Committee on Indian Affairs. *Hearings Pursuant to Senate Resolution 79 and Senate Resolution 308, Survey of Conditions of the Indians in the United States*. 16 vols. Washington, D.C.: Government Printing Office.

———. 1953. Committee on Interior and Insular Affairs. *Conferring Jurisdiction on the States of California, Minnesota, Nebraska, Oregon, and Wisconsin, with Respect to Criminal Offenses and Civil Cases and Action Committed or Arising on Indian Reservations within Such States*. 83rd Congress, 1st sess., S. Rept. 699. Washington, D.C.: Government Printing Office.

———. 1988. *Hearing before the Select Committee on Indian Affairs, on S. Concurrent Resolution 76*. 100th Congress, 1st sess. Washington, D.C.: Government Printing Office.

———. 1994a. Committee on Indian Affairs. *Hearings on Health Care Reform in Indian Country and the American Health Care Security Act.* 103rd Congress, 2d sess., 1994. Washington, D.C.: Government Printing Office.

———. 1994b. Committee on Indian Affairs. *Hearings on the Native American Free Exercise of Religion Act.* 103rd Congress, 1st sess., 1993. Washington, D.C.: Government Printing Office.

———. 1995. Committee on Indian Affairs. *Oversight Hearing on the Projected Impact of Proposed Rescissions for Fiscal Year 1995 and of Proposals to Consolidate or Block Grant Federal Funds to the States upon Programs Serving American Indians, Alaska Natives, and Native Hawaiians.* 104th Congress, 1st sess., 1995. Washington, D.C.: Government Printing Office.

———. 1996. Committee on Indian Affairs. *Hearings on Tribal Sovereign Immunity.* 104th Congress, 2d sess., September 24, 1996. Washington, D.C.: Government Printing Office.

———. 1998a. Committee on Indian Affairs. *Oversight Hearings to Provide for Indian Legal Reform.* 105th Congress, 2d sess., March 11, 1998. Washington, D.C.: Government Printing Office.

———. 1998b. Committee on Indian Affairs. *Oversight Hearings to Provide for Indian Legal Reform.* 105th Congress, 2d sess., April 7, 1998. Washington, D.C.: Government Printing Office.

———. 1999. Report 106-150, *Encouraging Indian Economic Development.* 106th Congress, 1st sess., September 8, 1999. Washington, D.C.: Government Printing Office.

U.S. Department of the Interior. 1889. *Commissioner of Indian Affairs: Annual Report for 1888.* Washington, D.C.: Government Printing Office.

Vanderwerth, W. C. 1971. *Indian Oratory: Famous Speeches by Noted Indian Chieftains.* Norman: University of Oklahoma Press.

Van Kirk, Sylvia. 1980. *Many Tender Ties: Women in Fur Trade Society, 1670–1870.* Norman: University of Oklahoma Press.

Vaughan, Alden T., ed. 1979–. *Early American Indian Documents: Treaties and Laws, 1607–1789.* 20 vols. projected. Washington, D.C.: University Publishers of America.

Veeter, William V. 1994. Doing Business with Indians and the Three 'S'es: Secretarial Approval, Sovereign Immunity, and Subject Matter Jurisdiction. *Arizona Law Review* 36: 169–94.

Wade, Mason. 1988. French Indian Policies. In *History of Indian-White Relations,* ed. Wilcomb E. Washburn, 20–28. Vol. 4 of *Handbook of North American Indians.* Washington, D.C.: Smithsonian Institution.

Wallace, Henry B. 1982. Indian Sovereignty and Eastern Land Claims. *New York Law School Law Review* 27: 921–50.

Wallis, Jim. 1994. *The Soul of Politics: A Practical and Prophetic Vision for Change*. Maryknoll, N.Y.: Orbis Books.

Wardell, Morris. 1977. *A Political History of the Cherokee Nation: 1838–1907*. 2d ed. Norman: University of Oklahoma Press.

Watson, Blake A. 1998. The Thrust and Parry of Federal Indian Law. *University of Dayton Law Review* 23 (Spring): 437–514.

West, Elliot. 1994. American Frontier. In *The Oxford History of the American West*, ed. Clyde A. Milner II et al., 115–49. New York: Oxford University Press.

Whaley, Rick, and Walter Bressette. 1994. *Walleye Warriors: An Effective Alliance against Racism and for the Earth*. Philadelphia: New Society Publishers.

White, G. Edward. 1991. *History of the Supreme Court of the United States: The Marshall Court and Cultural Change, 1815–1835*. New York: Oxford University Press.

White, Richard. 1991. *The Middle Ground: Indians, Empires, and Republics in the Great Lakes Region, 1650–1815*. Cambridge: Cambridge University Press.

Wilkins, David E. 1987. *Dine Bibeehaz'aanii: A Handbook of Navajo Government*. Tsaile, Ariz.: Navajo Community College Press.

———. 1992. Who's In Charge of U.S. Indian Policy? Congress and the Supreme Court at Loggerheads over American Indian Religious Freedom. *Wicazo Sa Review* 8(1): 40–64.

———. 1994a. GOP May Railroad Indian Interests. *Arizona Daily Star*, November 27.

———. 1994b. *Johnson* vs. *M'Intosh* Revisited: Through the Eyes of *Mitchel* vs. *United States*. *American Indian Law Review* 19(1): 159–81.

———. 1994c. The U.S. Supreme Court's Explication of "Federal Plenary Power." *American Indian Quarterly* 18(3): 349–68.

———. 1995. The "De-Selected" Committee on Indian Affairs and Its Legislative Record, 1977–1992. *Native American Studies* 9(1): 27–34.

———. 1997a. *American Indian Sovereignty and the U.S. Supreme Court: The Masking of Justice*. Austin: University of Texas Press.

———. 1997b. Convoluted Essence: Indian Rights and the Federal Trust Doctrine. *Native Americas* 14(1): 24–31.

———. 1998. Tribal-State Affairs: American States as "Disclaiming" Sovereigns. *Publius: The Journal of Federalism* 28(4): 55–81.

———. 1999. *The Navajo Political Experience*. Tsaile, Ariz.: Diné College Press.

Wilkinson, Charles F. 1987. *American Indians, Time, and the Law: Native Societies in a Modern Constitutional Democracy*. New Haven: Yale University Press.

Wilkinson, Charles F., and John M. Volkman. 1975. Judicial Review of Indian Treaty Abrogation: "As Long as Water Flows, or Grass Grows upon the Earth"—How Long a Time Is That? *California Law Review* 63: 601–61.

Williams, C. Herb, and Walt Neubrech. 1976. *Indian Treaties: American Nightmare*. Seattle: Outdoor Empire Publishing.

Williams, Robert A., Jr. 1990. *The American Indian in Western Legal Thought: The Discourses of Conquest*. New York: Oxford University Press.

———. 1994. Linking Arms Together: Multicultural Constitutionalism in a North American Indigenous Vision of Law and Peace. *California Law Review* 82: 981–1049.

———. 1997. *Linking Arms Together: American Indian Treaty Visions of Law and Peace, 1600–1800*. New York: Oxford University Press.

Wilmer, Franke. 1993. *The Indigenous Voice in World Politics*. Newbury Park, Calif.: Sage Publications.

Wright, Robin, ed. 1992. *A Time of Gathering: Native Heritage in Washington State*. Thomas Burke Memorial Washington State Museum, Monographs, No. 7. Seattle: University of Washington Press.

Yellow Bird, Doreen. 2000. Legal Warriors. *American Bar Association Journal* 86: 67.

INDEX